Angels Zero

ANGELS ZERO

P-47
CLOSE AIR SUPPORT
IN EUROPE

ROBERT V. BRULLE

SMITHSONIAN INSTITUTION PRESS

Washington and London

Copy editor: Therese D. Boyd
Designer: Janice Wheeler
Production editor: Ruth W. Spiegel

Library of Congress Cataloging-in-Publication Data

Brulle, Robert V.
   Angels zero:P-47 close air support in Europe/Robert V. Brulle
      p.   cm.
   Includes bibliographical references and index.
   ISBN 1-56098-374-4 (alk. paper)
      1.Brulle, Robert V.   2.World War, 1939–1945—Aerial operations, American.   3.World
   War, 1939-1945—Personal narrative, American.   4.World War, 1939–1945—Campaigns
   —Western Front.   5.United States.Army Air Forces.Fighter Group, 366th—History.
   6.United States.Army Air Forces—Biography.   7.Fighter Pilots—United States—Biography
   I.Title.

   D790.B686 2000
   940.54′4973—dc21   00-026765

British Library Cataloguing-in-Publication Data available
Manufactured in the United States of America

05 06 04 03 02 01 00   5 4 3 2 1

⊕ ∞ The recycled paper used in this publication meets the minimum requirements of
the American National Standard for Information Science—Permanence of Paper for
Printed Library Materials.

ANSIZ39.48-1984

For permission to reproduce illustrations appearing in this book, please correspond directly with
the owners of the works as listed in the captions. The Smithsonian Institution Press does not
retain reproduction rights for these illustrations individually or maintain a file of addresses for
photo sources.

To my many flying companions and good friends who paid the ultimate price, and to the World War II history buffs who preserve the documentation of their sacrifice

Contents

Foreword

For the men who came of age to join the armed forces and fight in the years 1939–45, World War II offered a once-in-a-lifetime adventure. Each veteran who fought saw everything through his own eyes and lived experiences peculiar only to him.

The young always consider themselves invulnerable and are therefore constantly brave and positive in their unhesitating action. They are mentally strong and thus able to accomplish more than they realize is possible. They form a close camaraderie with their fellow pilots, creating a tight bond of cooperation and teamwork that results in victory. Later, the survivors can reflect, with pleasure and pain, about the good memories and bad. They can express relief at being alive, yet remain remorseful about those friends and companions who did not make it back from that brutal conflict.

Bob Brulle's thoughts as narrated in this book are his own. As one who lived through the many months as a ground-support fighter pilot with the 366th Fighter Group, he is exceptionally qualified to tell about the way it was. He portrays accurately the hazardous days of ground-support fighter pilots who flew directly into the fire of the enemy's guns in their daily attacks on the enemy's fighting machine in France, Belgium, Holland, and Germany. He also provides a true glimpse of squadron life and the many antics and recreation pursued while living under the strain of combat flying.

Brulle's precision research to place in time the group and squadrons' missions, and relate them to the developing battle situation, are especially perceptive. The tally of the destruction meted out to the enemy, the group and squadrons' losses sustained, and other combat events described come from his attention to technical detail and lend credence to the historical validity of this account.

This is the story by one of our fighter group's pilots who survived and is able to tell how it was as only someone who was there can tell it.

Harold N. Holt
Colonel, USAF (Ret.)
Commander, 366th Fighter Group
World War II

Preface and Acknowledgments

World War II was an unprecedented struggle involving millions of people waging war on land, on and under the sea, and in the air. Many written accounts analyzing these battles are available. Some encompass the macro perspective view on the global tactics and strategy employed by the adversaries. Others cover a micro perspective study of the individual combatants, reflecting on their boredom, terror, savagery, and a host of other adjectives that describe the emotions of combatants. This historically accurate account supplements that storehouse of information by providing an objective examination of the front-line ground-support flight operations. It features the 366th Fighter Group in its attacks against the German war machine, with day-to-day combat missions, which are in turn related to the ongoing ground forces battle. The reader can visualize and tie together the ground assault with the air attack, thus gaining a perception and understanding on how the air attack impacted the overall battle situation. The 366th Fighter Group mission reports chronicle both the damage inflicted on the enemy and our aircraft and pilot losses. Air attack battle tactics, designed to maximize the enemy damage and reduce the losses, provide a unique look on development of the ground-support war. These facets, coupled with the pilots' thoughts, lifestyles, and anecdotes of squadron life, present a vivid picture of front-line air support in Europe during World War II.

Many misconceptions of the ground-support war are evident in many books and articles published, especially those written by front-line soldiers. This stems from the fact that front-line troops are only aware of our presence when we are overhead and actively supporting them. They do not realize that our battle area extends for hundreds of miles on either side and in front of them. Our destroying a supply dump fifty miles into enemy territory may not seem like support, but having the enemy running out of fuel or artillery shells will help them in the end. Many veterans of the European battles whom I have met lack an understanding what air force ground support was all about. Many soldiers thought that we should just loiter above the lines at low level, ready to pounce on any enemy soldier that showed his head. Except under unusual situations, such as when we provided column cover during the dash across France, this would be impractical (and suicidal in our case), since the enemy flak batteries would soon wipe us out. Soldiers also complained that they received no air support because weather grounded us, yet the weather was fine with a few clouds at several thousand feet and they could see at least 10 miles. Some even called us fair-weather flyboys. These implications are quite wrong, and reading this narrative should dispel those and many other notions about the ground-support flyboys' war.

Going to the European Theater of Operations was especially exciting for me. I am a native of Belgium, having immigrated to the United States with my parents in 1929 when I was six years old. The beginning of the war in 1939 severed communication with my Belgium relatives, and I was hoping for a chance to visit them. This eventually happened, and the narrative includes the many adventures on my trips to see them. I was also able to give them some exclusive buzz jobs in my P-47 that resulted in some hilarious and unexpected consequences.

Republic Aviation Corporation designed the P-47 Thunderbolt as a high-altitude escort fighter. It performed that task admirably by breaking the back of the Luftwaffe during the great air battles over Germany in 1943. American pilots flying the P-47 challenged the best of the Luftwaffe fighter force in their Me 109 and FW 190 fighters, and forced them to withdraw. Due to its rugged construction and highly reliable damage-tolerant Pratt and Whitney engine, the "Jug"—as we affectionately called it—then became the foremost ground-support aircraft of World War II. Why was it called a Jug? There is some controversy about that; some say it was shortened from "juggernaut," while others claim it came from its stubby profile being jug-like. No matter—we liked that reliable and sturdy Jug.

Front-line ground support of strafing and dive-bombing was the most hazardous of fighter operations, being equally dangerous to all pilots. Survival was not proportional to pilot skill, and many top-notch pilots in air-to-air combat succumbed to the murderous ground fire while strafing. Gen. James Doolittle, commander of the Eighth Air Force in England, admitted that the loss of experienced air-combat pilots in performing fighter bombing missions was intolerable. The Eighth Air Force abandoned fighter bombing except in rare instances.[1]

When reading the book by Jerry Scutts, *P-47 Thunderbolt Aces of the Eighth Air Force,* one is amazed by how many high-scoring aces finished the war in a POW camp or were killed while strafing.[2] Our fighter-group losses further exemplify the hazardous nature of ground support for the fourteen months we were in combat. During that time our group had seventy-one pilots killed, twenty-four imprisoned, and eleven shot down (who then evaded capture). An additional twenty-six pilots were wounded but managed to bail out or land their aircraft. This is from an average monthly availability of eighty-five pilots, so the group experienced greater than a 100 percent casualty loss. All told, 135 of our aircraft were shot down. The worst month was June 1944 when nineteen pilots and twenty-six aircraft were lost.

I titled this narrative *Angels Zero* after the way we identified a flight altitude. "Angels" expressed the altitude in thousands of feet, such as Angels 15, which meant 15,000 feet. Since altimeters show altitudes above sea level, theoretically, Angels Zero is flight at sea level. However, ground-level flight was always expressed as Angels Zero regardless of the height of the ground above sea level. Some fighter groups chose to add or subtract an arbitrary altitude to the Angels designation to prevent the enemy from knowing our altitude but we very seldom used this subterfuge. Since ground-support missions were, by definition, always conducted near ground level, *Angels Zero* is an appropriate title for this book. Throughout this book, I used both "Angels" and the normal numerical feet designation of altitude and hope it does not cause any confusion.

The events and mission descriptions are based on archive reports augmented with my own and other pilots' recollections on what occurred. The memories of these poignant events are awakened while reading the terse statements of interesting encounters recorded in a diary I kept during the war. Other memories are rekindled by the surviving pictures, combat film, archive records, and the spirited discussions and reminiscences at the reunions of our World War II organization. All these references serve to enrich the narration.

I tried hard to keep the account factual for use as a historical reference. With that in mind I verified the facts through archive records, with the people concerned, and from historical notes and books referenced in the text. So even though this story is written many years after it took place, it is probably as historically correct and true as if it were written when it occurred. A redeeming factor in writing the story in later years is that it allows a retrospective examination of the events that unveils interesting conclusions that might have been left in limbo if written earlier. It additionally allows these events to be placed in context with, and see how they affected, the overall battle situation. People seeing or participating in the same event will usually differ when relating the event. As such, if any of the people that are a part of this story do not agree with the happenings as depicted herein, I most humbly apologize and recommend they also write their story so history will be kept factual.

The 366th Fighter Group featured herein is still an active Air Force combat unit. Today's pilots are older, wiser, and much better trained. However, they are still just as boisterous, cocky, and "hot" as we were. The aircraft, missions, and operations have changed, but the pilots are still the same, the best of American youth.

The first two chapters outline the World War II pilot training program, detailing the accelerated pilot training syllabuses, for both learning to fly and then learning how to fight with the aircraft to become a qualified combat pilot. It is included for completeness, but may be skipped if one is interested in only reading about combat operations. Corroborating references are presented in appended endnotes.

I could not have written this book without the help of many people credited in the text. I do in particular want to thank Klaus Schulz, from Meerbusch, Germany. He is a Hürtgen Forest Battle historian and has guided many veteran units from that battle, both German and American, through the forest. They can now leisurely inspect that dark and dreary place, and reflect on that fierce battle so long ago. He supplied me with enumerable bits of information from both the German and American sides of the battle. These are incorporated in the narrative, making it more interesting and historical.

My most special gratitude goes to Therese Boyd who did an excellent job of getting my book together.

Angels Zero

1.　　　　　　　　　　　　Pilot Training

The Japanese bombing of Pearl Harbor brought America into the war. I was eager to help
defeat the enemy as a fighter pilot, but achieving that required some covert assistance to
bypass the bureaucracy. Wartime flight training is rigorous, demanding, and fun, but the
message was clear: make sure you fly "the Army way."

It was about 0300. The train jerked to another of its frequent stops. Along
with a couple hundred other tired, dirty, and sweaty men, I had been on the
train—my clothes and skin covered in steam-engine soot—for the better part of
a night. We were traveling from Nashville's Army Air Force Classification Center (AAFCC) to Maxwell Field at Montgomery, Alabama. It was my birthday,
31 May 1943. I was twenty years old.

An authoritative voice boomed out, "All right, misters—pop to—everyone
out—on the double." The voice belonged to some guy in an immaculate uniform carrying a large saber. This was my introduction to the upperclassmen who
would rule for the first month of our two-month preflight training. What was I
getting into? I wanted to be a pilot, but how did I get here?

From the time Hitler launched World War II in September 1939 with his invasion of Poland, I eagerly kept abreast of the war news on the radio and newspapers. Especially captivating were the fascinating reports by Edward R. Mur-
row from London. His descriptions of the German air blitzkrieg against England,
and the gallant combat and fighting spirit that the Royal Air Force (RAF)
fighter pilots displayed in thwarting the blitz, were spellbinding. His reports

convinced me that if the United States entered the war I wanted to enlist as a fighter pilot.

In the spring of 1942, with the United States now involved, I explored the requirements for an aviation cadet in the Navy Air Corps. It was no longer necessary to have two years of college in order to qualify for pilot training, so as a high school graduate I could qualify by passing the physical and written examinations. However, I could not meet one stipulation—they required a ten-year U.S. citizenship. I had been a citizen only five years, having immigrated from Belgium to the United States with my parents in 1929. My father became a citizen in 1937 and, since I was then below age sixteen, I automatically became a citizen with him. I asked about obtaining a waiver since we were now at war, but was emphatically told No! I could enlist in the Navy but could not become an officer and pilot. It was one of the lowest points in my life.

Although the U.S. Army Air Corps had the same qualification, I decided I had nothing to lose. (I should really say U.S. Army Air Forces, but it was so common to say "Air Corps," because of the popular Air Corps song, that the correct name of "Air Forces" was hardly ever used.) I secured an interview with the recruiting officer at the U.S. Army Air Corps recruiting center in downtown Chicago. To my surprise, this grizzled-looking second lieutenant with bright shiny bars on his uniform said, after listening to my story, "No problem. Just pass all the tests, then see me." Within a week I had passed the written and physical examinations. As he took the paperwork he said, "It will take a couple of months, but you're in." From his actions and no-nonsense approach to the problem I surmised that he was a former sergeant given a wartime commission.

The next few months went by slowly, but sure enough a letter saying that they had accepted me arrived. I was sworn in the U.S. Army Reserve on Thanksgiving Day, 26 November 1942, and was told to expect the call to active duty in about two months. The call came on 30 January 1943.

Army Basic Training in Miami Beach, Florida, was my first base, quartered in the Edison Hotel on Ninth Street between Ocean Drive and Collins. Introduction to Army life lasted six weeks. The usual initiation to military life occurred. We got jabbed (inoculated) for every conceivable disease, suffered through long days starting at 0500 (0400 when on KP), and had unforgiving corporals and sergeants who kept us hopping until every muscle ached and we wondered why we had been so eager to enlist.

I must inject a personal note. I was nineteen years old, small in stature, but street-smart, so I could handle myself in a crowd or on my own. Both my parents worked outside the home, so I had been taking care of myself since age nine. The street traits I picked up would be invaluable in coping with the people I met and worked with throughout my years of service. At the time I was inducted, however, I was naive and shy concerning girls and sex, not having attended many parties or dances or dated very much. I was a loner, content to go off by myself and do what I wanted, not what was in vogue or supposedly "grown up." Not liking the aftertaste of cigarettes killed my desire for them, so I didn't use them. Vulgar language was unknown at our house so I never acquired that habit.

Surprisingly, I found many friends who shared all or part of my convictions to govern their own lives. I got along well with most others, mainly by not butting into their business and having the discretion to look the other way on occasions. Most of all, I didn't make waves and tried to remain unobtrusive. This trait was extremely helpful in keeping me out of trouble. Sometimes I did not succeed, but then no one is perfect.

At the completion of Army Basic Training in the middle of March, they shipped about 200 of us, all with names beginning with *B,* to a Civilian Training Detachment (CTD) at West Virginia Wesleyan College at Buckhannon, West Virginia. I was the only Brulle, but there were bunches of Browns, Brooks, and several other names. To arrange us in alphabetical order was confusion galore, requiring a name comparison to the third or fourth letters and, for the more common last names, using first and middle names. We were at the CTD to learn basic physics and mechanics, a program initiated when the two-year college requirement was eliminated. For me CTD was a waste of time since I had mastered all the science, physics, chemistry, and related math courses that were available in high school. Fortunately, since they were greatly overcrowded, they shipped the thirty highest scorers of a surprise examination, including me, to the AAFCC.

AAFCC was south of Nashville, where the Sidco Drive industrial area and National Guard Armory now stand. The Battle of Nashville was fought there in December 1864, when Confederate forces under Gen. John B. Hood were soundly defeated by Union forces commanded by Gen. George H. Thomas. AAFCC, a temporary camp of tarpaper-covered barracks and buildings, surrounded by mud or dust (depending on the weather), administered the comprehensive tests and examinations to decide our fitness and the type of aircrew training we would pursue. About 60 percent of the accepted applicants entered pilot training, and 20 percent each were assigned to navigator and bombardier training. They fulfilled my wish by assigning me to pilot training as an air cadet. I was one happy person.

To earn both pilot wings and commission required four two-month periods of training: preflight, primary, basic, and advanced. The first month of each period we endured as underclassmen, having neither privileges nor liberty. On that dark, muggy morning heralding my twentieth birthday, our group quickly experienced the rigid rules we would have to abide by for the next eight months. The four toughest rules were:

1. Attention meant stomach in, kept there by upperclassmen cropping our belts. Our eyes had to be rigid and not wander.
2. Everything had to be done at double time. We had to follow a prescribed well-worn path (called a "rat line") when outside.
3. Shoes had to be shined, with polish, before we fell out for any function—even to just get a raincoat because of a uniform change.
4. The only three answers to questions asked by an upperclassman were: "Yes sir!," "No sir!," and "No excuse, sir!"

The tough rules worked, though. After one month the difference in appearance and bearing between our class and the new incoming class was startling. The gradual day-to-day change was unnoticeable, but very apparent under direct comparison.

The schedule was rigorous, from reveille at 0500 to lights out at 2200. We were perpetually tired. One week we would have schoolwork in the morning and military and physical training (PT) in the afternoon. The schedule reversed each week. Tuesday, Thursday, and Saturday we held formal parade reviews. Saturday evening and Sunday were usually free unless accumulated demerits required a cadet to "walk tours," which meant parading in full dress uniform back and forth in a specific area.

They occasionally called an unpopular somber muster of cadets at 2300 hours to expel cadets who violated the Cadet Code of Honor, usually for cheating or lying. It didn't do anything for our disposition being roused out of a deep sleep to listen to a list of names over the loudspeakers that never again were to be mentioned with reference to the Corps of Cadets.

Schoolwork consisted of subjects such as Morse code, ship and aircraft recognition, military subjects, aerodynamics of flight, navigation, and weather. It was hard to stay awake while sitting in a booth trying to decipher the Morse code dots (dits) and dashes (dahs) coming out of the earphones. Staying awake in a darkened room trying to identify an aircraft or ship projected on a screen for 1/50 of a second was even harder. Although I never used the knowledge, I will never forget the pagoda-type mast structure of a Japanese battleship.

PT consisted mostly of running. We also participated in the bend-and-stretch kind of exercise, but running was the main course. We would run around the country roads surrounding Maxwell Field for one and a half to two hours a few times a week. In between we would have to run the "Burma Road," a trail in the undeveloped region of Maxwell Field. It was over a mile long; each time we ran it, the required completion time was reduced. We hated it, as we hated all the running, but at least this was in the shady and cooler woods.

Our introduction to the altitude chamber came at this time. This was to test our physical suitability and adaptability to high-altitude flying. About twenty of us crowded into a steel tank and they started to evacuate the air. I didn't know what to expect. Going up was simple, as the air easily escapes from the middle ear and sinuses, and I experienced no trouble going to a simulated altitude of 35,000 feet. Coming down was another matter. To get air back into the middle ear requires flexing the Eustachian tubes, usually accomplished by simultaneously yawning and swallowing. Until a person develops the right sequencing of the throat muscles, it is difficult to get air back into the middle ear. I stopped our descent because I couldn't master the technique, but after a few tries I became acclimated and could clear my ears with very little effort.

We weren't sorry to leave Maxwell after those two months of preflight training. We were in the pink of condition, exhibited a confident military bearing, and were all anxious to begin the actual flight training. A nearly 24-hour train trip brought me and about seventy-five other aspiring pilots to Carlstrom Field, near Arcadia on the west side of Florida. Carlstrom Field boasted a distinguished history that dated from World War I.[1] It was just a one-mile-square open range with no runways and poor drainage. After a rain the field hosted many standing puddles of water.

After my upperclassman status the last month of preflight training, it was a rude awakening to be cast again as an underclassman. Fortunately, Embry Riddle Aviation, a civilian contractor, ran Carlstrom, so it was not a rigorous military installation. Even so, the upperclassmen required us again to toe the line and we were restricted to base for the month. All flight instructors were civilian employees of Embry Riddle, but several military check pilots, who had the final word on cadet washout for flying deficiency, conducted periodic flight tests. At Carlstrom we used the Boeing PT-17 Stearman aircraft, an open cockpit biplane trainer with a Continental 220-horsepower (hp) radial engine. The same airframe with a Lycoming engine was designated a PT-13; with a Jacobs engine it was a PT-18. The instructor sat in the front seat and the student in the back. Communications consisted of a gosport tube, rubber tubing connected to ear pads in the student's helmet, and a speaking tube (funnel) for the instructor. It was very unreliable and led to some amusing incidents due to misunderstood instructions.

What a thrill to be up for my first flight! My instructor, H. T. Rimmer, was a wiry, weathered old man (he must have been in his thirties). To the four students assigned to him he was the most important person and best pilot in the world. On my first flight, 2 August 1943, I was filled with apprehension; would I get airsick, how frightening would flying be? I need not have worried; flying was exhilarating and any thought of getting sick disappeared in the slipstream swirling through the open cockpit.

We spent a few minutes getting oriented and recognizing landmarks. Then I heard him say, "Okay, take the controls and follow through on some maneuvers." We practiced climbing turns, medium turns, and glides for thirty-five minutes; it was the most thrilling experience I had ever had. The next day, on only my second ride, he demonstrated two snap rolls and a slow roll. Boy, what fun! Throughout the next week spins, stalls, S-turns, figure-8 turns, and coordination exercises dominated my flights. His expletives, conveyed via the gosport tube, led me to believe I was all thumbs and that there was nothing between my ears except an extension of the gosport tube. Something was going right, however, since in the second week he started instructing me in takeoff and landings. After 8:05 hours dual instruction he climbed out and let me solo for three takeoffs and landings. It was Friday, 13 August 1943.

In those days, prior to soloing a pilot wore his helmet goggles dangling behind his neck. Therefore, when he returned to the main field with his instructor (practice takeoff and landings and first soloing were done at an auxiliary field), the other students watched for the goggles placed on the forehead, which signified soloing. With that signal they dragged the new student pilot out of the aircraft and dunked him in the swimming pool—a most happy occasion.

Over the next week the four of us being instructed by Mr. Rimmer soloed, but a noticeable number of cadets disappeared. The washout rate at this point was about 15–20 percent. In fact, Mr. Rimmer almost eliminated me. For the first three or four solo flights the instructor stands by, watching and supervising. Only after the instructor is satisfied with the student's flying skills will he authorize the checkout of a solo aircraft for an hour of air-work practice. I had completed two supervised solos from auxiliary fields and one from the main field, but was not yet authorized to take up a solo aircraft. A spot landing stage was the next dual-curriculum item, and I just couldn't seem to master it. I was really off that day, and the more he hollered, the more rattled I became. This disgusted Mr. Rimmer, so he grounded me.

After spending an apprehensive couple of days I repeated the spot landing stage with him. This time everything went better and he let me complete four solo spot landings. They were evidently satisfactory, since he then authorized me to take up a solo aircraft. My accumulated flying time stood at 13.5 hours at this milestone. I really practiced while solo, doing stalls, turns, coordination exercises, and spins. I was surprised to notice the aircraft spins differently without the instructor in front because the center of gravity is farther aft.

From this point on, flight instruction concentrated on precision and smooth flying. When the instructor said to level off at 1,500 feet, he meant exactly 1,500 feet. The student had to keep his head on a swivel and his sight outside the cockpit. Woe to the student who didn't see another aircraft close by, especially if it was behind him. This was an extremely frustrating flying phase—we had to watch our altitude, heading, airspeed, and rpm, and keep our heads moving. Mr. Rimmer stressed that watching everything would have to become instinctive as it was the key to survival in combat. This took a lot of concentration and hard work.

All flying objects in the atmosphere will experience wind drift. Pilots must gauge the wind-drift magnitude and correct for it when navigating cross country, bombing, firing guns, and landing. To instill a perception of wind effect the flight instructors made us fly around a rectangular field, tracing a track on the ground parallel to and equal distance from all four sides. Achieving this required that we "crab"—pointing the aircraft slightly up wind—to negate the wind drift. Performing S-turns across a road running crosswind, where the up- and down-wind S-turn were identical, served the same purpose.

I can still hear Mr. Rimmer bellowing in the gosport, "Stay coordinated, watch your altitude, you're drifting—can't you see—correct your drift!" It was a nerve-wracking experience. After 22 hours of flying, my next milestone—an Army check ride with Lieutenant Frisbee—rolled around.[2] I must have succeeded since I was continued in the program.

New maneuvers introduced after that included the lazy-8, chandelle, and pylon-8. Pylon-8s meant making an eight-turn over the ground while maintaining an altitude and airspeed combination that allowed the wing to aim at alternating spots on the ground, all while maintaining coordinated flight. Theoretically, it can be done; actually, it is a most difficult maneuver.

Although flying was the main part of our training, ground school and PT were not neglected. Ground school continued Morse code and aircraft and ship recognition, and introduced some new ones. One new subject was map reading (although we knew not to call it a map—it was a chart). We learned to lay out a course accounting for magnetic variation and deviation, and how to correct the compass heading and ground speed for wind using the E6B computer. The E6B was a circular slide-rule device with a sliding plastic plate on which we could draw our flight and wind vectors.

Our introduction to instrument flying began in ground school with the Link Trainer, a box with a hinged cover mounted on a pedestal that allowed a limited bank and pitch, and yawed 360 degrees. Some crude controls, consisting of a stick and rudder, and some flight instruments were mounted inside. The controls operated pneumatic valves that controlled the bank, pitch, and yaw. It was—at best—a crude simulation of an aircraft, but it did teach the fundamentals of instrument flying. When flying in a cloud, without reference to a horizon, a pilot cannot distinguish up from down and has to depend on instruments. This was difficult to believe and required proof.

Most of our aircraft had no flight instruments (artificial horizon and directional gyro) installed, and even if they did, we were not familiar with their use. One afternoon, with lazy, puffy clouds in the sky, I flew well away from the local field area and into the clouds. The first thing I noticed was that it was bumpy and cooler in the clouds. I could keep the aircraft reasonably straight and level for the one minute I was in the clouds, but when I tried to do a turn, I became completely disoriented and came out the bottom almost upside down. This convinced me and I needed no further encouragement to study and excel in instrument flying.

After a 45-hour Army pilot check ride, we entered the fun phase of flying—acrobatics. Instructions on performing the loop, half roll, slow roll, snap roll, and Immelmann were introduced in rapid order. These precision acrobatics were performed smoothly and gracefully. Snap rolls had to be stopped when the aircraft was exactly level. An Immelmann gave exactly a 180-degree change in direction, and during a slow roll the nose was kept on a point. Snap rolls to the right were easy since they required pulling on the stick to get it to the right rear position. A snap roll to the left required a push on the stick to an awkward left rear position, and it is harder to push than pull. The muscles PT developed over the past several months were put to work. After an hour of acrobatics we were well aware of the fatigue and ache in our right-arm muscles.

When primary training ended, we felt like the hottest pilots in the world with all of 65 hours flying time. The last flight in primary was a dual flight with the instructor in the rear. Flying from the front cockpit had a totally different perspective, which really affected me. From the front seat the pilot cannot use the upper wing as a reference plane, and that troubled me when doing some maneuvers. It was a harbinger of the future when I transitioned to the monoplane BT-13 at basic.

A two-day, one-night train ride brought us to Courtland Army Air Field, Courtland, Alabama, on 3 October 1943. After the relatively easy life at the civilian primary training school it was a shock to again come under tight military control. Hat bands were returned, which took away our "hot pilot" look, and shoes and belt buckles were polished again.

Courtland Army Air Base was a typical World War II–constructed field, with four concrete runways lined up with the cardinal compass directions (still there in 1986). Our quarters were the same type of tarpaper barracks we had at Nashville, but instead of an open barracks there were twelve roomettes, six on each side of the barracks, each housing four cadets. Each roomette had a study area about 10 feet by 20 feet and two bedrooms about 10 feet square. A small coal-fired stove heated each roomette. They were dingy and dark but clean—boy, were they clean. The strict enforcers were the second-lieutenant tactical officers stuck in the thankless job of instilling a military bearing on a bunch of couldn't-care-less cadets. We all took our turn washing windows, scrubbing floors, and polishing the brass in the separate latrine shack that served about eight barracks.

We continued the same alternating weekly schedule, one week flying in the morning with ground school and PT in the afternoon, followed by the reverse schedule the next week. We met our military pilot instructors and started flying on 5 October using the Vultee BT-13 and BT-15 aircraft. They used the same airframe with the BT-13 having a Pratt and Whitney air-cooled radial engine rated at 450 hp, and the BT-15 a Wright radial engine rated at 420 hp.

The BT-13/15 had a two-pitch propeller; low pitch was used for takeoff and high for general flying. Also installed were manually controlled wing flaps, cranked down at the rate of 2 degrees per turn, or thirty turns for a full 60 degrees of flaps. Elevator and rudder trim tab controls made flying easier, but they were very sensitive and required gentle application. A manually tuned low-frequency radio, having a range of about ten miles if tuned correctly, kept us in contact with the tower. The student flew from the front seat and he could easily hear his instructor in the back, and talk back if he wanted, through an intercom system. My instructor was Lt. Vincent Whibbs; however, different instructors conducted the various flight phases. Lieutenant Whibbs acted as the main instructor when a student had questions or problems.

My first ride in basic was spent getting used to flying without having a top wing to keep the aircraft oriented for level flight. During the second flight we started practicing stalls that confirmed the aircraft's nickname, "The Vultee Vibrator," because it shook so violently during a stall. The airplane wasn't too difficult to fly but keeping all the procedures straight became a chore. Rolling down flaps when they should be rolled up or vice versa, and turning the trim tabs the wrong way were common beginner's mistakes. Getting used to watching the airspeed on landing was also hard. Flying the Stearman in primary, a student could gauge the correct nose-down gliding attitude by keeping the upper wing on the horizon. From the vibration tone of the bracing wires, a student knew he was in the landing airspeed groove. With the BT-13/15 a student had to depend on the airspeed and acquire the habit of constantly checking it. After eight hours of dual instruction I soloed the BT-13/15. It was a great thrill to be flying solo again, but certainly not as eventful as the first solo flight.

A few cadets washed out during this time because they just couldn't make the transition. Strange, but a few cadets also quit; they just didn't want to fly anymore. One of my roommates quit. He claimed he was always getting a headache flying, but I believe it was just an excuse. He eagerly accepted a transfer to the Army Air Force mechanic training program. I was still as eager as could be—I wanted to be a fighter pilot.

After soloing and completing a few landing stages, we began instrument flight training. For those lessons a canvas hood covered the rear cockpit and we flew entirely by use of flight instruments, from takeoff to being guided down to flare out for landing by the instructor. We kept up with the other flying skills and learned a few new ones, but about every other dual flight was instrument training. The flight instruments available included an artificial horizon, directional gyro, and a turn-and-bank indicator. The turn-and-bank indicator was a gyro-driven needle indicator showing the rate of turn; a ball in a curved glass tube indicated coordinated flight or how good the turn was. A one-needle-width turn, defined as the standard rate, gave a three degrees-per-second turn rate. Also classed as flight instruments were the magnetic compass, airspeed indicator, altimeter, and rate-of-climb indicator.

Instrument flight instruction emphasized the use of the basic flight instrument group. This consisted of the turn-and-bank indicator, airspeed, altimeter, and compass. The reason for emphasizing basic flight-instrument flying was that the directional gyro and artificial horizon would tumble and become useless if a pilot exceeded a bank angle of 60 degrees. He would then be forced to rely on just the basic group to regain straight and level flight by centering the needle and ball and stabilizing the airspeed.

In a turn the magnetic compass behaved erratically, leading or lagging the actual direction by as much as 30 degrees. To roll out on a specified direction meant it was necessary to lead or lag the compass indication by an amount that depended on the turn direction and heading. I still recall the instructor's admonishments to "watch that damn needle," "center the ball," "correct your airspeed." The instructors made us practice combination maneuvers, where we made turns while changing airspeed or altitude, and we completed combination maneuvers in specific times. Also practiced was recovery from unusual positions. The instructor would put the aircraft in a steep climbing turn, tight spiral, or even upside-down from which we had to recover back to straight and level flight using only the basic flight instruments. Of all the flight training, instrument flying was by far the most fatiguing of all. There was no time to relax and we had to stay on top of everything or our aircraft would get away from us.

Also introduced was three-aircraft formation flying. This lasted a whole flying period of one hour, from takeoff to landing. It was not particularly hard except we had to keep our eyes on the lead aircraft and continuously make small throttle adjustments. Making steep turns in formation made me quite apprehensive, especially when I was the outside or upper aircraft in a flight of three in a vee formation. I had a tendency to hold top rudder and cross control, being fearful that I was going to slide down into the lead aircraft. This angered my instructor immensely and earned me a failing grade, or a pink slip, as we called it. He emphasized that the aircraft must always be flown coordinated with the ball in the center to perform smooth maneuvers. Holding top rudder could cause the aircraft to snap into a spin, causing a catastrophe. Coordinated flight in formation acrobatics was hard for me to master.

Another new flight phase introduced was night flying. My first night takeoff completely disoriented me. Fortunately an instructor was in the back seat to help me along. As soon as we took off, the ground and the lights disappeared, and darkness enveloped the aircraft. I realized why the instructor insisted that we pass a blindfold cockpit check, as the only lights in the cockpit were some dull fluorescent lights that just lit up the radium dial tips of the instruments. Instinctively we had to know where the instruments, switches, and controls were since we could barely see them.

They assigned all the night-flying aircraft orbit zones. North-south and east-west compass bearings bisected the field flying area into four quadrants. On takeoff they assigned a particular quadrant and altitude where we would orbit in a right-hand pattern. After takeoff we would clear the field area and climb to the assigned altitude and orbiting quadrant. We started orbiting at 5,000 to 6,000 feet altitude. Gradually we would be assigned lower orbiting altitudes at 500-foot increments. At 2,500 feet a pilot was then low man in the stack and cleared to enter the traffic pattern and shoot touch-and-go landings.

My initial disorientation in night flying disappeared and after about 45 minutes of flying I commenced landing practice. For these first landings a bank of flood lights lit up the runway. Landing was not at all difficult. When the aircraft landed and was under control, a runway control instructor would flash a green light. This cleared the pilot to take off to make another circuit and landing. After landing, but before the rolling takeoff, a pilot had to perform three very important procedures: push the propeller control forward to low pitch, roll up the flaps, and center the trim tabs. I experienced no problems shooting three dual and then six solo night landings.

Because of weather and other scheduled events, two weeks elapsed before they again scheduled me for solo night flying. After takeoff and orbiting in my designated quadrant for about an hour, they called me to shoot a series of fifteen landings. On my first landing the cadet following me was quite close, and as soon as I landed they flashed me the green light to take off again. The blinking green light momentarily confused me and I forgot to center my trim tabs. I knew only two of the three post-landing procedures were completed, but I just couldn't think of the third. The runway control instructor was furiously blinking that green light to get going, so I applied power and took off. Fortunately, the runway control instructor recognized that I was climbing too steeply because the elevator trim was rolled back for landing. When I heard on my radio, "Watch a stabilizer stall," I knew it was directed at me and took immediate action to prevent a stall and possible spin. I believe that was the closest I ever came to being killed while flying (excluding combat flying, of course). It was a lesson well learned which I would remember years later when I was a flight instructor. Prior to letting my students go solo to practice any recently learned maneuver, we would go over the procedures to refresh their memories.

Our instructors also stressed cross-country flying to sharpen our navigation skills. The BT-13/15 range was about 1,000 miles, so they scheduled several long cross-country flights. I remember one flight we took from Courtland to Smithville, Tennessee, to Crossville, Tennessee, and back to Courtland. This flight took us quite close to a prohibited flyover area near Knoxville, Tennessee (now known as Oak Ridge). They warned us not to stray into that area or we would be shot down with no questions asked. We didn't know or concern ourselves on what was there, but just heeded the warning.

Just prior to finishing basic training we were scheduled for a night cross-country. They divided the class into two sections of about 150 cadets, each to fly succeeding nights. I was scheduled for the second night. Just after the cadets took off, a deep haze descended over the area. Nineteen cadets got lost, and eight of them crashed and were killed. Aircraft were scattered at airports all over the southeast. Maxwell Field authorities, as headquarters of the Eastern Training Command, investigated the disaster and printed the results in a Montgomery newspaper article. The investigation board concluded that the main cause was the cadets' "failure to abide by regulations." In my opinion it was a whitewash. The exigency of war required the commander to make a decision between completing flying requirements and safety. Safety lost. The second night cross-country was canceled, delaying my participation in a night cross-country until I reached advanced flying school.

I was one happy cadet when told I was selected for single-engine advanced flight training. My wish to be a fighter pilot was one step closer. About seventy-five aspiring fighter pilots arrived at Craig Field, located at Selma, Alabama, on 6 December 1943. A flu-like infection temporarily grounded me, postponing my start of advanced flying of the North American AT-6 until 15 December. Boy, it was a sweet airplane. The only bad feature was its narrow landing gear, which made it tricky to land. A Pratt and Whitney 600-hp air-cooled radial engine powered it through a constant speed propeller, giving it a maximum level-flight speed over 200 mph. It sported hydraulic-operated wing flaps and a retractable landing gear. Even built in were provisions for the installation of two

.30-caliber machine guns, one mounted on the right side of the cowling shooting through the propeller and another in the right wing. After five hours of dual instruction and learning all the procedures (the hardest part), I was cleared for solo.

The first part of advanced stressed formation flying, where we each learned to lead a three-aircraft flight in precision acrobatic formation maneuvers. Also stressed was instrument flying, since graduation required passing the 50-3 instrument check (50-3 referred to the instrument flying regulation). My diligence in practicing instrument flying bore dividends as I completed the 50-3 check three weeks before graduation. This test included a complete flight under the hood from an instrument takeoff, a check on basic instrument techniques, and a radio-range orientation and low approach to the field. It was a great feeling when the instructor asked me to pop the hood and I saw the field right ahead of me. Several students were held back for the next class because they were unable to achieve the necessary proficiency. Several other unlucky ones were washed out.

The latter part of advanced was spent in day, night, and instrument cross-country flying, and simulated combat practice against our instructor. He would let us get on his tail and then try to shake us off by violent maneuvers of all kinds, called a "rat race." At first he was usually successful, but as we got better he had to give up. We checked out in ground gunnery techniques and tested low-altitude navigation procedures. A high-altitude formation flight to 21,000 feet indoctrinated us in the routine of flying an aircraft using oxygen.

On a cold January day we traveled 50 miles in a truck to Maxwell Field for another altitude chamber check. Again I experienced a problem at a simulated altitude of 35,000 feet; this time I got an excruciating toothache. They sent me to the dentist and, after taking an x-ray, he pulled the tooth. A wisdom tooth was impinging on a sinus cavity, and the pressure difference ascending to a high altitude irritated the tooth nerve. It was a miserable ride back to Craig in that cold truck.

Ground school continued many of the same subjects we had been studying since preflight. Graduation required passing Morse code by receiving 30 words per minute sent via the radio, and six words per minute sent via a light signal. Some fellows needed extra code classes, conducted in the evening, to pass. A new subject introduced was skeet shooting to practice leading a moving target. This was great fun, but competing against the Southern hunters in the group was futile; they outshot us all.

Finally the big day arrived—8 February 1944. We were roused as cadets at 0500 and marched to the theater. One hundred sixty cadets took the oath of office and were sworn in as second lieutenants in the Army of the United States. They then gave us pilot rating orders that allowed us to wear the coveted silver pilot wings. The ceremony took only ten minutes, after which we donned our officer's uniforms and ate our last breakfast in the cadet mess. To get my silver wings took 208.5 hours of flying, about average for the group.

Half of us left for a ten-day leave and the other half stayed at Craig to check out in the Curtiss P-40 fighter. They would go on leave when we returned to get our P-40 checkout. This was my first leave since entering the Army a little over a year ago. Boy, were my parents proud. Dressed in my new officer's uniform and pilot wings I was the star attraction in the neighborhood and found out the power of a snappy uniform. Neighborhood girls who would have nothing to do with me before now showed an interest. While I was on leave they drafted my brother, Albert, and I drove him to the Selective Service reception center to start his Navy duty.

Checkout in the P-40 started by shooting about twenty landings from the back seat of an AT-6 to get acclimated to the restricted visibility of the long P-40 nose in landing attitude. After studying the tech orders and pilot manual, and getting the usual blindfold cockpit check, they judged us ready to solo the P-40. The instructor helped start the engine, gave a good-luck handshake, and said, "Go."

The P-40 was still a front-line fighter but newer aircraft were rapidly replacing it. The P-40B and C series were called the "Tomahawk," the P-40D and E series the "Kittyhawk" and the P-40F series the "Warhawk." The Flying Tigers made the P-40 famous early in the war battling the Japanese in Burma and China. We flew the P-40F aircraft powered by a Packard Rolls-Royce Merlin, a twelve-cylinder vee in-line liquid-cooled engine generating 1,300 hp. It had a top speed of more than 370 mph. It was a formidable aircraft to fly solo the first time, especially with only 220 hours total flying time.

The main runway at Craig Field was about 300 feet wide, easily accommodating three-aircraft formation takeoff, and 4,500 feet long. For my first P-40 takeoff I used every bit of runway—from side to side and the total length. They sternly warned us that the P-40, because of its long nose and powerful engine, developed a large torque (left-turning tendency) on takeoff. Unfortunately, I neglected to anticipate the magnitude and did not use enough right rudder when advancing the throttle for takeoff and I violently swerved into a zig-zag track on the runway. Once I finally got control of its zig-zag track, I took off. After practicing a few stalls and simulated landings, and acquiring a feel of the aircraft, I landed safely. I must confess I shook like a leaf in a breeze after I was down. Quickly acclimating to the task, I was more composed on succeeding flights. I did not get by unscathed, though, managing a wing scraping on landing that tore a one-inch gash in the tip. In all, it was an exhilarating ten hours of P-40 flying.

On 10 March they bussed us to Auxiliary Field No. 6, Eglin Field, Florida, for gunnery training. It was back to flying the AT-6 to qualify in both ground and aerial gunnery using the .30-caliber machine gun mounted on the cowling. Firing the gun the first time was a revealing surprise; the control stick didn't shake as portrayed in the movies. We shot at a ground target that was about five feet square. In aerial gunnery we shot at a towed target that was about four feet wide by 30 feet long. Each cadet, in a flight of four all shooting at the same target, had a different color round loaded. On penetrating the target the bullet left a color smudge around the hole. A pilot's number of hits, from the 200 rounds loaded, coupled with standardized gunnery patterns and gun camera film, allowed analysis of our flying and gunnery mistakes. They required gunnery qualification, so we kept practicing until we qualified. I do not remember what qualification score was required, but my diary notes that I qualified by shooting a 46 percent in ground gunnery and a 40 percent in aerial gunnery.

2. Operational Fighter Training

Learning to fly was only part of the training. It was now necessary to learn how to fight with America's front-line fighter and finally become a "fighter pilot." Anticipation was accompanied with nervous excitement.

On our return to Craig Field after completing gunnery training at Eglin, most of us received orders to report to Richmond Army Air Base, Virginia. Richmond was the Eastern Training Command headquarters for fighter-pilot training. For traveling to Richmond, five of us pooled our money and bought a 1935 Plymouth sedan. The starter wouldn't always work, which required some pushing, and we had to stop a small gas-tank leak by rubbing soap on the hole, but other than that it was road-worthy. Although we acquired the necessary gasoline ration coupons for the trip, a couple of the fellows were adept operators and they procured gas most of the time without having to use coupons. It took four days to get to Richmond, having to stop early each day at a large city so my fellow travelers could pursue the local belles for the evening. I didn't care for their carousing lifestyle, so when we reached Richmond I sold my share of the car and parted company.

In Richmond we received orders assigning us to the Operational Training Unit (OTU) at Bradley Field, Windsor Locks, Connecticut. At Bradley we were going to learn the fighter-pilot trade while flying the best and most versatile American fighter, the Republic P-47 Thunderbolt. A friend invited me to drive to Bradley with him in his car. On the way we stopped in Washington, D.C., and

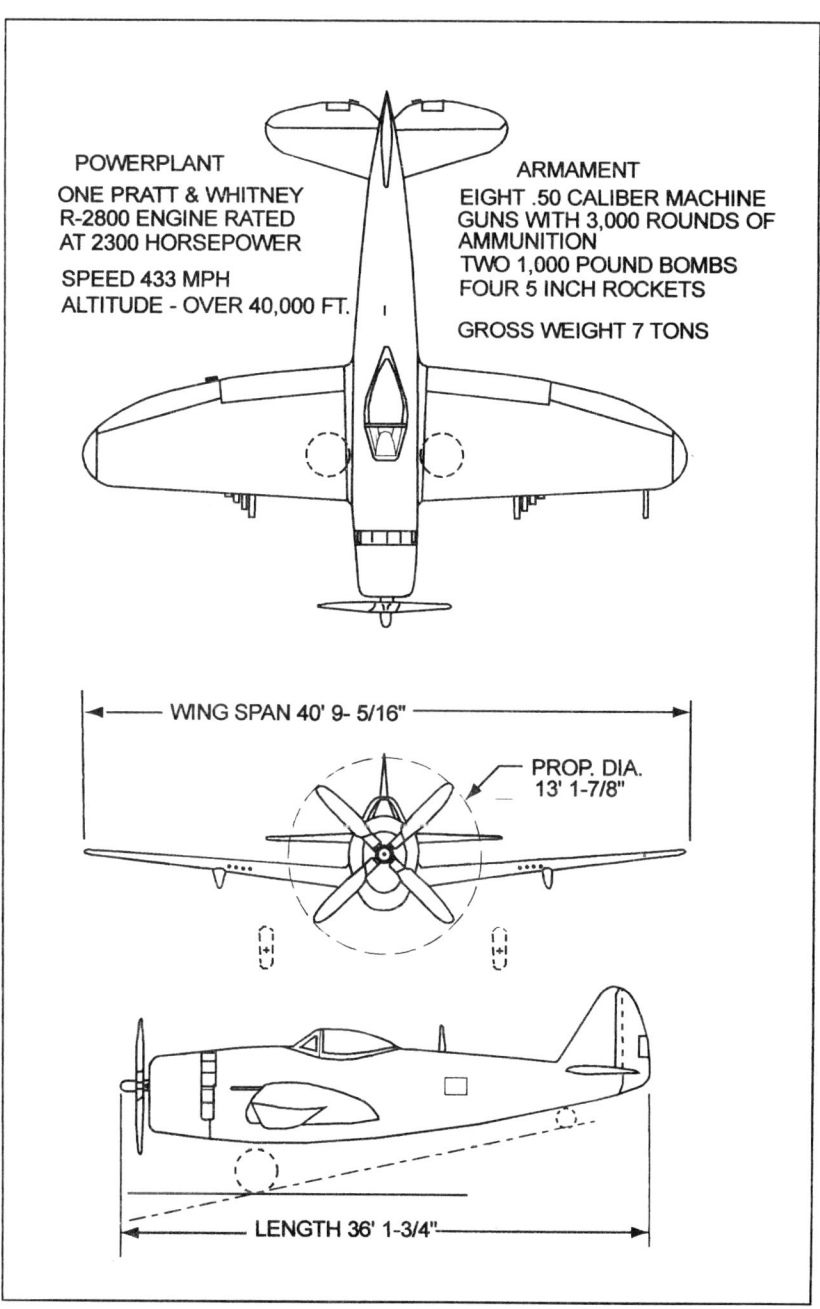

POWERPLANT

ONE PRATT & WHITNEY
R-2800 ENGINE RATED
AT 2300 HORSEPOWER

SPEED 433 MPH
ALTITUDE - OVER 40,000 FT.

ARMAMENT

EIGHT .50 CALIBER MACHINE
GUNS WITH 3,000 ROUNDS OF
AMMUNITION
TWO 1,000 POUND BOMBS
FOUR 5 INCH ROCKETS

GROSS WEIGHT 7 TONS

WING SPAN 40' 9- 5/16"

PROP. DIA.
13' 1-7/8"

LENGTH 36' 1-3/4"

Republic P-47D Thunderbolt

New York City. It was my first visit to Washington and the imposing government buildings overwhelmed me. While staying in New York we went to the top of the Empire State Building. Obviously, height doesn't bother me flying, but I don't like being in high buildings so I was quite uncomfortable on top. Two weeks later I flew over the Empire State Building, and at 10,000 feet I rolled over and looked down. I cannot resolve my anxiety when looking down from the top of a high building, but I have no fear at 10,000 feet, flying upside-down, looking at the same building.

Checkout in the P-47 followed the same procedure we went through for the P-40: read the tech orders, become familiar with the cockpit, and get the usual blindfold cockpit check and instructor help in starting the engine. The P-47 was the largest single-seat fighter in World War II. Yet it was the only airplane, up to that point, that I could adjust the seat and controls to fit my small stature without having to use the bulky leather Air Force cushions. A Pratt and Whitney R-2800, 18-cylinder air-cooled radial engine, rated at 2,000 hp, propelled the P-47 to more than 400 mph. With an exhaust-driven turbo supercharger installed, the aircraft could reach altitudes in excess of 40,000 feet. In training we could not utilize its full capability because we used 90-octane fuel instead of the design specification octane value of 100/130. It is interesting that a new airplane cost about $90,000 in 1942, which was a lot of money then.

Recalling the difficulty torque caused me on my first P-40 takeoff, I was determined not to repeat the experience. I needn't have worried. The P-47's tail wheel lock kept the aircraft rolling straight down the runway during takeoff. After getting airborne and retracting the gear, I started a turn to circle the field but, to my surprise, couldn't find it. The Bradley Field runways were green, with farm roads painted on them leading to dummy farm buildings built between the runways. Barracks and other buildings were also camouflaged. From the ground the camouflage appeared ridiculous, but from the air it was good. I spent five minutes looking before I detected the field. Camouflage does work.

After flying for about 45 minutes, doing stalls and simulated landings to develop the feel of the aircraft, I made a fighter landing pattern approach and peel-off. Peel-off was performed about a third of the way down the runway at an airspeed of 200 mph and 500 feet high, and consisted of a 180-degree turning pull-up to 1,000 feet on the downwind leg. As a pilot gained experience, he would show off by reducing the peel-off height and increasing the airspeed until he was flying 300 mph at 50 feet.

A flight of four in formation would approach in echelon left or right, depending on peel-off direction, and fan out to get landing spacing during peel-off. The plan is to get four aircraft on the runway, one pulling off, one in the landing roll, one just touching down, and the last one on landing flare-out. Peel-off should be smartly performed so that power is not required, except a burst to clear the engine, until touchdown. As the airspeed drops below 180 mph on peel-off, the gear is lowered and engine power and the glide angle adjusted to turn on base leg at 800 feet at 150 mph. The final approach turn is made at 500 feet with full flaps coming down at an airspeed of 130 mph. Final approach airspeed is 120 mph and touchdown is at about 100 mph.

For our first flight we were supposed to make one approach and then add power to go around for another approach and landing. My first approach was right in the groove. I said, "The heck with it," and landed with no difficulty. Trouble started as I turned off the runway to taxi back to the ramp. My knees were shaking so much from the excitement and stress on surviving my first flight that I couldn't taxi the aircraft. I pulled off the side of the taxiway, shut off the engine, and started walking the quarter mile back to the operations area. About halfway there I met the crew chief walking toward me. I told him the aircraft was okay and he should taxi it back. After drinking a cup of coffee and laughing about it with my instructor, I went up again and experienced no further problems. My total flying time was 230 hours. I spent the next several hours exploring the P-47 flying characteristics in dives and zooms, acrobatics and formation flying. Notes in my diary after six hours of P-47 flying say, "Goes down like a rock when put the nose down. . . . Controls are very sensitive. . . . Getting to like the aircraft okay."

My first high-altitude formation flight was a fiasco; I couldn't stay in formation at only 23,000 feet. It was my first opportunity to employ the turbo-supercharger and I didn't like it at all. The turbo control was extremely sensitive, causing the engine to surge intermittently. Discussions with the other pilots indicated they didn't have any problems and liked the turbo control. On a high-altitude formation flight the next day, the instructor happened to be flying the aircraft I had flown. At 28,000 feet we aborted the mission because the instructor was experiencing turbo problems. This time I had no trouble staying in formation. The turbo control worked beautifully and engine power control was smooth and positive. I was glad to find out it was a mechanical problem that plagued me the first time at high altitude, but I was chagrined that I didn't recognize the malfunction.

A note on high-altitude flying. It is very cold at high altitudes; in fact, the temperature decreases about 3.5 degrees Fahrenheit per 1,000 feet, so at 35,000 feet the temperature is –65 degrees Fahrenheit. The unpressurized cockpit was cold, so when we were scheduled for a high-altitude mission we dressed in winter flying gear. With temperatures in the 80s on the ground, we were sweating profusely dressed in our winter gear, before even getting in the aircraft. The sweat did not evaporate and we became clammy and cold. The cockpit had an exhaust gas air heater, but it was inefficient and it couldn't even keep our feet warm, much less warm the cockpit. I didn't care for high-altitude flying, although the view was spectacular.

P-47 training progressed rapidly with high-altitude acrobatics and simulated dogfights. Lowering the seat down and slouching over allowed us to simulate instrument flying. For these flights the wingman acted as a safety pilot. It was a crude simulation since we couldn't help but catch glimpses of the sky or ground, but it did instill confidence that the P-47 was stable and reasonably easy to fly on instruments.

A P-47 diving near vertical from over 30,000 feet can enter a compressibility dive, causing the pilot to lose control. Shock waves forming over the wing alter the aerodynamic air flow, which changes the control forces that effectively freeze the controls, leading to an uncontrolled vertical dive. In ground school we discussed the characteristics of this dive and found that we have only one method of recovery; we must let the aircraft descend to warmer air, to about 15,000 feet, where the shock waves disappear and we regain control for pullout. To explore this phenomenon, an instructor led us into a near vertical dive at 33,000 feet. Our instructions were to gently pull out the instant we felt the aircraft and stick start to shudder, indicating compressibility onset. I felt the buffet about 28,000 feet and gently reduced dive angle to prevent compressibility. It was scary but an essential part of training.[1]

An exhilarating low-altitude navigation flight nearly ended my flying career. On a four-aircraft low-altitude formation flight, each of us took a turn leading the flight for 50 to 75 miles over the Connecticut, New York, and Massachusetts countryside. Roaring over the ground at 200 mph at Angels Zero was really exciting. We saw startled people look up at us. Some even recovered enough to wave. The spectacle so engrossed me that I completely forgot to check my fuel. It was standard operating procedure (SOP) to take off on the 205-gallon main tank (increased on later-model aircraft to 270 gallons) and, when airborne, switch to the 100-gallon auxiliary tank. This tank lasted anywhere from 45 minutes to an hour or more depending on the power setting. A full auxiliary tank degraded the aircraft dynamic stability, so it was emptied as soon as possible. In the excitement of the flight I let the tank run dry and the engine quit. Fortunately the engine caught immediately as I switched tanks. Letting a tank run dry at a high altitude is no sweat; letting it run dry on the deck (ground level) is a situation I never want to experience again. An indelible lesson ingrained in my memory: flying continuously requires 100 percent concentration.

Another lesson learned during that low-level cross-country was that it is difficult to navigate accurately. When I led the flight I was supposed to intercept a small town on the Hudson River and then turn north. I knew I couldn't miss the river, but when I reached it we were several miles south of the town. Flying low takes more flight planning in order to mark clearly the prominent checkpoints that will be visible at low level. These are different from those usually selected for a normal height flight. Also, maintaining a desired ground track while weaving around high obstacles and hills is a difficult navigation problem. Flying on the deck over the Hudson River we came to a bridge spanning the river (I can't recall exactly where). I was leading and for a few moments entertained the notion to fly under it, but demurred since a couple of fellows had recently violated flying regulations and found themselves transferred to the infantry.

While flying we occasionally met some Marine Corps pilots flying F4U Corsairs who were training at Providence, Rhode Island. This was usually *raison de plus* to engage in a dogfight. The F4U used the same engine as the P-47, yet we would usually find ourselves being clobbered. They could climb and turn better, and all we could do was use our superior roll rate to prevent them from getting a good bead on us. My new roommate, Chuck Bennett (Charles E. Bennett from Janesville, Wisconsin), and I spent a weekend in Boston and met several Marine pilots training at Providence. We had a few drinks together and discussed our air encounters. We found that the Marines were using specification 100/130 octane fuel in training. To save 100/130 octane fuel for overseas use we used 90 octane in training. This limited the maximum power we could use, and the power differential made the Corsair more agile. We didn't feel so bad after that when they dominated the mock air battles.

After amassing 43 hours of P-47 flying they crammed fifteen of us in a Lockheed-Vega Ventura and flew us to Suffolk Army Air Base on Long Island for gunnery practice. We conducted ground gunnery on a range established a few miles from the air base in a (at that time) sparsely settled region of Long Island. Aerial gunnery practice was conducted flying along the Long Island coastline and firing out toward the Atlantic Ocean. For unknown reasons, I just couldn't get in the firing groove with a P-47 and barely qualified in aerial gunnery. I did well in dive-bombing exercises using 100-pound practice bombs, probably because I bored in low so I couldn't miss. This had consequences later in combat when twice I came home with bomb fragments embedded in the underside of my aircraft because I released my bombs too low.

We took turns towing the aerial gunnery target with a stripped down P-47 (guns and armor plate removed), and only the main tank filled with specification high-octane fuel. The ability to use full military power coupled with the light weight created the impression that the aircraft literally jumped off the runway. The expedited takeoff reduced the frequency of having a broken tow line because the target snagged on a crack in the runway. This led to a spirited competition between us to see who could be airborne in the shortest distance and pull up the steepest to get the target off the runway. Some takeoffs bordered on recklessness but no incidents occurred.

A surprise visitor woke me up on my twenty-first birthday, 31 May. It was my brother Albert, whom I had brought to the draft board in February while home on leave. They drafted him into the Navy. After only four months he was already a veteran of several Atlantic convoy crossings in a destroyer escort (DE). This ship was docked in Boston for installation of new equipment and he used the time to visit me. I arranged for his first airplane ride in a BT-15 used for pilot instrument checks and utility transportation. We flew around Long Island and did some acrobatics. He thought it was great but confessed he felt safer aboard his DE.

Once when returning from an aerial gunnery mission we observed several destroyers and destroyer escorts engaged in maneuvering exercises about 20 miles off the coast. This was too good an opportunity for a buzz job to ignore. For the next fifteen minutes we simulated dive- and skip-bombing and strafing attacks on the flotilla. They appeared to get into the spirit of the moment by maneuvering around. I'm sure the authorities did not condone this, but we never heard any repercussions about our actions.

On 2 June we were back at Bradley Field to complete our OTU training. During the last rush to complete all requirements the base loudspeakers blared out the news about D-day in Europe. By 8 June all training was completed, including three hours of night flying. By 10 June we were back in Richmond and received orders for shipment to England. By 16 June we were at the port of embarkation, Camp Kilmer, New Jersey, located about 10 miles north of New Brunswick. We received another round of inoculations and checked out our gas masks by going through a tear gas–filled room, and then going through it again without our gas mask.

On 22 June they herded us aboard the French liner *Louis Pasteur,* manned by Englishmen, and slipped past the Statue of Liberty on the way to Liverpool, England. Aboard the ship were about 120 fighter pilots, twenty nurses, an artillery battalion, and several other small units. Our unescorted voyage across the Atlantic took seven days. Spirited discussions with the artillery officers — mostly on which ground-support role is better, aircraft dive-bombing and strafing or artillery — enlivened the crossing. We would soon find out about our individual limitations but, as we learned to cooperate with the infantry and armored units, we would become an unbeatable team.

Our first base was Atcham Field near Schrewsberry in Wales. Atcham was a typical English wartime air station, having Nissen huts and a spread-out taxiway system for the dispersed aircraft. They issued bikes for transportation, and promptly we experienced a rash of skinned elbows and knees. We learned the hard way that it was more difficult to bike than fly in a tight formation.

Atcham was the final training base before assignment to a combat unit. The instructors were combat pilots on their way home for a thirty-day leave. While waiting for transportation back to the United States, they instilled the final rudiments of combat flying on a hot-shot bunch of neophytes. Four of us drew a captain flight instructor who had completed his tour with the 56th Fighter Group (I cannot recall his name). He related some of his combat escapades and then warned us to be prepared to fly like we never flew before.

For our first flight our instructions were to look over the area and get oriented with respect to the prominent landmarks. The instructions for the next flight were extraordinary; we were to do everything they told us not to do in training. Stall it going straight up, spin it, and in general kick it around to get the feel of it under all flight conditions. This was quite a revelation to us. Doing as ordered I found that the P-47 was a very forgiving aircraft. It could complete a vertical wing over at 50 mph. An extended spin was not very violent and recovered in about a turn. An important fact acquired, especially when performing violent maneuvers at low altitudes, was that the aircraft provided a strong warning shudder between 5 and 10 mph before encountering a high-speed stall. Even the snap roll was not too violent if done at less than 250 mph.

For the next flight the captain instructed us to follow him in a rat race. I never worked so hard in my life, finally having to use both hands on the stick because my right arm became completely fatigued. I followed him through most of what he called "stratagem maneuvers"; however, I balked at one. We were about 2,000 feet above the ground at 220 mph when he did a half roll and split-S out. Instead of following him I just spiraled around, keeping my eye on him to pinpoint his crash site. To my surprise he pulled out easily. I didn't think that was possible, but by getting the stick back in my gut it could be done. I tried it and sure enough I made it even though I blacked out for several seconds. It really surprised me that the aircraft could respond so well. Also unnerving was pulling negative Gs, even starting in an inverted dive. He lectured afterwards that when a "Jerry" (enemy aircraft) was on our tail, we should push the aircraft to and even beyond its limits. We might as well die in a crash as from German bullets.

A consequence of learning how well the aircraft responded and how easily it could be controlled occurred a few days later. Ground school briefed us on a condition called "rudder lock," where the rudder becomes locked in an unmovable hard-over position. We were told this could occur in the new bubble-canopy P-47 models just arriving. In an excessive side slip, the bubble-canopy turbulence is deflected to one side of the rudder, unbalancing the rudder air pressure and creating the rudder lock. To prevent it, a a small dorsal fin was being installed as quickly as possible; however, flying would continue. If we found ourselves in that predicament, we were to apply full power and let the propeller slipstream realign the canopy turbulence. Throughout my entire combat tour, I never flew a P-47 that had the dorsal fin installed.[2]

On my next flight after that briefing, I was engaged in a simulated dogfight flying a new bubble-canopy aircraft. In maneuvering to stay on the tail of the other aircraft, I cross-controlled and induced a large side slip while in a rolling dive. Suddenly the rudder pedals went hard over and the aircraft violently snapped to where the nose varied from horizontal to beyond vertical. I knew immediately what it was and applied full power. By the time I completed two radical snap rolls, rudder control returned and I recovered in a 45-degree dive, losing about 2,000 feet during the maneuver. I didn't stay on the tail of the aircraft in front of me but after the flight the pilot behind me wanted to know what I did to completely disappear from his view. I always considered that an excellent last-ditch evasive maneuver, but I never repeated it. Having just recently gone through the recovery from the most unusual aircraft maneuvers, recovery from this unexpected one was almost routine.

One very windy and stormy day my instructor forcefully brought home to me the fact that we were now in a wartime environment. I didn't get to the flight line on time for a scheduled flight because I didn't think we would get off. It cost me an embarrassing dressing down and admonishment that we flew when scheduled regardless of the weather. Another facet regarding the war was vividly displayed on a low-level formation flight over Wales, south to the Bristol Channel, and then east to near London, staying just north of a restricted flight area called "Diver Area." This was the start of the German V-1 buzz-bomb bombardment and the Diver Area was a designated zone where all low-flying aircraft would be fired on by a heavy concentration of antiaircraft batteries. It corresponded to the area where the buzz bombs started their terminal dive to the targets in southern England.[3] Flying over the English countryside I was absolutely amazed at the stocked war material. They crowded every road with parked vehicles, tanks, trucks, jeeps, ambulances, guns of all descriptions, and so on. Whole fields were covered with war material. The logistics of a world war were simply staggering. It was the most awesome display of equipment and material one can imagine.

We recognized that the lessons learned under the tutelage of these combat pilots were extremely important to survive the approaching combat environment. I, for one, am extremely grateful for their dedicated instruction. The lessons were also costly to our group of pilots. Within a week I know we lost several pilots due to crashes; nevertheless, training continued unabated. I acquired another 26 hours of P-47 flying and was finally ready for assignment to a combat unit. I had a total of 329 hours flying with 100 hours in a P-47.

Flying was not the only training continued. In ground school we discussed combat tactics, and reel after reel of combat film was viewed and critiqued. Most of these films showed that getting close and right behind the enemy aircraft resulted in a sure kill. We sat through briefings on air/sea rescue operations, emergency procedures, and escape and evasion. We practiced getting out of our parachute harness, inflating our Mae West life jackets, and deploying our dinghy in a swimming pool. They took escape and evasion photos, and all our equipment was personally fitted.

The escape and evasion lecture on the consequences and possible reprisals by the German authorities greatly concerned me because of my relatives in Belgium. I made some inquiries on what to do in the event I was shot down and captured. The response from the lecturers was not very encouraging, strongly recommending that under no circumstances should I admit I had relatives in Belgium. At that point in the war the German authorities were getting desperate and not living up to the fine points of the Geneva Convention. The best advice they could give was, "Don't get shot down," obviously not entirely under my control.

3.   Battle of France

Just as we arrived in France a massive air bombardment finally broke the German lines
hemming in the Normandy beachhead. We were finally ready to actively contribute to de-
feating the enemy. Training was fine, but this was the real thing!

During our year of training most of us cultivated a few special friends
and, as training ended, hoped they would assign us to the same fighter
group. The Air Force commanders understood the need to have a buddy to share
thoughts and dreams, so they devised a unique system to try to accommodate
most of the replacements; they used a drawing procedure for assignment to the
various Eighth or Ninth Air Force fighter groups. They posted the number of
vacancies in each group and drew names from a hat. Each pilot drawn could
then select the group he wanted and hope his buddy would also be drawn before they filled that group's quota. The Eighth Air Force groups were selected
first since most of us preferred escort and air-to-air combat over tactical ground
support. As it turned out, Chuck Bennett, Dick Tanselle, and I, close buddies
throughout our training, managed to remain together for assignment to the 366th
Fighter Group of the Ninth Air Force. All told, nine replacement pilots went to
the 366th Fighter Group, located at strip A-1 in Normandy, France.

On 30 July 1944 we said good-bye and good hunting to friends and class-
mates. Salutations such as "See you at Le Bourget" (the Paris airport) or "Tempelhof" (the Berlin airport) were common. A train ride to London, reeling under
a V-1 buzz-bomb attack, greeted our entry into the actual shooting war zone.

We spent one night in London, seeing the sights and hearing the explosion of occasional V-1 impacts. I was amazed at how calmly life went on under the attack, some people barely looking up to find the source of the staccato buzz of the V-1 racing overhead. The next day, 31 July, a short bus ride brought us to Croydon Field for the trip over the Channel to France in a IX Troop Carrier Command C-47. They required us to change our money into French francs invasion currency (to prevent black-market trading), and then we boarded an aircraft already partially loaded with cargo. It appeared that the C-47 was overloaded, carrying cargo and about fifteen of us with all our gear, each having a B4 bag, A3 bag of flying gear, and a personal footlocker. I guess flying overloaded was the norm at the time.

A solid cloud cover prevented our viewing the Normandy invasion beaches or France itself. The C-47 pilot let down through the clouds and drew antiaircraft fire (I didn't see it). Immediately he pulled back into the clouds and returned to England. We were weathered in for two days and finally landed on a dirt and grass landing strip in Normandy on 2 August. A short jeep ride brought us to strip A-1 hosting the 366th Group.

The 366th Fighter Group was part of the IX Tactical Air Command (TAC), commanded by Maj. Gen. Elwood R. Quesada. The 366th contained three squadrons, 389th, 390th and 391st. They assigned Chuck Bennett and me to the 390th squadron, Dick Tanselle and the others to the other two squadrons. The group commander was Lt. Col. Harold N. (Norm) Holt. Maj. Clure Smith, known to all as "the Chief," commanded the 390th squadron. Maj. James (Barney) Barnhardt, with whom I became well acquainted, was the operations officer. The 390th aircraft letter designation was B2, the 389th was A6, and the 391st A8.

The 366th Fighter Group had been activated at Richmond Army Air Base, Virginia, on 1 June 1943. They trained together the rest of 1943 and arrived in England in January 1944. Their combat base was Station 407, Thruxton, about 25 miles north of Southampton. During mid-February, six pilots flew combat orientation flights with the Eighth Air Force 353rd Fighter Group. Capt. Keith Orsinger, 366th Group Operations, was the first casualty when he was shot down and killed in aerial combat during these missions. Combat flying for the 366th commenced on 14 March with a fighter sweep over the Bayeux–St. Aubin area of France. On 15 March the 366th initiated the first tactical strike of the Ninth Air Force by dive-bombing the St. Valery airfield, located on the French coast between Le Havre and Dieppe. From that time onward they were heavily engaged with bomber escort, dive-bombing, and fighter sweeps over France, Belgium, and Germany. Several times they became entangled in dogfights with German fighters and shot down several. Losses were also sustained, bringing home the reality of war. Lt. Joe Hair from the 390th squadron was the first casualty after the 366th went active. He was shot down by an FW 190 on his second mission on 17 March 1944 and his badly mangled leg was amputated by German doctors. I first met him at our 1978 reunion, and even with an artificial leg he returned to flying and started his own crop-dusting service in Arkansas.

By D-day the 366th was an experienced combat group and played a major role during the landing by providing front-line support. On D-day itself, missions were flown from 0420 (a pitch-dark takeoff) until 0100 the next morning. They maintained this schedule during the crucial ground-forces buildup in Normandy. I recently had the opportunity to listen to the reminiscences of those missions by several pilots who were there. Norm Holt reflected on how the participating pilots seemed to feel more brave and were determined to destroy the assigned targets by dropping their two 1,000-pound bombs dangerously low.[1] The Chief recalled taking off for a mission in the fading daylight at 2230 hours and returning in the dark of the night near 0200. As a navigation aid, a searchlight near the airfield would point toward the runway; however, upon returning to England the pilots found dozens of searchlights pointing in all different directions. They were also assured that the barrage balloons would be down, but some didn't get the word and they had to wind their way around them to get home. The Chief said it was quite a day.

Strip A-1, home of the 366th Fighter Group, sat right on the channel coast overlooking Omaha Beach. It was located within the town area of St. Pierre-du-Mont and about one-half mile east of the heavily bombed prominent Pointe du Hoc, which jutted out into the channel. (Pointe du Hoc was immortalized in the D-day assault by the 2nd Ranger Battalion, who scaled the cliffs and routed the German defenders.) The 5,000-foot airstrip ran east-west and consisted of a heavy type of chicken wire that the British used in airfield construction. It was officially called "steel mesh Marston mat"; however, it will forever be known to us as "chicken wire." After the strip was abandoned the local farmers salvaged the wire, and even today fence lines of the wire mat abound along the regrowing hedgerows and fields, validating our name for the mesh.

The Ninth Air Force 834th Aviation Engineers built the strip. Sandy Conti, an 834th engineer who landed on Omaha Beach on D-day, told the following story of A-1's construction at one of our reunions. Units of engineers landed at D-day with very little equipment and none of the airfield material. To keep themselves useful until they could begin work on A-1, they scraped out an emergency 3,500-foot aircraft strip on the beach. Conti complained that "our biggest problem was first removing hundreds of mines and booby traps in the selected area." By D+1 the strip, christened E-1, was in use by C-47 aircraft bringing in emergency supplies and evacuating wounded soldiers. One of the first to land on the unplanned E-1 airstrip was General Quesada flying a P-38. Construction on A-1 commenced when the area was relatively free of the tenacious German defenders at D+3. Even then the engineers had to contend with artillery fire and snipers, but antiaircraft shrapnel, shot at attacking German aircraft, caused the most casualties. "That darn falling shrapnel cut some fellows up pretty bad," said Conti. Work on the strip went on day and night using floodlights since "the Germans knew exactly where we were." They leveled the hedgerows and laid the chicken wire. Again complaining, "We hated that damn Marston mat as we couldn't get it laid flat; the stakes would pull out and it would roll up again." When the strip was completed, about D+12 (18 June), the 834th moved on to build three more strips in Normandy and refurbished dozens of captured airfields as the front lines advanced.

They laid the Marston mat on bare ground that was eroded away by the prop wash in a monstrous dust cloud. To reduce the dust cloud, the hard-stand areas were refurbished by underlaying the mat with a heavy tarpaper. This allowed the crew chiefs to check out the engine while reducing the cloud of dust thrown up by the propeller. Some maintenance areas even had American pierced-steel planking installed.

The first Ninth Air Force mission was flown from the Normandy beachhead on 14 June when the 389th squadron landed at the partially completed strip A-1 to refuel and rearm their guns. For the next four days a squadron or two would land in Normandy and fly a mission from there. The majority of the 366th support personnel arrived at A-1 on 18 June, and on 19 June A-1 was fully operational. The 366th group and the 368th group at A-3 both became operational on 19 June.

Here we were—a bunch of newly minted pilots ready for induction into the fellowship of combat flying as a part of an illustrious unit. We were full of excitement tinged by apprehension to fly our first mission. I know I was nervous and scared, but I was going to do my duty. Colonel Holt gave us a pleasant, congenial talk where he warned us frankly that combat flying was indeed a dangerous profession. He emphasized, though, that defensive measures, learned by the group the hard way, were available which would increase our chances of making it through alive. Our flight leaders would teach those to us, so we were encouraged to listen to them and ask questions if we did not understand the instructions. With a handshake and hearty admonishment to uphold the excellence and traditions established by the group, he dismissed us to report to our respective squadrons.

As I became acquainted with and worked for him, I found that Colonel Holt was a dynamic leader and knew the hazards and risks inherent in performing ground-support missions. He was not content to lead from behind a desk and flew many missions with us, including some of the toughest. He amassed a total of 156 missions, more than any of us, and more than any of the other group commanders in the Ninth Air Force. It's no wonder he was selected to lead the 500 fighter-bomber aircraft strike heralding the massive air bombardment of the German lines to break out from Normandy.

The squadron quarters area was about one-half mile from the operations area. They put us up in an old bakery building with a wood-burning oven. It was a typical old, two-story building, with brick walls about two feet thick and heavy wooden floors. (That old building was still there when I visited the area in June 1995.) Four of us resided in the building, all other pilots being quartered in tents. The first night in France was peaceful until about 0200 when we were all awakened by the firing of a heavy artillery piece. A German air raid was in progress, and along the next hedgerow was a heavy antiaircraft battery. What a noise and spectacle as all the antiaircraft guns on shore and ships in the channel let go. The Germans dropped a few bombs in the channel and it was all over in just a few minutes. I noticed that many pilots, watching the spectacular show, congregated by the old building where I was quartered. The reason quickly became apparent as all the shrapnel shot up now came crashing down through the trees. It was an unforgettable introduction on my first night in France.

Over the next several days Chuck and I observed the operation of the squadron. The St. Lô breakout was in progress and the U.S. Third Army, commanded by Lt. Gen. George Patton, was starting an end run around the Germans, hemming in the Normandy beachhead. Weather permitting, missions were flown from dawn to dusk, or from about 0630 to 2200 during this late-summer period. The Air Force used British time. French time was one hour earlier since their time was based, by Nazi decree, on Central European time (Berlin time).

The P-47 had three bomb shackles, one on each wing and another on the belly. Each shackle could carry a 1,000-pound bomb, but the usual armament at strip A-1 were two wing-mounted 500-pound bombs. Sometimes various combinations of 500-pound bombs with 260-pound fragmentation bombs were carried, using all three shackles. Occasionally substituted were two fragmentation bomblets, each consisting of 24 ten-pound fragmentation bombs. This was in addition to 3,000 rounds of .50-caliber ammunition, which lasted 25 seconds. Missions of eight or twelve aircraft were the norm, lasting about one and one-half hours. Most of that time was spent over the battle area as the front lines were only a few minutes away. With four active squadrons occupying the field, we had aircraft landing or taking off continuously.

Flying from concrete runways in England pilots would carry two 1,000-pound bombs, usually enough to destroy a pillbox. During the battle for Cherbourg they found that a direct hit by a 500-pound bomb did not do the job. Strip A-1 was too short and bumpy to carry 1,000-pound bombs on the wings, and the fin dragged if it was mounted on the centerline. In desperation the fin was taken off but in the entire squadron only one bomb exploded. Another group cut one fin so it wouldn't drag, and that was successful.

By the time our group of replacements arrived, the prop wash had eroded the ground underneath the Marston mat, making the runway extremely bumpy. The loosened mat rolled up in front of the wheels, often causing a large stake to snap into the air as an aircraft took off. Unless a wind was blowing across the runway, the dust cloud following the first aircraft takeoff was so thick that the pilots of subsequent aircraft depended on instruments.

The 366th group, flying P-47 aircraft, occupied the Channel side of strip A-1. The 401st squadron of the 370th Fighter Group, a P-38 outfit, was temporarily stationed on the other side until their fighter strip was completed. I always wanted to fly the P-38 because it was such a sleek-looking fighter, while the P-47 looked like a pregnant guppy. But on 7 August I witnessed the belly landing of a badly damaged P-38 with the left engine feathered and the gear dangling halfway down, which changed my mind about flying the P-38. As the pilot touched down, the right engine's turning propeller broke off at the engine housing and walked its way right over the cockpit, narrowly missing the pilot. The aircraft skidded sideways, breaking the tail booms, and was a total loss.[2]

I had seen several P-47s belly in; each time the prop bent as the engine stopped and the aircraft slid to a gentle stop. It only required battle-damage repair and a new engine, prop, and belly-skin replacement to be flyable again. The additional security of having two liquid-cooled engines in a P-38 was more than offset by having one rugged air-cooled engine in the P-47. I saw a P-47 that sustained a 20mm antiaircraft shell hit in the engine, blowing off one cylinder and bending back two others which broke the piston connecting rods, yet the engine kept running with no oil to bring the aircraft home 50 miles. The pilot (I think it was Al Jennings) landed safely and even taxied to his revetment area. The more we flew the P-47 and saw the punishment it could take, the more we liked it.

After observing for five days, Chuck and I were scheduled for a flight. It was only a patrol orientation flight, not a combat mission. Wouldn't you know it, the first time I started an engine with the fighter group ground crew looking on, I forgot to energize the inertia flywheel first and switched the starter to engage. I, of course, corrected my goof the instant I saw the prop turn, but it was not an auspicious beginning to engender the confidence of the ground crew. We took off on a four-aircraft flight, both Chuck and I flying the wing of an experienced combat pilot. We did not carry bombs but were fully loaded with 3,000 rounds of ammunition. Being able to use full military power sure made a difference on takeoff and climb; the aircraft seemed to leap ahead. We flew around the entire Normandy perimeter, from Cherbourg to Caen to Mont St. Michel at Avranches. Twice more we flew orientation flights at Angels 15, listening and viewing the dive-bombing and strafing of our group over the front lines. Chuck and I were both anxious to prove our mettle with our first combat mission.

Radio call signs for the squadrons were: 390th, "Relic"; 389th, "Slipshod"; and 391st, "Foxhunt." On a group mission of more than one squadron the group leader's call sign was "Rupert." The lead flight of four aircraft in a squadron was coded "Red," the second flight "Yellow," the third "Blue," and the fourth "White." Our control tower was known as "Burdock." "Sweepstakes" was the IX TAC controller, and the IX TAC radar controller was called "Marmite." The group was supporting the First Army under the command of Lt. Gen. Courtney H. Hodges.

A squadron mission of twelve aircraft (three flights), escorting Martin B-26 bombers to a German supply dump located midway between Rouen and Amiens, introduced me to combat flying on 10 August. Flying as Relic Yellow 2, the wingman of the leader of the second flight, we provided top cover at Angels 15 to the B-26s bombing at Angels 12. Discounting my highly excited nervousness, it was a very uneventful mission except for bursts of heavy-caliber flak directed at us on retiring off the target.[3] The moment I saw the black puffs appear I applied power to get away. For a few moments I led the squadron until a gruff command from my flight leader got me back where I belonged. After landing, my flight leader explained that heavy-caliber flak was not a significant threat as long as we changed direction or altitude within as many seconds as we were thousands of feet high. Since we were at Angels 15, changing direction (15 degrees or so) or changing altitude (500 to 700 feet) every 15 seconds was adequate. No matter—it scared the heck out of me.

At debriefing the intelligence officer asked me several routine questions, if anything unusual was seen or did anything else happen. I was so excited about surviving my first mission, my mind was a complete blank and I could not remember anything. The squadron leader then recounted for the intelligence officer what had happened. The B-26s achieved a good pattern of bombs on the target, which caused several large secondary explosions, so apparently the B-26s hit a dump of some sort. The area of the heavy flak battery that shot at us was identified and carefully plotted on the intelligence officer's chart. I realized how much I had to learn. Afterwards the veteran pilots laughingly assured me they all were just as scared and confused on their first mission. I didn't tell them I even asked the crew chief how long we were gone to log in the form 1 (two hours).

When the group was based in England, the flight surgeon would place a bottle of whiskey on the table after a mission so that each pilot who wanted a calming drink could help himself. When the group moved to France, the front lines were only a short distance away and the missions became very short, so a pilot could fly three or four missions per day. Some pilots tended to overindulge, and by the afternoon became quite tipsy. They stopped the practice. Instead, the flight surgeon kept track of our missions and presented us with a bottle or two (supposedly at two ounces per mission) to take with us when we earned a combat leave. I sure could have used the calming effect of a shot of whiskey after my first mission.

At this time the group was busy supporting the U.S. First Army to contain the German Seventh Army's drive to retake the important road and bridge town of Avranches. Capturing that position would cut off the U.S. Third Army, led by Lt. Gen. George Patton, which had stormed through Avranches to fan out behind the German positions. The strong German attack, spearheaded by several Panzer divisions, reached beyond Mortain, but the First Army, helped by the fighter-bombers, soundly trounced them. The Germans were now being squeezed between the U.S. First and Third Armies.

The operations order for 12 August initially alerted our group for another B-26 escort mission, but at the last moment that was canceled. Apparently the German forces belatedly realized that they were in danger of encirclement by General Patton's Third Army end run and were recklessly taking to the roads in daylight, trying to escape. These enticing targets, a fighter-bomber's dream situation, were too good to ignore. So they ordered us on an armed reconnaissance of the battle area. This meant we were free to find and attack targets of opportunity within the area specified in the order.

I was wingman for Emil Bertza, a fellow of Hungarian parentage from Chicago. It was my first dive-bombing and strafing mission; in fact, they scheduled me for two ground-support missions that day. Emil told me to stay with him and bomb and strafe where he did. In order for us to claim a motor vehicle as "destroyed," it had to explode, burn, or be strafed twice. He therefore instructed me to strafe the same vehicle he did so we could claim it destroyed without having to set up a second strafing pass. If his strafing exploded or burned the vehicle, I should slide over and strafe an adjacent target. He also cautioned me to break (the turning pull-up from dive-bombing or strafing) in the opposite direction to him. This was to force the German flak gunners to swing their guns around which, he felt, improved our survival chances.

After reaching the Mortain/Domfront target area we found a column of German transport parked on the side of a road and in the surrounding fields. I heard the squadron leader notify Marmite that we were attacking and then he received a confirmation. We peeled off and I followed Emil down and dropped my two 500-pound bombs near his on the road. I know they impacted near a bunch of

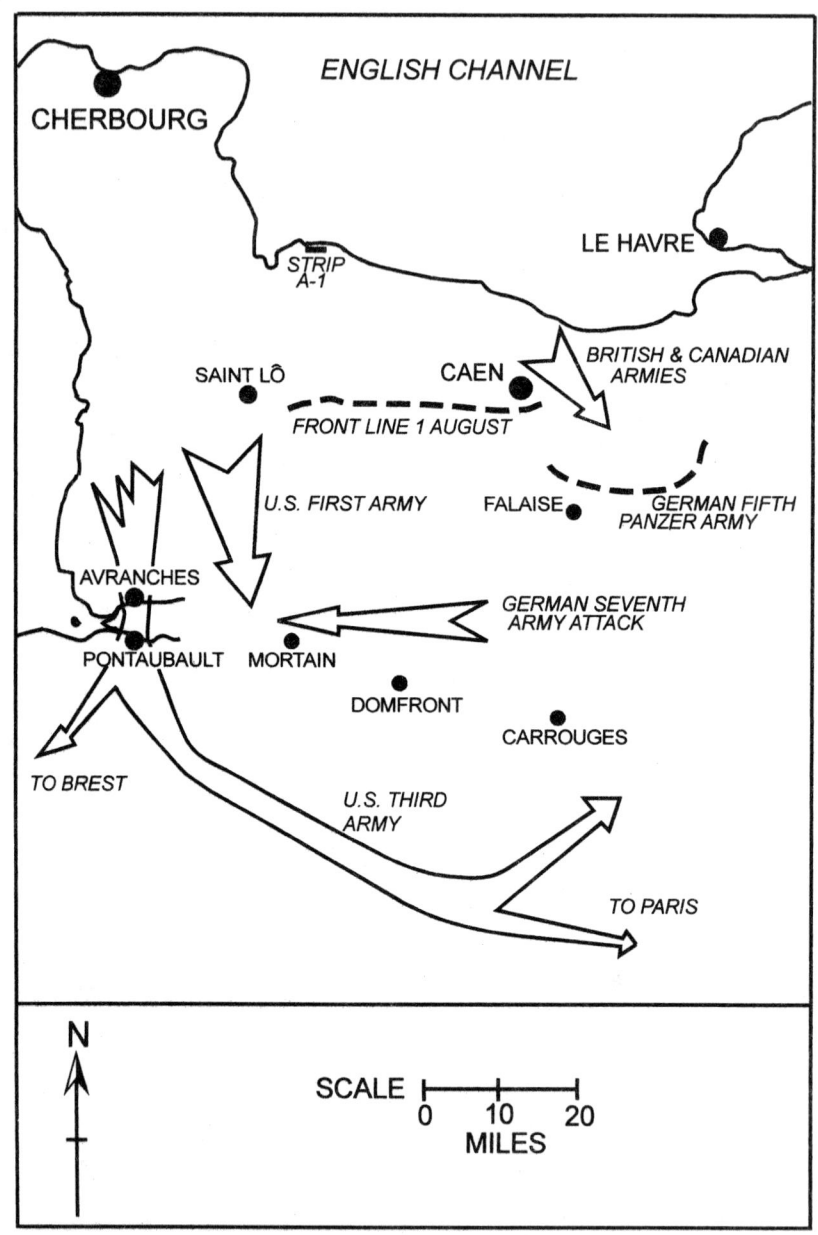

Normandy Battle Situation, 12 August 1944

vehicles stopped on the road, but in the high state of nervous excitement performing my first dive-bombing under hostile enemy fire, I don't know if we destroyed any. Emil then selected a stretch of road containing many vehicles jammed together in a massive confusing bunch. A strafing pattern on that bunch was set up. Dive down, line up on a vehicle, give it a short burst, and then make a turning pull-up to come around and attack the next vehicle in line. I followed him, slightly staggered sideways from his flight path, and strafed the same vehicle he did even though I was terrified from all the flying fireballs and explosions around us. When he broke to the right, I went left and vice versa. We would then join up for the next strafing pass, usually from a different direction. All around us were strafing aircraft, seemingly staking out their own stretch of road.

I received a reassuring surprise the first time I pulled the trigger and saw all the tracer bullets from the eight .50-caliber guns go streaming down. This was the first time I fired eight guns; in training we used only four. It gave me the feeling of power, being able to mete out such destruction upon the enemy. We were using an ammunition loading called 2-2-1, consisting of two armor-piercing, two incendiary, and one tracer. Therefore, between each tracer round that we saw there were four other rounds. Each of our guns was set to fire fourteen rounds per second, so there was a virtual explosion of fire from the gun barrels.

After completing a strafing pass while flying through a tremendous volley of flak and breaking in the opposite direction to Emil, I couldn't find him to join up for our next pass. Just then I heard the reassemble order to form up at Angels 10 at point A (a predesignated prominent landmark), I left the area and formed up with the squadron for the flight home.

Emil was an original member of the squadron, present since its formation in the United States. He was joyful and well liked. At debriefing I explained that I did not see him go down, or see a parachute or the aircraft on the ground. I just didn't know what happened to him. Emil had instructed me to change the break direction for my own safety. The German flak gunners did not lead their target aircraft enough, and while aiming at the first they usually hit the second if it was following the first in trail. Changing the break direction increased survival chances during the vulnerable low-altitude pull-up, but for perhaps 15 to 20 seconds we were not in visual contact. During that period he was shot down. Radio chatter (we had only four radio channels for a lot of aircraft) probably blocked out any quick report he might have made. The attitude of the original squadron pilots toward me—merely a squadron replacement—became very acrimonious, even though what happened to at least half the pilots shot down were complete mysteries.

When telling this story to others I am usually asked, "How can you not notice an open parachute and a crashed burning aircraft?" My answer to that is:

1. We maintained a high speed in that unfriendly environment and subsequently covered a lot of ground, quickly losing sight of the immediate area.
2. Visibility was restricted due to the smoke of many burning vehicles
   on the ground, making identification of a burning aircraft impossible.
3. This was only my second mission and I certainly wasn't yet combat
   hardened.

The situation was somewhat alleviated when six days later he showed up. What
an adventure he had.[4]

Emil was hit by ground fire just as he pulled up from strafing. His aircraft
started burning furiously, so he bailed out from 2,000 feet. He landed in an open
field, left his parachute, and sprinted to hide in some bushes. He shot at a German soldier with his .45 automatic pistol (and missed). When they returned fire
with automatic weapons he surrendered. His captors were an artillery unit attached to the 2nd Panzer Division. Several other Americans and an English
pilot, F/O Kilpatrick, 103 Squadron, 446 Wing were also captives.

That evening the prisoners were taken along as the artillery unit pulled out,
trying to make their way eastward. After traveling in a circle, at 0100 they ended
up in the same place they started. At 0600 they again hit the road and headed
east in a massive convoy of trucks, tanks, horse-drawn vehicles, and artillery
units. At 0930 they stopped and dispersed their vehicles in the fields and locked
the prisoners in a shed. At 1500 the P-47s found them and, as Emil described it,
"The bombing and strafing created havoc with the Germans. They seemed de-
moralized and scattered in all directions. In the confusion all of us prisoners escaped and headed northwest for about 400 yards and hid in a hedgerow."

While the prisoners hid in the ditch by the hedgerow, six Luftwaffe soldiers
led by a sergeant approached them. The German soldiers were friendly. Emil
could speak a little German and French, which helped him immensely during
this adventure. When he addressed them in their own language they wanted to
surrender to him. The Luftwaffe soldiers had a truck hidden away in San
Saveaux de Carrouges (about three miles away), but to get to it they would have
to go through the lines of an SS Panzer Division. (The unit was probably the
notorious 2nd SS Panzer Division, commonly known as the Das Reich Division.) The only way the Americans could get through the SS lines was for them
to be captives of the Luftwaffe soldiers. They all agreed to this deception and
approached the headquarters of the SS Division with the armed Germans escorting the unarmed prisoners. The SS officer wanted to take over the prisoners, but the Luftwaffe sergeant was adamant that he had orders to take them to
Luftwaffe headquarters. (Emil admitted this was the most frightening part of

the whole adventure.) After an antagonistic argument the SS officer finally relented and let them pass.

Near midnight they reached the truck, which was loaded with food, and they all ate a hearty meal. They slept there that night. The next morning they tried to get the truck started but couldn't, so they loaded up with food and started walking north toward Argentan. After going about four miles they took refuge in a barn. The lookout reported that a group of twenty-five German soldiers led by an officer was approaching. Emil figured the jig was up and he was about to be recaptured. However, he walked boldly up to the Germans and addressed the German officer, who asked if Emil was American. When Emil answered that he was, they exchanged name and rank and shook hands. On a hunch Emil asked if they were Austrians and they said they were. It turned out this group was also looking to surrender, so Emil brought them to the barn where the rest of the men were and fed them on German rations taken from the abandoned truck earlier in the day. While Emil was scouting the area shortly thereafter, he met a young French boy wearing the French tricolor and carrying a rifle. The boy told him a French armored column had just gone through the area. About an hour later Emil met the soldiers of the French 2nd Armored Division and turned over his prisoners to them. He then left his companions and started hitchhiking back to A-1, returning on 18 August. It took him three days, since he had to make a big loop traveling against the Third Army traffic streaming through the Avranches breach.

Emil's return somewhat exonerated me, but the group's animosity remained for quite a time until we (not only me, but also the other replacements) proved our mettle. The group had sustained heavy pilot losses during the past eight weeks of continuous combat, and from about ninety assigned pilots thirty-one had been lost. The staggering losses had shocked the remaining pilots, and their animosity and derision can be excused. Forty years later at a reunion when we were sitting around reminiscing, several of the original pilots apologized sincerely for the way they had reacted toward the replacement pilots. The apology was accepted as their behavior was understandable since we came into the group replacing their shot-down companions. The casualties during the June–July combat period were the most costly of the entire war. (The appendix shows casualty and other operating statistics for the 366th Fighter Group during their entire combat period.)

The next weeks' missions were concentrated attacks on enemy targets within what came to be called the Falaise pocket, formed by the American Third Army in the south, the First Army in the west, and the British Second Army in the north. The French town of Falaise gave the pocket its name. The carnage was unbelievable. Vehicles were jammed bumper to bumper on the roads and parked helter-skelter in the fields. Because of the many aircraft attacking within the small area, it was necessary to queue in line and take turns. We were the nemesis of the German forces and were creating hell on earth within this small area.

Emil had repeatedly emphasized that the German troops were "really scared of the Jabos." We knew they called us "Jabos" (shortened from *Jadgebombers,* or fighter bombers) and that the cry "Achtung Jabos" created an instant reaction. The foot slogger hit the dirt and scrambled for protection, the driver and passengers bailed out of moving vehicles into the ditches, and even armored vehicles raced for cover. Captured German soldiers claimed that the Jabos were "the most terrifying weapon on the Western Front—they are Eisenhower's secret weapon."[5] Even German Generalfeldmarschall Hans Gunther von Kluge, commander-in-chief in the west and Army Group B, complained, "The enemy air superiority is terrific and smothers almost every one of our movements. Losses in men and equipment are extraordinary."[6]

Missions were flown as fast as possible. Mission briefings were short since they were always the same. Every day a list was published of roads where any vehicles could be assumed to be enemy and could be attacked immediately. For example, the operations order for 11 August listed nine roads and crossroads in the Foret Des Andaines, located just east of Domfront, on which vehicles and troops could be attacked without further identification. This directive was applicable during the daylight hours through 12 August. The Report of Operations (record of mission results) shows that on a group mission of thirty-six aircraft dispatched to that area, they destroyed thirty-six vehicles, two Panther tanks, and five self-propelled guns on half-tracks, and damaged another thirty-three vehicles. Another report showed that twelve aircraft, armed with one 500-pound and two 260-pound fragmentation bombs, destroyed four tanks and nineteen trucks in the same area. These attacks were in the same area where I had lost Emil, my flight leader, who then experienced the shock and terror of P-47 fighter-bomber attacks from the ground. Our attacks were especially concentrated in the German escape-route corridor. The Germans referred to the escape corridor gauntlet as the "Jabo Rennstrecke" (fighter-bomber race course).[7]

The squadron leader announced during the mission briefing that one aircraft would be fitted with leaflet containers rather than bombs. A redeeming factor in carrying leaflets was that they were released at 3,000 feet to give the leaflets time to scatter, instead of the normal bomb-drop altitude of 1,000 feet. When I arrived at my aircraft, I found it was loaded with leaflet containers. It didn't particularly please me to have to experience that murderous flak just to throw some paper at them, but at least I could still fire my guns. During the mission I felt sort of hypocritical, tossing out leaflets urging surrender with guaranteed good treatment, and at the same time shooting at them. I wonder if those leaflets induced anyone to surrender.

I was flying Maj. Barney Barnhardt's wing when I made the mistake of trying to strafe all the vehicles lined up on a road in one pass, even trying to follow them around a curve. A stern rebuff from Barney to concentrate my fire on one vehicle at a time brought me back to reality. He explained afterwards that being sure of one vehicle destroyed was better than to throw bullets around and not know what was hit. We had to aim and fire at each individual vehicle, and not be influenced or aim with the tracer rounds. The tracers burned during their flight, which changed the round's center of gravity and could cause it to deviate in flight because of aerodynamic and gyroscopic force changes. I guess Hollywood films, rather than the reality of war, still influenced me. Despite Barney's admonishments, I found it rewarding to see the tracer rounds hitting the target, although I sometimes saw them diverge into a spiraling flight toward nowhere. I flew many missions on Barney's wing until he completed his tour and was sent home on leave a few months later. Throughout my combat tour I found that veteran combat pilots took newcomers under their wing. It wasn't planned or even encouraged, but just seemed to happen. Barney was my mentor, and I have always valued and been grateful for his stabilizing influence and timely advice as he acclimated me to combat flying.

Occasionally the squadron or the group would have a stand-down day to let the mechanics catch up on aircraft maintenance and the engineers repair our runway. Weather also gave us an occasional reprieve. With no place to go or anything to do, we started a sport of shooting at the beach obstacles topped by mines standing along the shore. Along the shoreline trenches and within the fortifications lay many German Mauser rifles, along with boxes and boxes of ammunition. We would sit on the cliff and fire away at the mined obstacles 300 to 500 yards away. I never exploded a mine, but occasionally a fellow would get lucky and explode one. This sport came to a screeching halt when the Navy complained that ricocheting rounds were upsetting the workers off-loading supplies from ships about a mile offshore.

The enlisted men of the squadron were a great group of fellows. We had very little contact with them, with the exception of whichever crew was tending our aircraft. They treated us with respect and consideration, not only because we were officers but because we were the ones actively engaging the enemy. I realized this one sultry evening after returning from a late mission. I was dirty, tired, and extremely thirsty. To my chagrin my canteen was empty, and when I walked over to the fresh-water tank to refill it, I found that it also was empty. Several enlisted men were lounging nearby and, when they saw I was out of water, offered to share some with me from their canteen. Accepting their offer, I then stood around and talked with them for a few minutes. I found they were genuinely interested in how I was getting along in the squadron and offered their help if I had any problems. I always thought that they were the best group of fellows and never had an altercation with them.

The food in our mess was typical Army, watery powdered eggs, hash, and other canned food. We ate a lot of bread with reverse Lend-Lease English marmalade, but waged a losing battle with the bees to get in a bite. Our mess tent was in an apple orchard and the bees were all over the trees. Those darn bees got into everything, but they really swarmed to the marmalade. We brushed them off the bread and hurriedly tried to get in a bite before they swarmed over it again. Several fellows suffered bee stings on the lips. On 12 June, six days after D-day, Generals Omar Bradley, George C. Marshall, H. H. "Hap" Arnold, and Dwight Eisenhower took a tour of the beachhead and had an impromptu lunch of Army "C" rations in an apple orchard here in St. Pierre-du-Mont. I often wonder if they, too, were plagued by the bees.

During a ten-day period we couldn't get bread and resorted to eating those hard Army crackers. It was the first time I ever developed a craving for a food item—I wanted a good piece of bread. Combat pilots were somewhat pampered and occasionally the flight surgeon would get us some real eggs and possibly an orange. Since I was required to eat what was put in front of me at home, I never complained about Army chow.

Flying combat is obviously a most dangerous profession. I admit I was scared and apprehensive during every mission. I did not realize, however, that that day-to-day pressure builds up an unconscious stress level that finally bursts out to the conscious mind. I reached my breaking point in the middle of the night when I woke up shaking in a cold sweat. My only thought was, "Boy, I can get killed in this war." We know death is the unavoidable fate of us all, but while flying combat it was a pervading menace, never far away. Fortunately I controlled myself and did not wake any of my tentmates. The next morning I was my normal self again. Having read many war stories, I now realize that this is a common occurrence with combatants.

In mid-August I received a large envelope in the mail containing a presidential ballot. I registered to vote when I reached age twenty-one so I could cast my first ballot in the 1944 election. Congress made it easier by passing a law that allowed registered servicemen stationed overseas to vote for president. I was one of several in the group who had completed the necessary paperwork to receive a ballot. To validate the ballot it was necessary to vote in the presence of a company commander or equivalent officer. The 390th squadron adjutant, Capt. Lawrence Keating, certified my ballot. It was my first presidential election.

Our primary mission after the Falaise pocket battle was supporting the First Army armored spearheads, primarily the 2nd Armored "Hell on Wheels" Division, as they drove across France. The emphasis shifted quickly, however, toward preventing the remnants of the German Seventh and Fifth Panzer Armies, which had escaped the Falaise pocket, from getting across the Seine River. We devoted several missions per day to interdicting barge and boat travel and attacking river-crossing ferry sites. Evidently reconnaissance aircraft discovered the ferry sites since they identified them in the operations order. They were well camouflaged, and only when boring in to bomb or strafe could we see the camouflaged boats and skiffs. From our vantage point several miles above the river, we could guarantee that no river traffic or ferries were in use during the day.

This period saw the initiation of a new war phase for us that we called "column cover." We would check in with the air/ground controller in a tank or half-track traveling with the armored spearhead. If they had a target for us, we would comply with their request for bombing or strafing. If they had no immediate target for us, we would roam, at a low altitude, in front of them, checking their advance route. We would investigate anything suspicious or threatening and attack if necessary. At first it made us nervous to be stooging around at low altitude and airspeed since that left us very vulnerable to flak. We then began to realize that the Germans were more frightened of us, and if they committed any overt action we could be on top of them with our bombs and guns in an instant. It was a very interesting and productive period for us, and made us feel good when we directly helped the ground forces by dive-bombing and strafing any German troops or vehicles that showed themselves. Since the ground forces were sweeping rapidly ahead, the Germans were forced to either travel by day, where we could see them, or be destroyed by the rampaging Allied forces. On most missions a respectable number of vehicles and troops fell victim to our guns and bombs.[8]

The weather was ideal for our hunting. Our tanks and other vehicles displayed bright cerise panels for identification that we could easily see from 12,000 feet. The contrast between the bustling roads filled with all kinds of vehicles displaying bright panels on our side of the battle line and the emptiness on the German side was startling. It was very obvious where the front line was and we could even watch its movement toward Germany as the armored column advanced.

Occasionally we would sight suspicious vehicles displaying the cerise panels or red cross markings. On one mission we sighted a column of vehicles displaying the red cross. A flight leader went to check them out and said there were several tanks, interspaced between other vehicles, all displaying the red cross. Not only that, the tanks appeared to be German. We circled them while the flight leaders and squadron commander discussed the situation. We finally left them alone but reported the encounter. Later in the war we found that the Germans were displaying cerise panels. This was countered by a requirement for our troops to display a specific combination of color panels.

Occasionally we would be unable to identify what the troops wanted bombed and would request artillery-fired red smoke shells to identify the target. This worked well for several months, until the Germans caught on and started firing red smoke shells, too. This happened during the Hürtgen Forest battle (see chapters 5 and 6). We also modified the practice to use different colors, and even combinations of colors. The air/ground controller would not mention the particular color or combination until the shells were on the way. So even if the Germans were listening to our radio conversation, they were unable to respond quickly enough to mark a bogus target with the specified smoke color.

We knew the Germans monitored our radio frequencies since they would occasionally talk to us. More frequently they would try, and sometimes succeed, to jam our transmissions. This was especially true when we flew deep into Germany and would get a modulated hum that sounded like, "go hommmmme, go hommmmme," coming out of our earphones.

The armored spearheads would sometimes advance so far and fast they would outrun their ground-communications capability. In a few instances, the morning mission was tasked to find where the armored spearheads were, not having stopped pursuing the Germans for the night. As they advanced, our flying distance to them lengthened, and our fuel reserve at landing lessened. We maintained continuous cover over the spearheads from shortly after dawn to about 45 minutes before dusk since it took us that long to return to base. Evidently German aircraft bombed and strafed some spearheads after the air cover left for home, so we were ordered to remain over the spearheads until dark. I was on one of these first late missions completed on 23 August. Both the 390th and 389th squadrons were involved.

Our mission was an armed reconnaissance supporting the 2nd Armored Division advancing north, toward Rouen, right across the British and Canadian army advance. The Americans undertook this mission in the British sector because the British and Canadians were, according to Field Marshal Montgomery, "beset by logistical difficulties."[9] This was a three-division effort, involving the 2nd Armored and the 28th and 30th Infantry Divisions. Their objective was to clear the Seine River from Paris to Rouen, forcing the 75,000 troop remnants of the German Fifth Panzer and Seventh Armies against the mouth of the Seine, where the river is wider and more difficult to cross. The American generals hoped that this pincers, created by American forces blocking the German access to the Seine and British and Canadian forces advancing from the West, would bag the German troops.

After reaching the battle area the 390th directly supported the 2nd Armored spearhead by destroying twenty-three German vehicles near the Seine River by the town of Elbeuf, just south of Rouen. They were offering stiff resistance to the 2nd Armored driving to clear the Seine. The 389th squadron was directed to bomb barges, boats, and ferry-crossing sites on the lower Seine River to keep the Germans from escaping the trap.

After completing our mission we set course for home at dark with our navigation lights on and many questions on our mind. Would our troops recognize and not shoot at us, would we find our strip, would the Navy have their barrage balloons down and not shoot at us (our landing traffic pattern went right over them), and, finally, would we have enough fuel?

About 10 minutes from base my fuel warning light came on. It was an annoying glaring yellow light that reflected brightly off the darkened canopy and could not be dimmed. The light signified that 20 minutes of normal cruise fuel remained in the tank. Burdock (the control tower) informed us that the night landing aid would be three burning barrels of gasoline placed alongside the runway, one at each end and one in the middle. We were to land to the right of the burning barrels of gasoline when landing from west to east. We all landed safely, with each of us registering empty gas tanks. Any slight delay or mishap could have been a disaster. I shut the engine off at 2215 hours and checked operations. They had scheduled me for the early morning mission. It was going to be a short night. The days get shorter more quickly in that northern latitude. A few months ago (D-day) missions were still being dispatched at our landing time, but now it was already dark.

The next several days we supported the 2nd Armored as they cleared the west side of the Seine. On 25 August 2nd Armored turned the captured territory over to the Canadians and British, who continued to clear and mop up the Germans west of the lower Seine. Our operations area then shifted with the 2nd Armored to expanded the bridgehead over the Seine at Mantes-Gassicourt.

The envelopment bagged a disappointing number of German prisoners on 28 August. The Germans fought skillfully and desperately and were able to evacuate the majority of trapped troops across the Seine. Prisoners reported that the British and Canadians did not push as hard as they might have, nor was the Allied Air Force as active as during the critical days of withdrawal.[10]

On 27 August the group transferred to A-41 at Dreux, France. What a relief to be on concrete runways again, away from the clouds of dust or knee-deep mud of strip A-1. Dreux airport is two and one-half miles south of the town. It has two runways, 4,300 feet long, connected by a taxiway and dispersal area. The RAF used the airfield until they elected to return to England in 1940 when the German air force took over. They improved the field and even erected permanent buildings. The airfield was heavily bombed, destroying 90 percent of the buildings and cratering the runways. The runways were so severely damaged that our move was set back two days to allow the engineers to complete the refurbishment of one runway. During the move we continued our scheduled missions.

We were at A-41 for only a few weeks since the whole Allied front was rampaging forward. In fact I flew only three missions from A-41, one of which was very memorable because I blew up my first, and only, ammunition truck. It was 31 August and we were supporting the 2nd Armored Division, now well east of the Seine in the area between Beauvais and Amiens. The supply situation became so critical that only two aircraft per squadron carried bombs; the rest had only their guns. I was flying Barney's wing as usual, and we were strafing a group of German vehicles camouflaged and parked under the trees lining the road. As I followed Barney, the vehicle he was strafing started burning with a satisfying explosion. I shifted my gaze and caught sight of another well-camouflaged truck. It was really hard to see, parked in the shade of the trees and covered with branches. I momentarily lost it as I swung around to strafe, but found it again just in time. A short burst from my eight guns produced a satisfying explosion and surprise when the ammunition truck blew up. Fortunately I was far enough away to allow a pull-up above the explosion debris. The only disappointment was that they lumped my destruction claim of an ammunition truck with the other twenty trucks destroyed on that mission.

The rampaging armored columns were meeting very little resistance and consequently were not asking for our help very often. This resulted in a change of missions; we were now to perform armed reconnaissances, where we made deep penetrations of the German lines and attacked targets of opportunity. On 4 September the mission was an armed reconnaissance in the Namur-Louvain-Liège area. Louvain, Belgium, is only 35 miles from my hometown of Oordegem. Anxiously I gazed in the direction of my hometown and wondered about the state of my relatives after living more than four years under German occupation. I hoped ground forces would soon liberate them so I could visit them. On that mission many of us viewed the Siegfried Line for the first time. We penetrated the German border near Aachen and saw the line of antitank dragon teeth snaking along the German border. From Angels 8 it appeared as a long ugly scar on the earth's surface. These missions resulted in only sporadic claims for destroyed vehicles as the Germans learned to hide and camouflage them. They weren't wasted missions, though, as we usually destroyed several trains.

At A-41 I bunked with some different fellows from the squadron, including 1st Lt. Lowell B. Smith (Smitty), a West Pointer. Smitty was the first person I knew who had graduated from West Point. Since it was starting to get cold, we used our ingenuity and built a small fireplace in the ground by the side of the tent using some scrap steel, rocks, and dirt, with a stovepipe leading outside. The fireplace worked well once a roaring fire was going but getting it started was difficult. One cold morning Smitty got mad because it wouldn't start, and threw a half-full helmet of gasoline on the smoldering wood. It immediately exploded with a roar and blew paper and wood scraps into the air through the stovepipe. No one was hurt but our tent suffered the consequences of many holes burnt in the canvas, the largest about four inches in diameter. The supply officer threatened to make us pay for it, but nothing came of it. I don't know what happened to the holey tent when we moved from A-41. We didn't get the small pot-belly stoves for our tents until early December after we moved to Belgium.

On 5 September they granted Chuck Bennett and me our first operational combat leave for five days. Along with us were Major Barnhardt and Lieutenants Claude Halterman and Harry Wildhaber. Each of us carried a bottle of Canadian Club, courtesy of the flight surgeon, Capt. John Clark (Doc), in payment for missions flown. This bottle was worth more than gold in liquor-starved London. We hitched a ride to England on a B-24 that was being used to ferry fuel for the rampaging armored spearheads. Making our way to London, we checked in the Cumberland Hotel located just off Marble Arch.

Sightseeing, meeting people from around the world, and partying took up our days. One evening Chuck and I were taking some girls home in a taxi; it was the only way to get around after 2300 (or was it 2200? I can't remember anymore) since the Underground (subway) and buses stopped running. Their apartment was on the second floor of a building having iron stairs in front leading to their floor. We escorted them up the stairs after telling the taxi driver to wait. When we were at the top of the stairs, the taxi driver took off. The meter had showed we owed quite a bill, and we wondered why he would leave us stranded. Then we remembered—about one-third of a bottle of Canadian Club was left in the back seat. He would rather have the whiskey than the fare. We were lost in blacked-out, fog-shrouded London in the middle of the night. A friendly bobby finally oriented us and hailed a taxi to take us back to the hotel. When relating this episode to others who had been in wartime London, it always brings a leery look and questions about our misuse of a perfect excuse to ask the girls if we could stay overnight. For one, these were nice girls (and there were plenty in London, contrary to popular belief), and two, neither Chuck or I was a carouser.

While on leave Chuck and I met some flying companions who went to the Eighth Air Force. Conversation with them revealed that they only completed about six missions to our fifteen in the same time period. This showed the more frantic pace of ground-support air combat with the Ninth Air Force, as opposed to the Eighth Air Force's escort of heavy bombers. None of us, yet, could claim a shot-down enemy aircraft; in fact, most hadn't even seen any.

Getting back to France was difficult since all transport aircraft, and many temporarily converted bombers, were being used to ferry fuel and other priority cargo. After waiting two days we finally squeezed aboard a flight and made our way to Dreux only to find our group was no longer there. Our only recourse was to go to Ninth Air Force Headquarters in Paris and find out where our unit was. We hitched a ride to the western outskirts of Paris, and from there rode the Metro (subway) to the Arc de Triomphe station. As we climbed the stairs to street level, we were swept away by the liberation celebration still in progress. The liberation of Paris, by the French 2nd Armored and the American 4th Infantry Divisions, happened only two weeks ago, and the people were still ecstatically celebrating. We checked into a hotel and, armed with a couple of bottles of champagne, joined the celebration. I believe my most enjoyable part was riding around Paris in a horse-drawn carriage, toasting with champagne all the French mademoiselles riding by on bicycles with their skirts billowing around them. Viewing the show at the Folies Bergère closed out the evening. The next morning we found our group was now at A-70, by Laon, France. A Ninth Air Force weapons carrier and driver delivered us to our new base. A five-day leave lasted nine exciting days.

Laon airfield is situated about six miles northwest of Laon and consists of two concrete runways in a sort of wide V, only one which was usable. The taxiway from the runway is long and curved, providing access to the dispersal area. Heavy bombing damaged the field's hangars and buildings, but we made several sections of a building into a lounge and operations office. A large bomb-storage area littered one side of the field. In it were many types of German bombs and other equipment. We carefully avoided it, although the temptation to investigate once brought me to its fringe where I warily looked at some odd-looking German bombs. In 1940 Dornier (Do) 17 bombers used the airfield during the Battle of Britain. Later Junkers (Ju) 88s were in residence. It was last used by fighters that were withdrawn prior to D-day. Several partially destroyed aircraft provided attractive projects for souvenir scavenging and curiosity exploration.

My first mission from Laon was a complete fiasco. It was 17 September 1944 and we were supporting the airborne attack in Holland. The operations order specified that we neutralize ground fire and suppress flak for the southern route Troop Carrier Command C-47 stream. Our allocated area was a 45-mile stretch of the route from the initial point to the drop zone, or from 10 miles southeast of Antwerp to Eindhoven. Orders specified we were to remain with the tail end of the stream to the drop zone and escort them back to our lines.

We met the troop carrier and glider stream right on time and provided flak-busting support by weaving below and to the side of them. The weather was clear but a heavy haze restricted visibility to about five miles. To weave below the stream we descended to only a few hundred feet above the ground, providing very little maneuvering room and hardly enough altitude to identify the flak guns and strafe them. So many aircraft were buzzing around, I spent most of my time trying to avoid a collision. Every time I spotted a flak position, three or four aircraft were strafing it before I could get there. At the drop zone (Eindhoven) it was quite a sight to see hundreds of parachutes both in the air and on the ground. Some troops started bailing out over us, causing a mad scramble to get out of the way. I saw several crashed C-47s and saw one on fire. I didn't fire my guns throughout the mission, but some pilots claimed several gun positions and German vehicles destroyed. There were so many aircraft, in poor visibility at low altitudes, that flying was downright dangerous.

The British finally liberated my hometown in Belgium. This lifted my burden of keeping my relatives from being implicated in case I was shot down. Oordegem is on the main highway between Brussels and Gent and about 100 miles due north from A-70 at Laon. Chuck Bennett and I set out to hitchhike our way to Oordegem when we both had a stand-down day. What we hadn't counted on was the difficulty of hitchhiking between the American and British zones, which was across the prevailing traffic. It was late afternoon before we reached Brussels. Obviously we weren't going to make it and reluctantly turned back. In the center of Brussels we took the southbound tram to Waterloo. To be sure we were on the right tram I asked the conductor, in Flemish, if this tram went to Waterloo. He became so flustered having an American officer speaking Flemish he dropped his money box. Everyone helped him pick up the change but about half had rolled into the street. We tried for about four hours to get a ride south from Waterloo to no avail. During that time we became well acquainted with the statues commemorating that famous battle. Rather than spend a lonely night on a roadside corner, we took the last tram back to Brussels and spent the night in a hotel. We returned to base the next afternoon. Fortunately we did not miss any scheduled missions.

A few weeks later we tried again. This time we were lucky enough to get a ride to Brussels from our supply officer, Tommy Thomas, who was going there on official business. We arrived in Oordegem about noon.

Though I was only six years old when I left Belgium, I recognized many landmarks. As Chuck and I walked the two kilometers from town to the old house, many memories returned. The old windmill, where my uncle brought me to watch his wheat being ground into flour, was still there. So was the brook where I had spent hours trying to catch the minnows. We passed the big meadow that usually flooded during the winter, making an ice pond where my older brother pushed me around on a battered chair. A contingent of Canadian troops now occupied the soggy ground trudging around in that miserable muddy field.

The old house finally came into view. I recognized several relatives standing in front, talking. They turned and looked curiously at Chuck and me as we approached, wondering why American officers would come there. They obviously did not recognize me, since I had changed considerably since they last saw me 15 years ago.

As we came closer, I addressed them in Flemish, still tinged with the local dialect, "Ik ben Robert Vanden Brulle van Oordegem en bringen ju vele complementen van myn famalie in Amerika" ("I am Robert Vanden Brulle and I bring you many good wishes from my family in America"). Boy! That sure did cause a commotion. They couldn't believe that I was Robert. In their eyes I was still a little boy and I must be Albert, my older brother. With many gestures accompanying my halting Flemish I finally convinced them who I was. Shortly the whole community was there, asking questions and wanting to meet me.

Every one of my relatives had survived the war, although American aircraft bombed one uncle's family out of their home (they lived near the Gent railroad marshaling yard). The Germans early in the war captured another cousin, a Belgium soldier, but after a six-month imprisonment he escaped. The Germans did not bother him as he helped my aunt and uncle tend their small farm. When speaking of Germans I noted my relatives used the derogatory expression, "expletive, expletive Deutsche Boche." My relatives looked healthy, and stated that they had survived well during the war since they grew most of their own food. My aunt and uncle, with whom I lived the first five years of my life, looked just like the farm couple in the painting *The Angelus* by Jean Francois Millet, even wearing their wooden shoes. In fact, most of my relatives wore wooden shoes since that was the common footwear for working in the fields, and shoe leather was unobtainable. This meeting with my relatives finally relieved my parents' five-year anxiety and concern about what was happening to their family in Belgium.

My relatives were surprised that I was a military officer. The class system still existed in Belgium, and as common Flanders peasants they could only expect to be privates. They thought there must be some mistake since even the burgomaster's son was only a sergeant in the Belgium army and I came from a peasant family. I finally convinced them that in America things were different and a person could rise above a peasant status. Having an officer as a relative increased tremendously their local status. A curious thing, they took up a collection to give me some money. They expected that all soldiers couldn't live on the pay they received since that was the situation they experienced in the Belgium army. I had a difficult time convincing them I didn't need their money since the American army paid me very well. They were, however, horrified to learn that I was a fighter pilot and couldn't understand why I wanted to do such a dangerous job.

I became a local celebrity and, when able, I would request a few days' leave to visit them. On one such visit my cousin Emil (he was the Belgium soldier captured by the Germans early in the war) made me accompany him to every tavern in the area. Only vaguely do I remember coming back from that tour of taverns, riding a bicycle with two flat tires along the cobblestone streets in the middle of the night. (Thirty-four years later I visited several of the same taverns with the same cousin, and people still remembered me.) Also very popular when I visited was the musette bag full of American cigarettes, candy, gum, and other goodies. I brought them the first coffee they had in five years. My cousin Madelyn, on opening a bag I gave her, let each person smell the "real coffee" aroma. She then made a pot of coffee, but couldn't force herself to use only her treasured coffee, making it instead with mostly ersatz coffee, and then adding one scoop of the real stuff. It was a great homecoming.[11] I wrote my mom and dad about my visit and it was written up in the *Chicago Tribune* newspaper with the byline, "This Pilot Gets Home the Hard Way, Via D-day."

Returning from the first visit to my relatives, Chuck Bennett and I hitched a ride on a Red Ball Express gasoline-truck convoy. The Red Ball Express was a long-distance highway system inaugurated late in August to support the rampaging American forces. It was a most dramatic logistical development to get supplies to the front from the Normandy beaches. The express route we were on was not that Red Ball but was named the ABC Route (Antwerp-Brussels-Charleroi). It was customary, however, to call all the express routes Red Ball; therefore, it became a generic name.

The gas-truck convoy sped along in the middle of the road at 40 mph and maintained a spacing of about 200 feet. Escorting squads of military police cleared the road and intersections of all traffic. It was in the middle of the night, and this large gasoline tanker-truck convoy was barreling along the middle of the highway with bright headlights on. It was either very foolish or a very trusting display of confidence in our roving night fighters' ability to prevent any German aircraft from getting through to strafe and bomb the convoy.[12] It was against regulations for the drivers to pick up passengers, but it was the middle of the night and the drivers enjoyed our company as we helped keep them awake. The MPs just looked the other way and even accommodated us by driving Chuck and me to our Laon airfield from the gasoline storage dump near Laon.

4. German Border Stalemate

The halcyon days of pursuing the German armies defeated in Normandy came to a screeching halt at the German border. Our missions became dull, boring, and monotonous as no tangible results could be seen.

We moved to A-70 in Laon, France, just as fall was approaching, which brought the notorious European winter weather. Nearly every morning, just before dawn, the cold sky would be absolutely clear. The familiar constellations of stars, memorized in Boy Scouts in Chicago only a few years earlier, would be shining brightly but noticeably displaced in the sky due to the further northern latitude of Europe. By the time the sun was up, fog and/or low clouds settled in. The battle line, now more than 100 miles away, made some missions last close to four hours. We carried a 150-gallon belly tank and instituted a cruise-control procedure to and from the battle area. This procedure was developed by Charles Lindbergh in the Pacific theater. The throttle was reduced to idle, and then the propeller control retarded to 1,400 rpm (normal cruise was at 1,850 rpm). Manifold pressure (throttle) was then slowly increased until the engine felt like it was ready to break off the mounting. Manifold pressure was then reduced by two inches of mercury. That gave a cruise speed of 160 mph and used about 50 gallons of gasoline per hour. For comparison, combat power burned over 300 gallons per hour at 2,700 rpm.

We were lucky when we could run two missions in a day. Individual mission count went up slowly at the rate of two or three per week. At least I had graduated from just being a wingman and would occasionally lead an element, making me feel I was beginning to pull my weight. However, it didn't alleviate the fear and respect for all that flak.

In September a subtle change in the missions became apparent. Instead of flying most missions in direct support of the ground troops, we started to perform interdiction-type missions. We attacked railroads, river barges, and bridges, and performed armed reconnaissance missions, shooting up targets of opportunity. We even escorted medium bombers attacking transportation targets well inside Germany. The change in mission priority was due to the resurgence of the German army as it deployed into the West Wall (Siegfried Line) defenses. Attacking transportation targets was an attempt to inhibit their buildup and supply. We still performed ground-support missions but not on a continuous basis. Occasionally we even strafed airfields. In my own case, they always scheduled me on the rail-busting missions or other operations, and I never strafed an airfield.

An extensive rail-busting campaign began on 25 September. Group missions of thirty-six aircraft concentrated on cutting rail lines and strafing trains along the Moselle and Rhine River valleys, reaching from Trier to Koblenz to Cologne. The next four days we returned to the same area, doing the same thing, before they reprieved us by scheduling a ground-support mission. For the next month they called on us to cut the same railroads again and again. These missions didn't stop until we became heavily involved in the Hürtgen Forest campaign at the beginning of November.

Dive-bombing left only individual craters in the rail line, which the Germans would have repaired by the next day. To make the railroad cut more difficult to repair, we employed a new tactic using 11-second time-delay fuses. The bombing technique employed four aircraft in line zipping over the railroad at Angels Zero, each aircraft dropping its bombs in the same place. The delayed action fuses allowed enough time for a four-aircraft flight to drop its bombs in the same spot and get clear before the bombs exploded. Bombing at a lower altitude also increased the accuracy and resulted in a cluster of bombs impacting one small area. This resulted in a larger and, we hoped, harder-to-repair crater. It was a hair-raising experience, especially for the last aircraft (Tail-end Charley), who had to roar clear of the target area before the first aircraft's bombs exploded. I don't recall ever losing a pilot due to the explosion, but there were some close calls. The Germans were masters of construction, and by using foreign workers and slave labor they kept critical railroads repaired, no matter how often we repeated the missions. We tried clustering three or more craters within a one-mile section of railroad, and tried to make a larger crater by having each flight bomb the same spot. All to no avail—the next flyable day the railroad would be in business.

These rail-busting missions along the Moselle River are most vividly engrained in our minds. The Moselle River valley is an especially picturesque area, with green, quite steep ridges flanking the river. The railroad snakes its way alongside the river, occasionally disappearing into a tunnel. Here and there, perched on the hilltops, are the remains of medieval and other era castles. The serene picture was very deceptive, though, as the tops of the ridges were lined with flak emplacements embracing both light- and medium-caliber antiaircraft batteries. When we skimmed over the railroad to cluster our bombs in one place, the flak batteries from both ridges would be firing down at us!

That picture of the flak arching down and forming a large V over the railroad while we dove into that apex of fire to drop our bombs will forever remain in our minds. At our reunions, whenever someone asks about the most terrifying missions conducted, those low-level Moselle River rail-busting ones are rated at the top. We all recalled how a collective groan emanated from us when we were briefed for that mission. We also remembered how we ducked behind our armor plate and used full power with water injection (used synonymously with war emergency power) to get away fast from that railroad. As bad as the flak was, I cannot recall seeing an aircraft get shot down over the Moselle River railroad, although the German flak gunners usually damaged several on each mission. After bombing we usually performed an armed reconnaissance, shooting up trains or any other target of opportunity which, we felt, was more effective and productive in disrupting the German Siegfried Line buildup.

War emergency power, or water injection, involved injecting a water and alcohol solution directly in the cylinder to boost engine power. This prevented detonation at high power settings and allowed an increased manifold pressure. The P-47 had a 30-gallon tank, which was a 15-minute supply of the water and alcohol solution. A throttle-mounted switch activated the injection system and provided a 15 percent increase in power. The additional power really gave the aircraft a boot in the pants, which surprised me the first time I used it.

It is interesting to recall how things were done in wartime. I was stationed at Wright Field, Ohio, after the war and found out how the war emergency power setting was determined. They tested five production engines and gradually increased the manifold pressure until the engine blew up. The five destruction manifold pressures were averaged, reduced by two inches, and that was the value specified. It was an expensive way to work, but they got an answer.

Reports surfaced that the Germans were arming their trains with multiple 20mm quadruple-barrel flak guns on flat cars, interspaced between the other cars. Thus, if we concentrated on firing at the train engine, a formidable fusillade of antiaircraft fire greeted us from accompanying flak cars. To counter that, we started having several aircraft simultaneously attack the train, one to strafe the engine and the others to strafe the flak cars. They told us to be careful until the train was verified as not transporting ammunition. Blowing up an ammunition truck was spectacular, but it was puny compared to exploding an ammunition train. If a pilot was too close there was very little chance of surviving the flight through the explosion. Not many of us saw an ammunition train explode, but many of us saw or blew up an ammunition truck and knew what it looked like. We received reports on the destruction caused by an exploding ammunition train and needed no further convincing to be wary. One of our pilots blew up an ammunition train while dive-bombing, and the blast disabled his aircraft, requiring him to bail out even though he was at 5,000 feet when the massive explosion occurred. (His story is told later.)

On 30 September another group of replacement pilots reported for duty and the first group of pilots to complete their combat tour were sent on their well-earned thirty-day leave. Pilots were rotated home for a thirty-day leave after completing at least 100 missions, or flying 200 hours combat. The 390th squadron contributed six of the lucky pilots: Maj. Barney Barnhardt (I was losing my mentor), Captains Mack Strohm and Steve Van Buren, and Lieutenants Al Merz, John Stonnell, and Bayard Taylor. In aggregate they completed 638 missions and flew 1,516 hours of combat. For the departing pilots we had one wing-ding of a party. It was the first time that the fellows got me stinking drunk, on champagne, no less.

The party broke up with everyone staggering back to their tent or, like myself, to the latrine to throw up. At the latrine were several fellows in the same shape; however, two others with flashlights and tent poles were poking down one of the holes. Bob Goff had lost his teeth (partial plate) while throwing up his party spirits, and they were trying to retrieve them. The next day I learned they were successful, but Bob soaked them for ten days in every antiseptic the doc could provide before he used them again. Over the years we've had fun teasing Bob, and at our reunions we usually have a good laugh over a few drinks and toast the successful recovery of his teeth under aromatically trying conditions.

The next morning in the chow line (we had only one line for both officers and enlisted personnel), the enlisted boys insisted I go ahead of them and get some coffee because I looked so bad. They also suggested that I sit in an aircraft and breathe some pure oxygen for a few minutes. I took their advice and it seemed to help enough that I did it several more times after other parties.

Capt. Maurice L. (Marty) Martin encountered an unusual situation on 2 October while leading the 390th squadron escorting ten groups of B-26s bombing targets north of Aachen. They intercepted a British Mosquito bomber loitering in the area and ascertained it had German crosses on the fuselage. Marty proceeded to shoot it down. I know it caused a controversy but the participants remained adamant about the markings.

On the same mission a box of B-26 bombers hit the wrong area, 27 miles from the intended target. Marty and the other fighter-squadron leaders attempted to contact the bombers before the bombs were dropped, but they were not successful. The air/ground controller, Decline, ordered our aircraft to stop the bombers even if they had to shoot them down. By that time, of course, the damage had been done. Thirty-five Belgium civilians were killed in the mishap.[1]

My first deep penetration of Germany occurred on 7 October, on a mission to Wiesbaden and Frankfurt to dive-bomb railroad marshaling yard chokepoints (where the main line first starts to branch out into the yard). We obtained several good cuts, destroyed some locomotives, and set a gasoline tank car on fire. A typical (sort of) boring mission.

A Jewish pilot named Saul Faktorow came into the squadron. He had the dubious distinction of becoming the pilot with the most shot-up aircraft. It seemed that on every mission he would come home all shot up, some even ending up classed as junk. Those pilots assigned an aircraft dreaded him flying their aircraft since it was almost sure to be hit. At this time I had about thirty missions and had not yet been hit. One evening, sitting in the lounge we had created in a bombed-out building, Saul made the comment, "Do you think the Germans know I'm a Jew flying that aircraft?" He was serious. He survived the war but I'm sure he holds the group record of getting the most aircraft shot out from under him. I now wish I had kept count. I finally met Saul again at our 1995 reunion in Seattle. He stayed in the Air Force after the war and retired a full colonel. I related what I said about him in this book, and his remark was, "I only got them [the aircraft] damaged; I never got one shot down."

A stagnated front line made it appear we would be stationed at Laon for some time. With cold winter weather upon us we winterized our tent, putting in a door and even some windows. It made it quite homey. Our lounge had a small stove but it was still cold and damp, not the kind of place someone would want as a lounge during winter. The building had a heavily damaged fireplace so we hired French bricklayers to repair it using salvaged brick. It was finally finished and we christened it with a roaring fire. Shortly we heard a shot and a couple of fellows swore that a bullet came zipping between them. Then several more shots rang out. We simultaneously realized that the fireplace bricks were exploding. The workers did not use firebrick in the hearth, and brick chips were assaulting us, whizzing around the room. We beat a hasty retreat from our cozy lounge.

Since there was time for only one or two missions per day it became common to have group missions of forty-eight aircraft. On one such mission we were on course to the target area and were busy forming up into flights and squadrons as we climbed through several thousand feet of clouds. After about 15 minutes a most peculiar radio conversation came from the 391st Foxhunt squadron. "Foxhunt leader, this is Foxhunt Red 4—my eyes are crossed and I can't uncross them." We all looked at each other and tapped our ear phones to be sure they were working okay. "This is Foxhunt leader—say again," came the reply. Much more frantic he came back, "My eyes are crossed and I can't uncross them!" Red leader told him to return to base and Red 3 to accompany him in case of an emergency. About 15 minutes later we heard him call for landing instructions and a short while later heard, "Burdock, tell me if I'm lined up with the runway since I'm coming in on one eye."

It was a humorous incident and those of us who flew in the large formations of World War II can easily visualize how that can happen. We had our eyes on the leader to stay in tight formation (at least until we approached the front line). Occasionally we would glance at our instruments to assure all was well, all the while observing, from the corners of our eyes, other aircraft above and below us sliding into formation. The constant eye movement and trying to notice everything probably cramped one of his eye muscles. The flight surgeon restored his normal vision, but the affected pilot had lost his nerve and refused to make a dive-bombing run. They quietly transferred him from the group.

We received the first assignment to bomb barges on the Rhine River on 11 October. A group mission of thirty-six aircraft initiated several weeks of alternating missions between bombing railroads and barges. A few escort missions were mixed in, but nothing we felt worthwhile. On that first barge-busting mission on 11 October heavy flak batteries constantly tracked and fired on us. It was very intimidating to see those deadly black bursts around us no matter which way we turned. The flak hit Lester Swanke's aircraft and he spiraled out of the formation. Fortunately his aircraft was just damaged and he limped back to base. We found a large cluster of barges around Cologne and proceeded to sink about twelve and damaged many others.

My good friend Dick Tanselle was killed in a midair collision with his wingman, Lt. Joe C. Meyer, in the vicinity of Marche, Belgium, on 15 October. Dick and I had been friends throughout our training and received our wings together at Craig Field. The 389th squadron was on the way to the target when they encountered heavy inclement weather. Dick and his wingman became separated from the rest of the squadron and were last seen skirting a cloud layer, trying to rejoin the formation. The lousy European weather we were flying in claimed several more victims.

The Laon city railroad marshaling yard was a mass of rubble from bombing and strafing that left several locomotives tossed around. On a stand-down day several of us went there to examine the damage. We first noted that the cab had two inches of thick steel plates welded around it to protect the engineer. It obviously was not armor as several .50-caliber bullets pierced it. I also followed the path of a .50-caliber armor-piercing round that went through the steel drive wheel several inches thick, ricocheted off the lower flange of the engine I-beam structure, and imbedded itself sideways in the upper flange. I had a hard time prying the round out for a souvenir, and it didn't have a scratch on it. (I still have it.) It was an amazing revelation of the power of a single armor-piercing round.

My turn for another five-day operational leave rolled around in the latter part of October. The leave group included Chuck Bennett, Claude Halterman, Duane Lund, Homer Schaeffer, Lester Swanke, and me. Within the next few months everyone but me would be shot down. Halterman, Schaeffer, and Swanke would be killed, Duane Lund made a POW (although we didn't know it then), and Chuck Bennett badly wounded. However, that was in the unknown future. We set out planning to spend our leave in Paris. But after one night the Parisians completely disillusioned us. Their attitude had changed from one of cordial friendship, which we experienced our first time there, to one of exploitation. Champagne was five to six dollars per bottle (five times the going rate) and everywhere they were looking for tips. Their attitude also left us with the feeling that now that we had liberated them we should get the hell out, which we did as quickly as possible. At Le Bourget airport we hitched a ride back to London. I vowed then that I would never again visit Paris. I kept that vow for forty years but then relented when we had our reunion there in 1984. Also a little pressure from my wife, Marge, helped sway me.

After staying in London for a night, I decided to try a rest home set up for pilots near Oxford that I heard was really first class. I took the train to Oxford and called them from the station to see if there was room for one more. Their answer was "Yes" and I was told to wait there and they would send a car. About twenty minutes later a limousine pulled up for me.

What a place! It was undoubtedly the home of a wealthy family that had been turned into a rest home where a soldier could live a life of luxury for a few days. There were about twenty of us, quartered two to three in a room. At 0800 the maid woke us with a glass of orange juice. If we were downstairs before 1000 we could have breakfast; otherwise, we would have to wait for lunch. Local girls, acting as hostesses, took us around to see the local historical sights and on a picnic. In the evenings there was always a party with a dance. One day we even went horseback riding. I had never been on a horse but, after half an hour of instruction, went galloping across the fields with the rest of them. When we came to a hedge, the girls sailed over effortlessly. About half the pilots tried to jump, with mixed results. Luckily we incurred no major injuries and we all laughed heartily at the comical antics that occurred as the horses approached the hedge with mostly neophyte riders in the saddle. I chickened out and went around the hedge. We even got caught in a typical English afternoon shower and took refuge in a barn. It was the most relaxed and enjoyable leave one could hope for.

When we returned from our leave it was back to the same old routine—go bust up some railroads, sink some barges, or perform an armed reconnaissance, shooting up targets of opportunity. The aspect of these missions was that we saw no tangible results from our efforts except to see our companions shot down. My friend Chuck Bennett expressed the attitude succinctly when he returned from a mission and I asked him how it went. "Oh, the same old crap. We bombed a railroad track, shot up a train, and probably scared some Germans, but nothing worthwhile." The monotony of the missions became wearisome and a workday-type atmosphere of a daily grind permeated the group.

They introduced a new way of bombing as a fallback when the weather at the primary target precluded dive-bombing and strafing. Occasionally, when weather over our base was clear enough for takeoff and landing but the enemy targets were completely socked in, "pickle-barrel missions" (sometimes called "blind bombing" or "SCR 584 missions") were scheduled. Col. Blair Garland, the IX Fighter Command signals officer, came up with the idea. He married the microwave early warning radar with an antiaircraft SCR 584 gun-laying radar. The SCR 584 was an accurate close-range radar. Using a scrounged computer from a Norden bombsight, the system duplicated the flight of the aircraft on a chart spread out on a table. The radar operator acted as bombardier, correcting the heading of the squadron and counting down to bomb release. Pickle-barrel missions were experimented with during the Normandy campaign. Since then further refinement supposedly made them a potent strike force.[2]

We flew in a tight formation 200 feet behind a lead aircraft. This aircraft would have its radar transponder turned on to give the ground radar operator a good reference to guide the squadron on a bomb run.[3] We flew at a constant 220 mph indicated airspeed and a specified constant altitude between Angels 10 and 15. All we did was follow the directions of the radar operator and drop bombs on cue. Most of us felt these missions were a waste of resources, putting up twelve aircraft to drop twenty-four bombs.

Flying from a concrete runway, even a crudely patched bumpy one, was much better than the Normandy strip. We were again able to make formation takeoffs, which expedited a group mission. Seeing the three majestic squadrons in a compact formation on their way to do battle was a quite thrilling sight. We knew the ground crews were delighted because we could see and hear them send their chargers on the way with a salute and exclamations as "Go get 'em" and

"Give 'em hell." This must have made an impression on our commander since he called a pilot meeting and directed us to spiff up our formation flying. We had to admit, we had became sloppy.

As it turned out, a sort of competition developed between squadrons, and woe to the pilot who spoiled the formation. The squadron commander or his designee also rated us on our formation takeoff. At first this was a great sport, but with flying close to four-hour missions it became a chore to get in close when we returned. We were tired, usually very thirsty (from breathing dry oxygen), and just wanted to get down and off that very uncomfortable dinghy we sat on. Our spiffed-up formation must have worked since we got comments from the crew chief like, "You guys sure looked good coming in."

One time, on takeoff, the lead pilot slammed the throttle full forward instead of feeding it slowly so that I—his wingman—could keep up with him. Since they were rating us on takeoff I wasn't going to be left behind, so I flipped on water injection to catch him. I brought it in close and just as I switched off the water injection a severe vibration developed. By the time I realized it we had flying speed and lifted off. Instinctively, I tapped the brakes to stop the wheel rotation and raised the gear. The vibration stopped and, since everything was normal, I continued the mission. On my return, I found out what had caused the vibration; I had blown a tire on takeoff. It's frightening to think on what could have happened if it had blown before I reached takeoff speed.

Our ground crew was top-notch and took special pride in keeping the aircraft in tip-top shape. We trusted them completely with the aircraft and almost never had to abort. If they said it was ready, we didn't doubt them. They usually pointed out that some minor discrepancies existed, like the compass needed swinging, an engine inspection was overdue, or some other mundane thing. I never flew an aircraft that wasn't entirely fit for combat. Of course, we occasionally had system failures. The P-47 is a complicated piece of machinery, and failures are to be expected. Most are not life-threatening, just a nuisance. I experienced several such failures during my combat period; in fact, during my flying career I had my share. One of the most annoying occurred shortly after the blown tire instance. On takeoff I attempted to raise the gear but felt no response. The hydraulic fluid pressure was zero. I had a pump failure.

That's no big deal, I thought, I'll just pump the gear up by hand. We were almost to the battle area before I had the gear up and locked. The hand pump is on the left of the seat and requires a great deal of exertion. Pumping with the left hand and flying with the right sets up a symptomatic motion in the right hand, which causes the aircraft to porpoise. The other flight members moved aside to give me room to wander around, and then made laughing fun of my predicament.

My first major accident occurred after a group mission at Laon. When we were taxiing, our crew chief usually rode on our wing to direct the way. The long large nose of the P-47 in a three-point attitude precluded seeing straight ahead, so we continually S-turned to see where we were going. This took a lot of taxi room and time. With the crew chief riding the wing and communicating with simple hand signals, we could taxi straight ahead.

The 390th was the first squadron to land that day, and the crew chiefs had not yet arrived at the end of the runway. We were taxiing slowly to our revetments, S-turning as we went. Engineers filled and concreted the bomb craters on the runways and taxiways; however, one bomb crater that impinged about three feet into the taxiway had been filled with only dirt. I was just at that point when another squadron roared overhead at treetop level. I glanced up to appraise their formation flying, and I zigged one wheel right into the dirt-filled crater. Recent rains had turned it to mud, and the wheel sank in, causing me to nose up the aircraft, a quite embarrassing situation. Newly promoted Maj. Maurice L. Martin, the new squadron commander, immediately grounded me for the length of time it took to get the aircraft repaired with a new engine and propeller. This took several days since it had to wait its turn with the other battle-damaged aircraft.

My first flight after grounding was to ferry a P-47 to a boneyard field at Reims where war-weary aircraft were collected and stored. The one I brought to Reims was an old razorback that just wouldn't stay trimmed, making flying quite fatiguing. One wondered how many wings and other parts had been changed on that aircraft during its one year of combat flying. A secondary objective was to restock our supply of champagne. The jeep driver picked me up at the boneyard and on the way back to Laon stopped at Pommery Champagne in Reims. My specific instructions were to get the champagne that had been marked in German, "For Luftwaffe use only." At an equivalent price of $1.10 per bottle I bought several cases. It kept us supplied for a few weeks, and going to Reims to stock up became a regular event. Just before leaving Laon the champagne became less tasty; either Pommery was marking inferior bottles with the Luftwaffe stamp, or we were just getting too much of a good thing. That supply dried up when we transferred from A-70 to Y-29 in Belgium in November, just after we had winterized our tent with walls, door, and window.

Since I could speak Flemish, I asked and received permission to go with the advance contingent to our new base Y-29. I could help recruit local labor to work for the squadron as general helpers in the kitchen and other odd jobs. Another important assignment was to find and contract with some washwomen. Having dependable washwomen to keep us in clean clothes was an invaluable luxury. It didn't cost much, a few Belgium francs and a bar of soap, but kept us feeling so much better with clean clothes, especially clean socks, which meant warm feet.

The advance contingent was led by West Point graduate and now Capt. L. B. Smith (Smitty). Since I was not trained in engineering to set up a base, it turned out to be a very enlightening adventure for me. I was amazed at all the details that need to be considered. Where should the kitchen, latrines, operations, communications be set up, where should the roads be built? A West Point engineering training was obviously a prerequisite to commanding an operation of that sort.

The Ninth Air Force engineers built Y-29, and it consisted of one pierced-steel plank runway, 120 feet wide by 5,000 feet long, running in a northeast–southwest direction. It had 150 hard stands and a perimeter strip circling the runway. The center of the runway was at K-488633 (map coordinates, Nord De Guerre Zone) or 50° 58' 22" N. latitude, 05° 35' 00" E. longitude, about midway between the towns of Genk and As (or Asch). The people in the area have since erected a stone monument memorial where the center of the runway was located. I recently visited the area and found the monument in the center of a new cultivated forest. It was hard to believe, standing in the midst of the large trees, that a bustling and important airstrip had been located there.

Twenty of us were in the advanced contingent. On the day before Thanksgiving Smitty and I, with a driver, went to the big supply dump near Aachen, Germany. There we picked up several frozen turkeys with all the trimmings needed for fixing a traditional turkey dinner. Our cook went all out the next day and, with his makeshift oven and stove, prepared a delicious meal for lunch. Major Martin, still at Laon and wanting to make sure we enjoyed the traditional dinner, sent another one, already cooked, to us in a truck. A jury-rigged stove on the truck kept the meal hot while traveling. It arrived in the late afternoon, so that evening we enjoyed another full-course dinner. It was a Thanksgiving to remember, being able to literally stuff ourselves twice.

The day after Thanksgiving the remainder of the group moved to Y-29. Greeting my friends, I assured them I had several washwomen lined up ready for business. Asking about the latest happenings on the war front, I learned that on 21 November the 389th squadron of sixteen aircraft had a donnybrook of a battle with sixty Me 109 aircraft northeast of Cologne. They claimed the destruction of fifteen German aircraft, losing only one P-47 and having several others damaged. They surprised the enemy by attacking them out of the sun in a perfect setup (more on this later). They were the envy of the other two squadrons, as most of us hadn't been in a dogfight. In fact, I still had not seen an enemy aircraft in flight.

With the group now in Belgium the fellows drafted me to teach them a few key phrases in Flemish. Some knew a little French or German, but I was the only one who knew Flemish. The main key phrases they wanted to learn were, "Will you sleep with me?," "How much?," "Can I buy you a drink?," and "Will you do my wash?" I repeated the lessons several times. Although Y-29 was in the Walloon, or French-speaking area of Belgium, most people could speak Flemish. I experienced no difficulty, except for my limited Flemish vocabulary, in conversing with most local inhabitants.

Y-29 was in a clearing surrounded by cultivated pine trees. The low-level ground bordered on being swampy. At least they made this runway from American pierced-steel planking (probably required on that swampy ground), and it seemed quite a bit sturdier and smoother than the British chicken wire used at A-1. This first impression was corrected as this runway also became very bumpy from hard use. It also had the same tendency as the Marston mat to roll up in front of our wheels, literally snapping the two-foot-long steel stakes out of the ground. Many of us again experienced the sight of a steel stake flying by on takeoff. On the well-used dirt roads and paths mud soon became a major problem. A jeep in four-wheel drive and low-low gear could just get through with mud up to the running board. Fortunately the mud was sandy and did not stick and cake on our shoes. With all the mud around it was bound to get into the cockpit and caused a dust and dirt storm whenever we pulled negative Gs. To help keep our aircraft cockpits clean, and earn the gratitude of our crew chiefs, we would occasionally open the canopy and roll over, letting the dirt blow and fall out.

All aircraft that had undergone major repairs required flight testing prior to combat commitment. Pilots often volunteered for this duty since it usually was a relaxing flight. Depending on the type of repair, the aircraft was wrung out by performing some violent maneuvers and acrobatics, and dived to at least 450 mph. If they installed a new engine, it was flown for 10 hours at reduced power to break in the engine. Since my Belgium hometown was now only 70 miles away, I volunteered quite often to test aircraft since I could then buzz my relatives. My first hometown buzz job was remembered by many people, some not too happy about it.

With a slow-time aircraft I flew to Oordegem. Since I flew with reduced power, I really couldn't give them a good buzz job but just flew around the area at 500 feet, sightseeing and rocking my wings at relatives and other people waving at me. I circled my aunt's home where I used to live, over several cousins' homes, the old windmill, and other boyhood landmarks I remembered. Later I found out the consternation I had caused in the entire neighborhood. My relatives surmised it was me since I had warned them to expect me, but the rest of the residents had absolutely no idea what was going on. The commuter train had stopped and the people scrambled into the ditches, thinking I was a German aircraft looking for a strafing target. Several factories in the adjacent town of Wettern shut down as the workers scrambled to the air-raid shelters. The teachers (Catholic sisters) let the children out of school, but in this instance it was to let them watch the "flying fool." My young cousins circulated news of my impending visit in school, and all the students had been anxiously anticipating the air show. I certainly made a name for myself, and everyone now knew about the local boy fighter pilot.

An incident occurred upon landing that exemplified the excellent pilot training we received. We always flew a tight landing pattern so we could reach the runway for a normal landing without using the engine from peel-off to touchdown. This was continually stressed because we never knew when an engine that may have been abused in combat would quit. This training paid dividends when my engine quit on peel-off. One magneto had burned up during flight, meaning I had only one magneto and a set of plugs keeping the engine running. When I retarded the throttle to idle on peel-off, the set of working plugs fouled and the engine quit. Luckily I had not retarded the throttle during my buzz job over Oordegem, since I would have had a hard time explaining, at my court martial, what I was doing 70 miles from base. Slow-timing an aircraft is supposed to be done near the base to accommodate just such emergencies. My guardian angel was with me again during that flight.

We soon learned our Belgium airfield was in "Buzz Bomb Alley." The Germans were conducting a concentrated V-1 attack against Antwerp, launching them from a dense wooded and hilly area southeast of Aachen, Germany, known as the Eifel. A straight line from there to Antwerp went right over Y-29, so we had a continuous stream of them overhead day and night. Several V-1s impacted in our area, and we wondered whether the Germans were targeting us or if they were malfunctioning V-1s. Foxholes sprouted and were covered with trees cut down to make room for the tents but soon filled with water. As long as we heard the staccato buzz from the V-1 pulse jet, we knew we were okay. The dilemma came when we heard one cut out and knew it was on its way down. During the day we could see it start its dive, but at night or when it was cloudy and foggy, when most seemed to come over, we couldn't. The V-1 pulse jet-engine exhaust plume lit up the night sky, but when it cut out we had no way of knowing where it would go. The question was, should we get in a water-filled foxhole or take a chance? Most of us started to ignore them, especially at night while sacked out. To storm out of our tent into a soggy foxhole was too unappetizing; however, some fellows would do so. Sometimes we would hear several buzz bombs go overhead as in formation. Antwerp took quite a beating from the buzz bombs.

Mission time, which lasted about three hours each from A-70, suddenly was halved. We were about 10 minutes from the front lines again and were in the

British sector, right on the boundary between the British and American zones. The next strip over, Y-32, about seven miles away, hosted a British Spitfire group. We were set for the winter and ready for everything it would bring. Little did we know that the most severe fighting of the entire war was going to engulf the U.S. Army in Europe.

5.   The Hürtgen Forest Campaign

Initial Attacks

Supplies were finally adequate to resume the offensive into Germany. The First Army attack to reach the Rhine River lay through the Hürtgen Forest. Our optimistic expectations to break through to the Rhine River were dashed by the terrain, desperate German defense, and atrocious weather that stifled our attacks.

The Hürtgen Forest covers a nearly rectangular plot of ground about 30 miles long by eight miles wide, the long axis oriented in a northeast/southwest direction. It is part of the hilly tree-shrouded region that runs the entire length of the Belgium-German border. The Hürtgen Forest is quite dense, with only a few open areas sprinkled about, and contains many sharp ridges, steep ravines, and streams. The hills, some of them quite steep, rise to 1,500 feet. Closely spaced large pine trees provide an impenetrable canopy that allows almost no sunlight to get through, creating a perpetual twilight below. The trees and the tangled underbrush restrict ground visibility and limit the field of fire to only a few yards. With very few landmarks, getting lost is easy. The weather is perpetually wet and cold. Worst of all, for us in the war, part of the Siegfried Line fortifications ran through the forest. It is a terrible place for a war, especially for the attacker. The resulting ground battle to push through that forest was vicious and debilitating, wearing out several divisions of ground troops.

For us, as pilots, the forest was a beautiful green carpet studded with a few small villages. Here and there a short section of a road was detectable, but only if we looked almost straight down. All that was visible for any oblique view was the green carpet. We very seldom saw any ground activity with the exception of smoke rising from something exploding or burning underneath that carpet. A hundred vehicles could be parked on the side of a road, only visible to us if we buzzed the area. Few landmarks were apparent, and unless we were tasked to attack a town or another prominently visible feature, we couldn't be sure of the target. Winter weather added its contribution of low clouds, haze, rain, and snow.

The battleground conditions were obviously not conducive for war. The American superiority of fire power and air support would be of very limited use. To those who fought on the ground there, I have this to say: we hated the Hürtgen Forest as much as you did and we tried our best to support you. The missions required a major effort on our part and we were admonished to do everything we could do to help. The November-December casualties reflect the consequences of our effort. During that two-month period our group lost thirty-six aircraft and twenty-six pilots, a 50 percent loss of aircraft and a 30 percent loss of pilots (see appendix).

Many World War II soldiers believe that the fighter-pilot air war was glamorous and chivalrous combat. That statement is somewhat true, but applies only for the air-combat scenario, with its one-on-one combat between aircraft cavorting about the sky. The mundane ground-support air war was a different story. We were forced to fly in an environment that pitted the impersonal antiaircraft ground fire against our luck, and that was never more true than in the Hürtgen Forest battle. The fighter-bomber effort during that battle is a story that should be remembered. As such, I have chronicled the Hürtgen Forest missions to present an accurate account on six weeks of combat with a fighter-bomber group in our battle against the Germans and the weather.

During the halcyon days of August advancing almost unopposed through France and Belgium the U.S. First Army troops reached the German border in the middle of September. There they ran into the Siegfried Line fortifications. With the German army in disarray, the lightly held Siegfried Line was penetrated in several places around the German city of Aachen. Unfortunately the American troops ran out of gas—literally. The troops that had reached the Hürtgen Forest between Monschau and Roetgen mounted some battalion-size attacks but were repulsed. The front there stagnated while the limited resources were used to capture Aachen, which fell on 21 October. The First Army center of attack then shifted to the Hürtgen Forest region to capture Schmidt, which controlled the approaches to the Schwammenauel and Erft dams on the Roer River. From that point on, our group was tasked to help the troops push through the Hürtgen Forest.

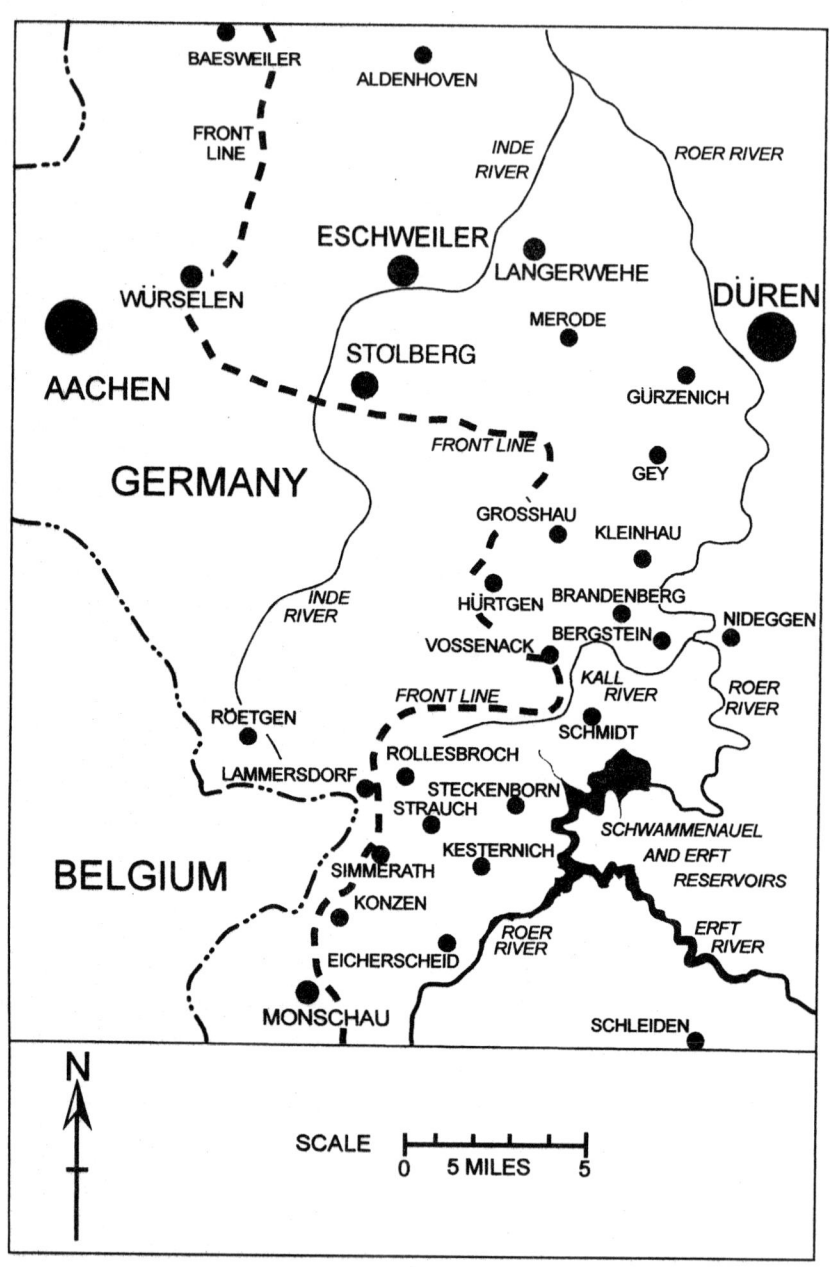

Hürtgen Forest Area, Front Line, 16 November 1944

We were still at A-70 in Laon when we started to support the American First Army troops slogging through the Hürtgen Forest.[1] Our first mission was 3 November, tasked to support the 28th Infantry Division in their drive to capture Schmidt, on one of the high ridges on the southeastern fringe of the forest and a crossroads town that controlled several roads through the forest. It was the key position for controlling the approaches to the Roer River dams, although the U.S. Army commanders initially overlooked that strategic function.[2] The oversight and resulting consequences still generate active debates within the military history community. We, of course, knew nothing about that at the time, and just bombed and strafed the enemy positions while trying to help our troops get through that forest.

Three squadron missions of twelve aircraft were scheduled. Half the aircraft were loaded with two 500-pound general-purpose bombs, and the others with two 260-pound fragmentation bombs. Fragmentation bombs were especially effective against troops because they exploded when they hit the trees and spewed their lethal shrapnel downward. We also carried a 150-gallon belly tank of extra fuel since the battle line was 150 miles from our base. Unfortunately, the usual fog and low clouds at our Laon base delayed the first squadron takeoff for three hours, allowing only two missions.

The twelve aircraft of the 390th (including me) flew the first mission, taking off at 1155 and reaching the target area at 1235 for an armed reconnaissance of all roads leading from Schmidt, with the exception of those from the west. We checked in with "Hopcraft," the 28th Infantry Division air/ground controller near Schmidt. He advised us that German troops and vehicles were congregating in the northeast and he wanted us to discourage them. Knowing where to look, we sighted tanks and other vehicles clustered on the roads (more aptly called trails or fire breaks) and in the woods. After Hopcraft confirmed that as the target, we bombed and strafed it. We claimed three tanks destroyed and three more probably destroyed. Also destroyed were five trucks, a motorcycle and rider, a barracks, and radio tower. In addition, we damaged several flak positions firing at us. We advised Hopcraft that another large concentration of German tanks and vehicles was congregated in adjacent woods, but Hopcraft denied us permission to attack since they were too close to our troops. Hopcraft complimented us on the good job we did.

As we were returning to base, the 391st squadron, with twelve aircraft, reported to Hopcraft. They were told to continue the destruction of the assembled German troops by bombing and strafing. Three motor vehicles and six horse-drawn vehicles were claimed destroyed. In addition, they strafed several houses in the town of Vlatten since they appeared to house a command post. Communications were hampered by the Germans jamming of C and D channels with a loud siren sound. The American tanks in the fields they reported seeing near Schmidt were probably the Sherman tanks led by Lt. Raymond E. Fleig, 707th Tank Battalion, in a drive through the Kall trail to attack Schmidt.[3]

Our group received a commendation from Maj. Gen. Leonard T. Gerow, Commander V Corps, for breaking up and stopping a large concentration of German forces on the 28th Division front. General Quesada, CG IX TAC, endorsed the commendation, noting that it was accomplished in adverse weather.

It didn't seem like we did that much but it is hard to assess the destruction from fleeting glances as we roared by at 400 mph. Perhaps the weather lulled the Germans into thinking it was too cloudy to fly and they were out in the open instead of in their foxholes when our bombs came thundering down. The ceiling was at 2,500 feet with a visibility of five miles. The ground elevations in the area range up to 1,500 feet, which allowed only 1,000 feet for maneuvering. This low-altitude operation presented both a flak and mountain hazard. Little did we know that was going to be the normal scenario in this battle. The 390th had one aircraft heavily damaged and five others lightly damaged from flak, while the 391st had one aircraft heavily damaged.

The German units attacking the Americans near Schmidt were the 275th Infantry Division with attached tank units of the 116th Panzer Division. We chased the 116th Panzer Division out of Normandy, but it was reconstituted and again was going to be one of our antagonists in the Hürtgen Forest. The division contained many new troops who weren't aware of our capabilities, which is perhaps why we caught them out of their foxholes. They must have learned fast, though, because their defense of Schmidt was successful, and the American forces didn't capture the town until February 1945. The long quasi-static battle line allowed elaborate foxholes and bunkers to be constructed. In 1995 my grandsons, searching the foxhole remains still visible in the area, found several corroded rifle bullets and my son the remains of a teller mine.

The next several days our group was tasked to destroy ammunition and supply dumps that supported the German troops fighting in the Hürtgen Forest. This was a nasty assignment. We wanted to destroy the dump, but we didn't want it to explode under us at a low altitude. Consequently we dropped our bombs at a higher altitude and then immediately turned and clawed for altitude using war emergency power.

A group mission of thirty-six aircraft, twenty-four carrying bombs and twelve flying top cover, attacked an ammunition dump in Bruhl, just south of Cologne. We dropped all bombs on the target and observed five big secondary explosions. On our withdrawal we saw black smoke and fire covering the whole dump. Scratch one dump.

The group did such a good job on that dump that for the next several days they targeted us to hit several others. After bombing we were released to conduct reconnaissance missions, strafing targets of opportunity in the rear of the battle area. An ammunition supply dump south of the Hürtgen Forest by Schleiden was the next day's target for thirty-six aircraft. Unfortunately we bombed the wrong target. A factory building that we thought was the dump was bombed instead. Several large fires were set within the factory, and several errant bombs that hit in the bordering woods produced a large, satisfying secondary explosion. This led us to believe the well-camouflaged dump was in the woods.

The armed reconnaissance following the bombing was very fruitful. We caught and destroyed five locomotives, some pulling a long column of boxcars. I discovered and accounted for two of the locomotives. It was my first experience strafing a locomotive, previously only having the opportunity to strafe the train cars. It was exhilarating to see the steam billowing out of the numerous holes punched through the boiler by my .50-caliber guns.

For the second group mission of the day, thirty-five aircraft went to an ammunition storage dump located between Trier and Koblenz on the railroad the group was trying to interdict. All bombs impacted within the target area and left it exploding and burning, with smoke billowing up to Angels 10. The armed reconnaissance following the bombing was again very fruitful. The group discovered several clusters of vehicles parked in adjacent towns. A Tiger tank was disabled by repeated strafing, and twelve trucks and a staff car were destroyed. As a bonus, several houses were set on fire by the parked vehicles.

The reader may wonder how strafing a tank could disable it. Recall that our .50-caliber armor-piercing rounds packed a wallop that could penetrate several inches of soft (not hardened) steel. (Recall the story on our visit to the Laon railroad yard, where I followed the path of a .50-caliber armor-piercing round that went through a locomotive drive wheel.) During the war we thought the penetration power of our armor-piercing round was sufficient to disable a tank by shooting off the tank tracks. To research this issue and keep the record factual, I contacted several armored vehicle historians and specialists. Their collective views on this issue are summarized below.[4]

The .50-caliber armor-piercing round fired from fast-moving aircraft does indeed have a high momentum but the German tank armor was very hard and massive and the round only dinged the armor. The most vulnerable area (least armor thickness) is the rear deck engine compartment and the top of the turret. The tracks are extremely hard steel and .50-caliber rounds were shrugged off with little damage. A lucky hit was possible that might cause the tank to throw a track, but if they were on a hard surface they could just keep moving on the road wheels. The Germans in 1944-45 had three main battle tanks in use. They were the Mark IV which was a medium tank comparable to the American M4 Sherman tank, and two 50-plus-ton heavy tanks, the Mark V Panther and the Mark VI Tiger. The Panther and Tiger tanks completely dominated the M4 Sherman.

The Mark IV had a lightly armored rear deck that could be penetrated by our .50-caliber rounds and set the engine on fire, but the Panther and Tiger were mostly impervious to our strafing. In those tanks the tank crew would button up and hope we wouldn't call in some aircraft that had bombs since that would finish them. There is a case on record where a Panther tank was strafed by P-47s for an extended time. The massive strafing shot off all the equipment parts carried outside the tank, and entombed the crew by dinging the hatch lips, essentially welding the hatches closed. If we could catch the tanks while on a road march far from the front lines they sometimes carried extra fuel and ammunition strapped on the outside. In those cases strafing could ignite the fuel or ammunition, possibly destroying them. Although we couldn't be sure of damaging or destroying a heavy tank, our strafing was sure to affect the crew psychologically, having to stay cooped up and hear the constant rattle of our rounds hitting the tank and not knowing when a bomb or other heavy gun would finish them off. In summary, strafing a tank could do nothing or it could destroy them, depending on the circumstances.

Lest anyone think that it was all fun and games on our part, the next several missions should dispel any such notions. The objective of the group mission on 6 November was to destroy a fuel dump about five miles northeast of Düren. All bombs from the thirty-six aircraft landed within the target area and exploded six small roofed huts, producing restrained explosions as if they were underground. One bomb hit directly on a zig-zag covered trench but produced no explosion. Bombing also destroyed one large building and two smaller ones, one of the smaller buildings exploding in a large boiling fire. Strafing after bombing destroyed two small locomotives and a large one pulling at least twenty-five cars. They thoroughly strafed the cars but results were unknown. The cost was three P-47s badly damaged and one lost. Heavy flak hit Lt. Bob Hogue's aircraft as he pulled up into a cloud. A short while later a part of the tail was seen fluttering down, but no one saw the rest of the aircraft or a parachute. Postwar records indicate Hogue's body was found in the crashed aircraft. Some aircraft strayed over Düren and experienced a murderous barrage of flak.

The excellent working arrangement developed by our air/ground team allowed us to exercise considerable leeway to carry out air support. One of these was to provide emergency aid to anyone in dire need. I recall a mission where we had completed our scheduled dive-bombing and were returning home. Over the front lines we received a call from an air/ground controller (I cannot remember the name or place) asking for some emergency help from P-47s flying over the area. The squadron leader verified the air/ground identity with Sweepstakes, and then asked what we could do to help. They asked us for assistance in breaking up a strong local attack by the German forces. We told the air/ground controller we had no bombs but could provide some strafing support. After identifying the target we proceeded to strafe vigorously for several minutes. A grateful thanks from the controller made us feel good.

During the Normandy invasion and the battle of France, the 366th Fighter Group was attached to IX TAC, which was the air support command for General Hodges's First Army. Right after the Normandy breakout, General Patton's Third Army and the accompanying XIX TAC air support command became operational. The 366th, although assigned to IX TAC, would occasionally be loaned out for a few days to support the Third Army. At mission briefing they told us we would be under this or that TAC's control, but it really didn't matter to us as we went where ordered to help the ground forces. In fact, we felt special being switched from one TAC to the other, like firefighters rushing from one hot spot to another to contain a persistent and difficult fire. For administrative control and logistical support we were under the jurisdiction of the First Army IX TAC. In early October they officially transferred us to XXIX TAC, the air-support TAC for the newly formed Ninth Army commanded by Lt. Gen. William Simpson, but the transfer was not implemented until February. We therefore remained under IX TAC during the Hürtgen Forest and the Battle of the Bulge campaigns, and even flew a few for the Third Army XIX TAC. It can truly be said that our group covered a substantial portion of the front line and saw a lot of Europe while strafing.

For example, on 8 November, they temporarily assigned the group to Gen. Otto P. Weyland's XIX TAC for two days to support General Patton's Third Army attack to encircle the French fortress city of Metz, an offensive code-named Madison. This was the first assault of a double-prong offensive coordinated with General Hodges's First Army attack, called Queen. Queen, scheduled to begin a few days later, was to reach the Rhine River in the vicinity of Cologne.

An attack on a major German unit headquarters in the village of Kemplich, France, was the mission for 8 November. Kemplich, located about 18 miles southeast of Luxembourg, was right in the middle of the defunct French Maginot Line. According to the operations order, the whole village consisted of a major unit headquarters and we were to aim at the center of the village and let the normal bomb dispersion produce the desired results. This was a coordinated *coup de main* by a dozen fighter-bomber groups against identified major enemy unit headquarters and coincided with the start of Patton's offensive. The bombing, carried out by forty-eight aircraft, leveled the small village.

World War II historian Klaus Schulz concluded that we had probably bombed the headquarters of the German 19th Volksgrenadier Division in Kemplich.[5]

They were defending against a crossing of the Moselle River by the American 90th Infantry Division north of Thionville. Interrogation of captured German officers revealed that the disruptions caused by the fighter-bomber attacks on major unit headquarters delayed the enemy response several days. This allowed Patton a good jump forward in his latest assault. The Germans complained that the attacks were very unsportsmanlike.[6]

The armed reconnaissance, conducted in the Saarlatern-Trier area after bombing Kemplich, accounted for ten locomotives, four trucks, one staff car, three horse-drawn vehicles, and a streetcar. The cost was the loss of two fine officers: Capt. Al. Jennings and Lt. Lester Swanke. Al had completed his 100 missions and was under orders to go on a 30-day leave. He volunteered to lead one last mission and was shot down and killed. This initiated an immediate edict that anyone with orders to go home was grounded. Lester Swanke was the first to be lost from those I had gone on leave with just a month ago.

After again assisting in Patton's offensive by bombing a fuel storage dump at Bingen, 10 November brought us back to the Hürtgen Forest. The second prong of the simultaneous attacks by the Third and First Armies, Queen, was scheduled to begin on 11 November, or when the weather cleared, but no later than 16 November. The First Army attack was to drive to the Rhine River near Cologne. This meant pushing through the Hürtgen Forest and the Stolberg Corridor from Aachen to Eschweiler to Düren, and then across the Roer River leading to the Rhine River plain. Unfortunately, weather did not cooperate and they postponed the start of the attack. They needed clear weather because a massive bombardment by the Eighth Air Force and the RAF was planned to kick off the ground attack. This bombardment was several times larger than Cobra, the air bombardment that precipitated the Normandy beachhead breakout in July. It is interesting now to read the top-secret operations order and note with hindsight the great plans that were too ambitious for the forces involved, and the fact it was the worst time of the year to carry out such an operation in that rugged terrain.[7] From a fighter-bomber standpoint we were going to be busy.

Although the weather was too foul for the heavy bombers, they deemed it clear enough for our missions. Railroad bridges on the main double track line between Cologne and Düren were the targets for 11 November, with the 366th tasked to destroy two bridges in the middle of the line. Forty-eight P-47s participated in the raid and were very successful, destroying both bridges and an additional overpass a short distance further up the track. The Germans did not expect an attack in this area, so the flak was sporadic and ineffective. We enjoyed putting our full concentration on destroying the targets and it showed by the excellent bombing results.

The weather finally cleared enough to initiate Queen, and the massive bombardment by both the RAF and the U.S. Eighth Air Force was initiated on 16 November. Twelve-hundred heavy bombers from the Eighth Air Force dropped 4,000 tons of bombs on Eschweiler, and the RAF unloaded another 5,500 tons on Düren and several other Roer River towns. Low clouds at their base grounded the medium bombers from the Ninth Air Force. Low clouds and low visibility similarly hampered us, but we were able to mount two squadron missions in support of the 4th Infantry Division.

The 391st squadron mounted a morning strike of sixteen aircraft on the town of Gey, bombing on artillery-fired red smoke shells. The results were not observed with the exception of several houses on fire. One P-47 was lost, Lt. Vince Kramer bailed out over friendly lines, and another P-47 was heavily damaged. The weather was very bad, having an overcast at 2,000 feet with a visibility of five miles.

The 390th mounted an afternoon strike of sixteen aircraft bombing on artillery-fired red smoke at Hürtgen and Hamich Ridge just south of Eschweiler. Results were not observable but Organ, the 4th Infantry Division air/ground controller, said it was a good job. Four RAF Lancaster bombers were seen going down over Düren, and four B-17s down at Eschweiler. In spite of a ragged broken cloud ceiling, ranging between 1,000 and 2,000 feet, and a visibility that was at best five miles, they strafed and destroyed three locomotives and a truck.

The operations order specified continued support for the 4th Infantry Division for 17 November. If close support was impossible, we were to bomb bridges, cut tracks, and prevent any movement on railroads between the 4th Infantry Division front and the Rhine. Squadron missions of sixteen aircraft, all loaded with two 500-pound bombs and a 150-gallon belly tank of fuel, were specified. The order specified continuous missions at 1.5-hour intervals throughout the day.

First light on the seventeenth revealed that the weather was still bad, with a ragged cloud ceiling that varied between 2,000 and 4,000 feet and an associated visibility of about one to two miles in light rain and fog. The prognosis was for continued slow improvement during the day, so the group commander decided to go as scheduled.

The first squadron off that morning was the 389th, at 0941. They reached the target area at 1037 and Organ told them to bomb the town of Hürtgen, where red smoke would mark the target. Bombs smothered the target, but they could see no tangible results, although Organ reported the results were good. Then they complied with an urgent request by Ballard, the 4th Infantry Division frontline air/ground controller, to strafe the town of Gey, but again they observed no results. Pilots reported a continuous barrage of light-caliber flak over the target area, which damaged several aircraft.

The second squadron mission of sixteen aircraft from the 391st squadron was off at 1124 and also bombed Hürtgen as directed by Organ. They also could not observe any results. They were then released to perform an armed reconnaissance. Because of the marginal weather, a ceiling of 4,500 feet, and visibility of five miles, they split into separate flights to strafe targets of opportunity. Four horse-drawn wagons full of troops, a staff car, two trucks, and a motorcycle and rider fell victim to their bullets. Unfortunately, they lost four aircraft but one of the four pilots lost returned to base later. The three pilots killed were Lt. Rufus Barkley Jr., Lt. Dick ("Red") Alderman, and Lt. Gus Girlinghouse.

Remarkable coincidences and happenstance occurrences have uncovered the full story of that fateful mission. Historian Klaus Schulz and I have uncovered many interesting connections between our Hürtgen Forest missions and the German and American ground war accounts. Schulz interviewed a former flak platoon leader, Leutnant Eberhard Kabitz, from the 16th Panzer Regiment, 116th Panzer Division. Kabitz fought in the Hürtgen Forest and claimed to have shot down two P-47s on 17 November. The aircraft crashed close by and he wrote down the pilots' names from the crashed aircraft. Klaus traced the names, Alderman and Girlinghouse, and found they were from the 391st squadron of our 366th Fighter Group. I did additional checking with members of the 391st squadron, and pieced together the American side of that mission. Klaus did the same in Germany and thus we reconstructed the mission from both the German and American eyewitness accounts.[8]

During this mission the 391st squadron became embroiled in a battle with a 116th Panzer Division flak unit dispersed around Merode Castle. Merode is in the northeastern fringe of the Hürtgen Forest, about eight miles west of Düren. Leutnant Kabitz was in charge of two flak wagons armed with four-barrel 20mm guns. He related that the 116th Panzer Division was being withdrawn from the Schmidt area of the Hürtgen Forest to München Gladbach for a welcome rest and refit and had paused at Merode Castle. Unknown to Leutnant Kabitz their refitting was to get them ready to participate in the upcoming German Ardennes offensive, known now as the Battle of the Bulge.

Leutnant Kabitz described his journey for refitting.

From Schmidt we proceeded to Merode where parts of the 2nd Battalion, 16th Panzer Regiment was concentrated at the park of the castle. We took up positions located in the orchards between the houses of the town and waited for departure of the panzers which we were to follow. Because of continuous bad weather, we did not expect any enemy air activities. However, in the late hours of the morning on 17 November, two Thunderbolts flew very low over the town, from the southwest. We rushed to clear our guns for action. Only a few minutes later the two aircraft returned flying at a height of

30 meters [100 feet] in the opposite direction. We fully hit both planes during their approach and flyby. Both came down aflame at the southern end of Merode. One crashed on a field, the other one into a stable where a German artillery element had billeted its horses. One of the pilots, presumably catapulted from his cockpit, lay mortally wounded not far away from his wrecked aircraft. The other burned in his plane.

Shortly after the air attacks the panzers were on their way. Thus I personally preferred to stay with the platoon to be in place in line forming the end of the battalion which had commenced their move to Langerwehe. Therefore, I dispatched a sergeant who was in charge of one of my guns to the crash scene. He reported to me and handed me the pilots' papers including a receipt for an amount spent at a Parisian bar dated the preceding day. The papers from the pilots were subsequently passed on to our headquarter's company. The artillery unit on site promised the sergeant that the pilots would receive a proper burial.

For subject action the NCO's in charge of the guns, the gun layers, and myself were awarded the Iron Cross, 2nd Class.

The shot-down pilots, Alderman and Girlinghouse, while looking for strafing targets had stumbled upon the juicy target of a parked and clustered panzer unit. Because of the low ceiling the pilots were probably unsure of their exact location to report their find and, since they drew no flak on their first pass, went back for another look at low altitude which was fatal for them. The weather had caused the squadron to split up so no one from the squadron saw them being shot down.

The battle continued with occasional flights of Thunderbolts roaring over Merode Castle and strafing the parked vehicles. According to Klaus Schulz, the strafing P-47s were also engaged by a local flak unit stationed at Merode Castle and led by a flak officer known only as Leutnant Kind, who fired at the aircraft with a mobile MG 42 antiaircraft machine gun he set up on the castle bridge. Many Merode civilians had taken refuge in the castle's deep cellar to escape the heavy bombing by British Lancaster bombers the previous day on the nearby town of Düren. Many bombs impacted in the Merode area and severely damaged the town, killing over sixty people. Among the civilians taking refuge in the castle's cellar was a young boy named Albert Trostorf, who, with a friend, had crept up to the cellar door to peek at the battle raging around the castle. The boys learned that P-47 fighter-bombers were attacking German armored vehicles around the castle and were curious. Young Trostorf saw Leutnant Kind firing at a strafing P-47 and saw the shells hit the aircraft, which started burning and crashed into the forest south of Merode.[9]

The aircraft that Leutnant Kind shot down was piloted by Rufus Barkley Jr. and crashed in a swampy, nearly unaccessible area of the Hürtgen Forest. Lt. Henry Collins, Lieutenant Barkley's flight leader, described the incident.

Lieutenant Barkley was leading the second element in my [Yellow] flight. We had just strafed three horse drawn supply wagons moving into the woods in the vicinity of Düren, Germany, and had set course for our rendezvous point at Eschweiler. Lieutenant Barkley apparently, but without a call to me, sighted an enemy target and made a strafing pass. We saw his tracers hit a vehicle just outside a chateau on the edge of the woods, but he never recovered from the dive and crashed in the forest. The loss of Lieutenant Barkley left all of us stunned. He was an excellent pilot, a super young man and was very well liked by the others.

Another pilot, Lt. Stan Sobek, remembered that mission, which was his first combat mission.

I vividly remember that mission in the Hürtgen Forest because it was my first one and I was flying as wingman to my flight leader, Lt. Henry Collins. We were at squadron strength of four flights [sixteen aircraft] under a low ceiling and strafing tanks and motorized and horse drawn vehicles. The flak was heavy and accurate. I observed Lieutenant Barkley's aircraft crash and burn, and saw two other P-47s burning on the ground. When we formed up there were only twelve of us left to return. The experience completely shocked me and I resigned myself to a two-week longevity in that environment. As a replacement pilot I did not know Girlinghouse or Alderman, but was acquainted with Barkley as he took me "under his wing." He was also a Pennsylvanian, living about 20 miles from me in Uniontown.

It is interesting to note that Lieutenant Collins's flight of aircraft flew over the parked panzers and only Rufus Barkley caught sight of them. The Germans were masters of camouflage, by necessity facing an enemy that had air superiority, and were so good that even when a pilot strafed a target many other pilots still could not recognize it. This was especially true in the Hürtgen Forest because of the dark shade under the trees.

   Lt. Quentin Aanenson flew the other aircraft that was missing. His aircraft was heavily damaged during his dive-bombing pass but he nursed it to an emergency crash landing at a forward American fighter base.[10] As he related the mission:

As we approached the target area, we had to come in under an overcast at 4,500 feet. Everything was so dark and eerie, and we could see flashes of the big guns on the ground and the flak explosions in the air. It was as if we were looking into a segment of hell. They hit me in the canopy right behind my head as I rolled into my dive-bombing pass, and [I] was hit again as I was pulling off the target. I headed for the American lines, and out of pure luck found a forward American fighter base where I crash landed. Several hours later when I returned to our field, they listed me on the scheduling board as "Missing in Action."

   Both "Red" Alderman and Gus Girlinghouse lived in my tent, "Duffy's Tavern," along with Johnny Bathurst and me. The night of November 17th was a terrible night for us as we started preparing their footlockers for shipment home. Johnny and I lost four pilots from "Duffy's Tavern" during a three-week period, and we were the only ones left. We decided we needed to protect ourselves emotionally, so we refused to let anyone else move in with us. We kept it that way until we all moved to Y-29 at Asch, Belgium in late November.

Quent is more emotional than most of us were in coping with our companions' loss. It was a way of life at the time and we just took it in stride. We grieved for the pilot and his family, but were resigned that some of us would be killed.

While researching the facts for the Hürtgen Forest battle I received a fortunate piece of information from Stan Sobek. Stan found Mr. David Barkley, younger brother of Lt. Rufus O. Barkley, still residing in Uniontown. I contacted David Barkley and he related a touching story that the research of this story finally closed. Rufus Barkley's crash site was in an almost inaccessible area of the Hürtgen Forest The location was identified by Lieutenant Collins in the operations report, but it remained hidden until a young boy, Josef Schell, who was gathering firewood, stumbled across it in 1946. The American graves registration unit officer who responded to the reported discovery to retrieve the remains was able to identify them from recovered dogtags and clothing as belonging to Lieutenant Barkley. Coincidentally he was acquainted with the Barkley family, so he encouraged Josef to write a letter to the father of the deceased pilot, Rufus Barkley Sr., to release their anguish of not knowing what happened to their son. This correspondence continues today. David also related that he was drafted and sent to Germany in 1955. He arranged a meeting with Josef Schell and they visited his brother's crash site, even retrieving some small pieces of the aircraft still there.

The fortunate meeting between Klaus Schulz and Leutnant Eberhard Kabitz led to the final conclusion of how and where Lt. Rufus Barkley Jr. was killed in action. The family eventually returned Rufus Jr. for burial in the family plot at Uniontown, Pennsylvania.

The Barkley family was extremely appreciative of finally knowing the full story, especially Lieutenant Barkley's niece, Mrs. Marcia Barkley Ross. She was so overwhelmed she arranged to travel to the Hürtgen Forest and Merode Castle, meet Klaus Schulz and Josef Schell, and stand in the place where her uncle was killed. From her letter to me after her trip to Germany, it was apparent that it was a highly emotional experience for her.

The 390th squadron followed the decimated 391st into the cauldron of the Hürtgen to maintain the assault, but could only muster twelve aircraft instead of the requested sixteen. Some well-aimed bombs cratered two crossroads, one by Kleinhau and the other by Stolberg, blocking traffic until the roads were re-paired. The squadron was unable to see any other bombing or strafing results, but reported seeing American troops in Eschweiler. Several German armored vehicles spotted were painted white, probably from the 116th Panzer Division being refitted in the area. The white paint was to camouflage them in the up-coming Ardennes offensive, slated to start in December, when snow was expected.

The 389th squadron sent out another mission, but the weather was so bad they returned to base with their bombs. So ended the first day of the long-awaited major attack to push through the Hürtgen.

6.   The Hürtgen Forest Campaign
A Slugging Match

The first two weeks of the battle showed it was going to be a long, brutal, and frustrating campaign. The slugging match decimated the attacking American ground forces and devastated the fighter bombers helping the ground troops push through that damn forest.

In the first two days since Queen was initiated, the group lost five aircraft and three pilots. We also had six aircraft heavily damaged to require maintenance group repair and about a dozen aircraft damaged that the squadron maintenance would repair. It was not an auspicious beginning and we started to be concerned about having to go to that embattled forest and its heavy flak. We hoped the weather would clear so that we could increase our flight altitude and escape the lethal 20mm flak batteries set up throughout the forest. That was a forlorn hope, as winter was upon us. We would just have to do our duty.

The squadron commander called a pilots' meeting to pass down several new directives. Because the Germans started firing both red and white smoke rounds, hoping to confuse our attack, a new smoke-marking procedure to prevent bombing our own troops was implemented. Instead of the target being marked with only red smoke, starting immediately the artillery would use different colors or combinations of colored smoke shells to mark the target. They were to broadcast the colors only after they fired the shells. Also, to allow bombing and strafing closer to our own troops, the air/ground controller would specify an approach direction. This, it was hoped, would minimize the chance of errant bombing or strafing of friendly troops.

Since most supplies were still being brought to the continent through the Normandy beaches, the supply situation had become desperate. We had depleted the bomb dump supply of fragmentation bombs, and belly tanks were almost gone. The situation was so bad that a IX TAC directive ordered us not to drop our empty belly tanks before dive-bombing. We did not like that edict because we believed that the residual fuel and fumes in them were a very real explosion hazard if they were hit by ground fire. Regardless of our concern, we complied. The directive also told us to ignore the 250-mph speed restriction when carrying a belly tank and to dive as fast as needed since a ripped-off tank would probably not damage the aircraft.

I dived close to 400 mph many times with a tank on and never lost one. I also can't recall anyone ever mentioning that they saw a belly tank explode when hit by flak. It therefore appears that the gamble was appropriate over our objections and concern.

The next day the weather was clear and would not be a factor in the missions for our continued 4th Infantry Division support. Once over the battle area the air/ground controller released the 390th squadron to perform an armed reconnaissance, and they went at it with determination. Three trucks, three locomotives, and four railway cars fell victim to their bombs. They then strafed twenty-five to thirty railroad cars with four flak positions firing at them. Light-caliber flak was intense and accurate over the entire area. Lt. Duane Lund was shot down and two other aircraft were heavily damaged. Pilots reported that Lund bailed out successfully near Euskirchen and was seen landing in his chute on the ground. Duane was the second to be lost from the fellows I went on leave with in October. He became a POW and was liberated by American troops in April 1945.

The 391st squadron was directed to bomb an enemy command post in the center of Kreuzau, on the Roer River just south of Düren. They reported excellent bombing results with the center of the town in shambles. Flak was heavy and intense, damaging three aircraft so badly they departed early to struggle for landings at fields nearer the battle area. They were at first listed as missing in action, but all pilots returned to base.

We always posted an "alert" flight of four aircraft near the runway, ready to scramble into the air to repel an air attack. We all took turns at that boring duty but the German Luftwaffe very seldom contested our air dominance. In an unusual occurrence, they scrambled the alert flight to investigate bogeys (unidentified aircraft) in the area. The patrol was uneventful.

Sixteen aircraft from the 389th squadron were next to challenge the flak-infested Hürtgen battle area. Eight aircraft bombed on red smoke near Eschweiler and lost Lt. William Phillips in the process. His aircraft was set on fire but they

1. Brand-new pilot 2d Lt. Bob Brulle, trying to look like a
"hot" pilot. (Brulle collection)

2. World War II primary fighter trainer, the Boeing PT-17. (USAF Museum)

3. Lieutenant Brulle with a North American AT-6 advanced trainer at Eglin Field Auxiliary #6, Florida, during aerial gunnery training, March 1944. (Brulle collection)

4. P-47D-2 razorback canopy aircraft. (USAF Museum)

5. P-47D-26 bubble canopy aircraft. (USAF Museum)

6. Strip A-1 at St. Pierre-du-Mont, overlooking Omaha Beach, Normandy, France, July 1944. Pointe du Hoc is on the upper left and supply ships are in the English Channel. The 366th group (P-47s) is on the channel side; 370th group, 341st squadron (P-38s) is on the near side. (USAF)

7. Lt. Emil Bertza being welcomed back by his crew of B2-U after his sojourn in the Falaise pocket. Shaking hands with Emil is the crew chief, S.Sgt. Leighton Moore, and beside him (*left to right*) are assistant crew chief Sgt. Glen Ogelvie, Sgt. Bob DeVilbis, and Cpl. Isaac Brock. (USAF)

8. Finally, a fighter pilot in combat. (Brulle collection)

9. Chuck Bennett, a training buddy and lifelong friend, in flying gear ready to go on a mission. (Brulle collection)

10. Major Barney Barnhardt's B2-B, named *Gentleman Jim,* in a revetment at strip A-1. This was a P-47D-27 and one of the first bubble-canopy aircraft assigned to the group. (Brulle collection)

11. P-47 flying column cover for an armored spearhead. (USAF)

12. P-47 eliminating a German roadblock. (USAF)

13. Some of my relatives in Oordegem, Belgium, my hometown. My Aunt Alice and my Uncle Peter (holding his grandson) are on the far left; the others are cousins. I visited them as much as I could when I was overseas. Note the wooden shoes. The home in the background is 200 years old. (Brulle collection)

14. The fighter-bomber's nemesis, the German Zugkraftwagen eight-ton, two-centimeter Flak-Vierling, or (as we called it) the flak wagon. Most wartime wagons did not have the armored cab but just a canvas top. (Courtesy Bundesamt für Wehrtechnik und Beschaffung-Wehrtechnische Studiensammlung)

15. Chuck Bennett's aircraft, B2-BAR, ready to go on a mission, January 1945, at Y-29. Note the wide paddle-blade propeller (installed on some model P-47D-28-RA aircraft). (Brulle collection)

16. Lt. Karl Hallberg, 389th squadron, survived the explosion of a 500-pound bomb that dropped off his aircraft on landing at Y-29, 31 December 1944. He sustained head wounds and a concussion that hospitalized him for a while. He was bestowed the title of "Luckiest Pilot in the 366th." (USAF)

17. Jack Kennedy, posing by his shot-up rudder after the 1 January 1945 air battle. The right wing was in worse shape. (Jack Kennedy collection)

18. B2-J being rearmed and fueled in a 30-minute mission turnaround. Men in the foreground are loading a 500-pound bomb. S.Sgt. Al Czaplicki is filling the oil tank. S.Sgt. Jim Hizer, on opposite wing, is fueling the aircraft. Not visible is Sgt. Ray Johnson, the armorer, who is cleaning the right wing guns and loading ammunition. The bomb-loaders and the armorer will swap sides when done to complete the job. (Brulle collection)

19. Lt. Claude Halterman getting ready to take B2-J on a mission. He was killed in action on that mission, while strafing about 20 miles northeast of Cologne, Germany, 28 February 1945. (Brulle collection)

20. S.Sgt. Jim Hizer, performing routine engine maintenance on B2-J no. 3 at Y-94, Münster, Germany. (Brulle collection)

21. I was photographed so I could remember the ad hoc installation of our high-velocity aircraft rockets underneath the ejection chutes for the shells and belt links. We could not fire our guns until the rockets were fired since the ejected cases and belt links could break the rocket firing wires. (Brulle collection)

22. The end of the war brought military spit and polish back into our lives. Fred Keys (*left*) portrays the lackadaisical attitude and dress during wartime, while Don DeWyke (*right*) shows the attitude now expected. He couldn't wipe the smile off his face. (Brulle collection)

23. 390th Fighter Squadron, 366th Fighter Group officer personnel as of May 1945, at Y-94, Münster, Germany. (*Left to right, front*): Lackey, Ewell, Jones, Brulle, Sills, Gibson, Eddy, Hawkins, Cronk, Crowell, Eltz; (*second row*): McCarl, D. J. Ross, Paisley, Kiebler, Ray Kennedy, Davis, Mohns, Bernard, Golden, Conger, Gimill; (*third row*): Riek, S. A. Ross, Pendergraft, Stewart, Brotten, L. B. Smith (CO), Keating (XO), Crawford (Communications), Clark (M.D.), Lieberman (Supply), Lundi, Benton; (*back row*): Farnall, Picton, Barrett, DeWyke, McLean, Ebright, Coyne, Keys, Staz, Johnson, Wozniak.

24. F-15Es of the 391st Fighter Squadron refuel from a KC-135R of the 22nd Air Refueling Squadron, both a part of the Air Force 366th Air Expeditionary Wing, carrying on the tradition set by the World War II 366th Fighter Group. (Courtesy Boeing)

saw him bail out successfully. He became a POW and was liberated by American troops in April 1945. The remaining aircraft bombed a marked artillery position, hoping to silence the heavy guns, and then cratered a road intersection near Merode Castle.

The heavy flak over the Hürtgen took its toll, limiting the 390th to only nine serviceable aircraft for the next mission. I was the odd man and attached to the lead flight. Grosshau was our bombing target. On the bombing run I heard a quick call by Homer Schaeffer, who was bombing just before me, "Hit bad—bailing out." He didn't have a chance since he was much too low and heading down in a 45-degree dive. His aircraft exploded in front of me on the ground and left a P-47 impression on the ground. I saw the location of the flak position that hit Homer and after I finished my bombing performed a quick chandelle and strafed the gun position. It was well camouflaged, but I kept my eye on it and knew exactly where it was. I only reported it strafed, not knowing what damage, if any, I inflicted on the position. It felt good to shoot at one of those ubiquitous flak positions that always seemed to have us in their sights. Homer was the third to be lost from the fellows I went on leave with in October.

After our bombing, the air/ground controller reported that enemy activity was reported east of Grosshau. Investigating, we discovered a column of German horse-drawn vehicles hiding alongside a hilly and wooded country road. What happened next gave me a taste of the gory business of war. As I pulled up from making a strafing pass on a parked wagon, I caught sight of a large gun being pulled by a double team of horses. The horses had bolted from the gunfire noise and roaring of our aircraft and were galloping down the road. I banked around, keeping my eye on them, but when I lined them up in my gunsight, I had second thoughts. I didn't want to kill the horses, but how else could I destroy the gun? I gave them a short burst and as I banked over them saw the gory sight of the horses and gun all tangled in a big ball, tumbling down the road. I was glad to be fighting the war in the air where one was usually spared such sights. We destroyed at least eleven horse-drawn vehicles including several that were pulling large guns.

It may seem strange that I would be concerned about killing some horses, while every mission I went on had a high probability that I killed or wounded some humans. I never had any reservations about shooting at anything or anybody in Nazi Germany. Although I never strafed a lone farmer tilling his field, I don't think I would have hesitated if given the chance. He could have been growing potatoes that they distilled to make the alcohol that powered the V-2 that was devastating London. Nazi Germany was an evil place that plunged the world into a conflagration of unprecedented proportions, and they deserved to reap what they started. This was the general feeling of most other pilots as well.

One thing many (but not all) of us vowed not to do was to shoot at a German pilot floating down in his parachute.

The 391st was prowling the battle area when a front-line tank air/ground controller called Bronco requested immediate assistance to destroy a Tiger tank near Grosshau. They spent some time looking, but it was finally found. Four aircraft bombed and probably destroyed it with well-directed bombs that impacted on or near it. Sweepstakes interrupted and directed the immediate bombing of a castle-like structure near Grosshau. The rest of the squadron bombed and reported it heavily damaged or destroyed. So ended another day over that flak-infested forest.

A clearing of the weather allowed the carnage to continue on 19 November with the launch of six squadron missions. Although the operations order specified support for the 4th Infantry Division, we were vectored throughout the battle area, responding to whomever had a worthwhile target. The supply services had replenished the stock of fragmentation bombs, which allowed all missions to carry a 50/50 split of either two 500-pound bombs or two 260-pound fragmentation bombs per aircraft as specified in the operations order.

The six missions were all typical; dive-bomb a target we could not see within the confines of that dense forest or strafe a few vehicles we could see and get our aircraft shot up. On this day we had one pilot of the 389th squadron get wounded by a fragment of glass in his eye when he was hit in the canopy, and the 390th lost Lt. John Gallagher. He was last seen strafing three miles northeast of Düren. No calls from him were received and no one knew what happened to him. Postwar records indicate that he crashed into a railroad yard while strafing and the aircraft disintegrated over a wide area. His body was never found. He is listed on the Wall of the Missing, Netherlands American Cemetery.

A welcome day off because of fog at our field gave us time to reflect on our operations over this new battle area, and it was grim. During the preceding three days, supporting the First Army's major attack through the Hürtgen Forest, the group lost seven pilots. That is almost a 10 percent loss of available pilots, and at that rate none of us would be around by Christmas. In addition we were getting low on serviceable aircraft to meet our commitment.

The next week a low overcast prevented us from completing many of our troop-support missions, and we fell back on performing pickle-barrel missions. We also ran several escort missions. The 389th did get into a good dogfight. They sent up sixteen aircraft to escort B-26 bombers striking rail bridges in the Cologne area, but the bombers did not show up (probably because of the inclement weather). That was lucky, because the escorts were then vectored by Marmite to the Dusseldorf area to investigate bogeys coming in from the east. They climbed to 18,000 feet and identified over sixty Me 109s below them at

13,000 feet. They attacked out of the sun in a perfect setup, and in a ten-minute dogfight claimed ten enemy aircraft shot down, with three others probably shot down and three more damaged. Capt. Henry Struth was shot down in the dogfight and another P-47 sustained major damage but returned to base. Captain Struth was killed and is buried in the Netherlands American Cemetery.

The weather was marginally better on 25 November and each squadron launched a ground-support mission. Each bombed and strafed what little they could see but they could make no significant claims. The 389th caught flashes of a German artillery battery in action and bombed and strafed it, but could not observe any results.

At the completion of this day's missions the aircraft landed at our new base, Y-29 in Belgium. Other aircraft were also flown over and C-47s brought the remaining pilots and ground crew. Truck and rail brought additional equipment. We did not miss a single scheduled mission during this change of base.

On 26 November we started flying from Y-29. Belly tanks were removed since we were now only 10 minutes from the front line. Being so close we could also look forward to flying more missions to that dismal forest. We were starting to hate those missions and what the Hürtgen Forest stood for. It again became not only a daily grind, but also a dreaded one.

The 389th flew its first mission from Y-29, but the battle area was completely socked in so the air/ground controller released the squadron to find their own targets. They found an open area around Cologne and bombed the town of Horrem, but were unable to claim any tangible results for their effort. Returning to base they noted the weather was moving out of the battle area toward the southeast.

The 390th was next and launched a strike of twelve aircraft. I was flying Red-3 with Smitty leading the squadron. This was the first mission that Smitty and I had flown in 10 days since we were at Y-29 setting up our new base. The consequences of this mission dispelled any ambition I harbored to lead a squadron mission. The weather was marginal for dive-bombing, but we did manage to find and bomb Grosshau and Gey as requested by Stanza.

Completing our mission, we formed up into a tight formation and set course to our new base at Y-29. I pocketed my charts and wasn't paying much attention to where we were going. In a tight formation pilots concentrate on the leader and don't really keep track of where they are. We were close to base when suddenly I heard Smitty say, "Okay, Bob—take them home." Here I was leading the squadron and I didn't know where we were so, obviously, I didn't know where to go. Now this was also Smitty's first flight from Y-29, and I always felt he wasn't quite sure of the field's location either. It took several homings from our radio direction finder station located on our field before we found it. They did not intentionally camouflage Y-29, but new green pierced-steel planking laid on green grass between two groves of green pine trees was difficult to spot for someone who did not know exactly where to look. After landing I knew they would never give the me the chance to lead a squadron, even though I felt it was not completely my mistake. I toyed with requesting a transfer to another group, but I shrugged it off by reminding myself that this was just a temporary job. I knew I would miss the many friends and lose the kinship cultivated these last few months, so I just swallowed my disappointment and dismissed the thought.

The remainder of the missions that day were routine weather frustration of low clouds and a hazy fog. We bombed and strafed on a smoke-marked target in that green carpet, and tried to prevent getting shot down by the flak that was always tracking us with puffs of white smoke. Lt. Wallace Dunton was the unlucky one when a hit started his aircraft burning. He was seen getting out of the aircraft, but his parachute did not open. I remember Wally quite well since he was the first member of the 390th squadron to introduce himself to me.

A major catastrophe was narrowly averted when a heavily damaged B-17 made an emergency landing at our just-activated field. We were watching a bomber stream of B-17s returning from a strike flying overhead. Suddenly we saw three other B-17s come into view, flying only a few hundred feet high and heading directly at our field, opposite the takeoff direction of P-47s going on a mission. The three B-17s started to shoot off red flares, which alerted the P-47s just in time to avoid the bombers with some radical evasive maneuvers. We then noticed that one B-17 was flying with three engines feathered and was attempting an emergency landing with only the left outboard engine running. The other two B-17s were obviously shepherding him. Just as the damaged bomber was about to touch down, the right wing dropped, and we all gasped in horror, waiting for the bomber to cartwheel in a ball of flame. By some miracle the pilot recovered and landed safely. Our crash truck and ambulance were quickly on the scene. The B-17 was from the 92nd Bomb Group, 327th squadron, stationed at Podington, England. The ball-turret gunner had been killed and several other crew members wounded by German fire.

For the rest of November almost all missions were directed toward supporting the 8th Infantry Division assaulting Brandenburg and Bergstein. From five to seven missions were run each day, most of them bombing and strafing the two towns and the high prominence just to the east of Bergstein, officially known as Hill 400 (its height in meters), but we usually called it Castle Hill because of the castle-like structure perched on top. We bombed and strafed it regularly since it was a German observation post. Also regularly bombed and strafed were several German heavy gun batteries situated around Gurzenich, a western suburb of Düren. The guns were well situated so their field of fire covered a large portion of the forest and were well camouflaged so we couldn't see them. This made it necessary to bomb on map coordinates although sometimes our artillery marked them with smoke.

Klaus Schulz sent me a map showing where those batteries were located. It is interesting to note that the coordinates we were given to bomb were about one-half mile from the actual position of the guns. They were, of course, well camouflaged, and unless they were firing we couldn't see them. No wonder we were asked to bomb them repeatedly with no tangible results.

The repetitive and frustrating missions to the same place day after day with no noticeable ground-force advance caused us some concern. Would we ever get out of that forest and its murderous flak? Until we did, all we could do was continue our ground-force support missions fighting the weather and Germans. Samples of the more productive or exciting missions we flew during that period are detailed.

On one mission we plastered a barracks just to the northwest of Brandenburg. Just as we were starting home I caught sight of several vehicles parked on the side of a small secondary road or fire break. I reported the find and since no one else could see them they ordered me to "go get 'em." On diving down I ascertained that there were five vehicles and they were buses. I got a good burst into two of them and ran my bullets through the other three. At interrogation I claimed two probably destroyed and three damaged. The fact that they were buses, showing the desperate plight of the German army transportation system, was carried on the news the next day. It is interesting that the officials inflated my claim and credited me with two destroyed and three probably destroyed.

The 390th squadron was spared the Bergstein-Brandenburg flak inferno and sent south to Kall on the Erft River. A reconnaissance pilot evidently uncovered a train loaded with military vehicles in the marshaling yard. The 390th found the camouflaged train unloading about sixty tanks, and in the gathering twilight they bombed and destroyed six tank-laden flat cars. The Ardennes offensive jumpoff point for the 12th SS Panzer Division, part of the I Panzer Corps offensive, was in this area, so those were probably their tanks getting into position for the attack.

Unfortunately it was in the gathering twilight when the train was found and too late to launch another mission. The next morning the 389th squadron was tasked to find and bomb the train again. They found the train, but the Germans had unloaded and hidden all the tanks. They reluctantly returned to bomb and strafe Bergstein and Brandenburg. One aircraft was shot down by flak, but the pilot bailed out safely over American lines and returned to base in a few hours.

Again the boring duty of being on the alert flight became interesting. Two aircraft each, from the 390th and 391st squadrons, were sent aloft to attack German aircraft strafing our troops. By the time they reached the area the enemy had departed. A short time later they scrambled a second alert flight of two aircraft each from the 389th and 390th squadrons to intercept strafing German aircraft. Again, by the time the flight reached the area, the FW 190s were gone. Having the Luftwaffe intervening on behalf of their own troops in battle was extremely unusual. It caused us to wonder what was going on.

As the gun batteries at Gurzenich were being bombed and strafed, Sweepstakes requested the 390th to break off and bomb and strafe Merode. The Germans had surrounded an American unit and they desperately needed help.[1] The four remaining aircraft with bombs complied and bombed where directed. All aircraft then strafed the area. Flak heavily damaged one aircraft and it barely got back to base.

The 389th squadron of twelve aircraft identified their Brandenburg target and started their dive-bombing run. At that moment Sweepstakes ordered them to break off the attack and contact Marmite for a high-priority target. Reconnaissance aircraft had discovered another train loaded with tanks and Marmite sent them to Euskirchen to attack the juicy target. They destroyed eight tanks with six direct hits on the camouflaged train. An errant bomb impacted a large adjacent tank, causing a satisfying explosion that marked the target for another arriving P-47 squadron to continue the destruction. This is an excellent example of the control and quick reaction the Ninth Air Force had developed, being able to render an immediate attack on a just-discovered opportune target.

Nideggen, a town just across the Roer River from Bergstein, was the target for ten of the twelve aircraft sent up by the 389th squadron. Red smoke marked the area of Nideggen they wanted bombed, and as the aircraft pulled up from bombing, the other two aircraft swooped down on an adjacent woods. These woods harbored several medium and light flak batteries that continuously harassed our attacks on Bergstein and Brandenburg. After randomly dropping the four bombs in the woods, the whole squadron repeatedly strafed it. It was payback time that made one feel good, at least for a short time. They also strafed some horse-drawn vehicles. One was evidently carrying ammunition and as it blew up it heavily damaged Lt. Jim Taylor's aircraft when he flew through the explosion. Fortunately, he nursed the P-47 home and landed okay. In March 1945 Captain Taylor was killed strafing Tiger tanks attacking to eliminate the American bridgehead over the Rhine. He was flying his 102nd mission. I wonder what happened to the edict that when a pilot reached 100 missions and was due for a thirty-day leave he was grounded?

The 391st squadron received a very unusual request during their mission. While they were circling to identify targets at our old stomping ground of Brandenburg and Bergstein, they were directed to bomb and strafe a just-identified artillery position in a haystack. It took some time to identify which haystack to attack, but they did so under difficult conditions as the deteriorating visibility was one mile. They did not know the results of the attack.

The first two days of December rolled in with more fog, snow, and low clouds, allowing the launch of only a few pickle-barrel missions. On 3 December the weather was still bad, but they ordered us to run our specified missions in spite of it. It was a good call, since the weather in the battle area was clear, being within the cold Siberian high-pressure area that moved in. The four missions completed that day in support of the 8th Infantry Division were all very productive. The 390th squadron with eleven aircraft was airborne at 0815 and reached the target area of Brandenburg and Bergstein at 0830. Stanza, the 8th Infantry Division air/ground controller, turned us over to a 5th Armored Division forward tank air/ground controller called Adolph Able. He was in a lead tank with Task Force Hamberg, part of Combat Command R from the 5th Armored Division. Task Force Hamberg was spearheading a determined attack in company with the 28th Infantry Regiment of the 8th Infantry Division to capture Brandenburg. Our task was to neutralize three specific fortified houses on the north edge of Brandenburg. These houses contained heavy-caliber antitank guns covering the attack approach and required neutralization to give the ground attack a chance of success. The ground troops would launch their attack the moment we started our dive-bombing. We circled as Adolph Able identified the strong points and we apportioned the three houses among ourselves and assured ourselves we each knew the specific house we were to bomb. Our dive-bombing was excellent and we achieved several direct hits on all three houses. Adolph Able was ecstatic. "We got 'em—we got 'em," he yelled. "Now strafe the bastards." We strafed the other houses and wooded areas next to the town, roaring in over the heads of our troops moving into the town. Even after we had used up our ammunition, Adolph Able exhorted us to keep buzzing the Germans to keep their heads down. Fortunately, the twelve aircraft of the 391st arrived to continue the support. The ground troops finally captured Brandenburg.[2]

This mission was the culmination of close air support development during the past year of combat and is a classic example of what close air support could do. We bombed and strafed so close to our own troops that I'm sure they vividly experienced the concussions from our bombing, and we probably pelted them with the shells and casings ejected from our guns as we roared over them strafing. One of my proudest moments was to be part of the team that finally broke the stalemate to capture that stubbornly held town.

As mentioned, the 391st squadron continued the close support, to the gratification of Adolph Able who was extolled by his tank company commander to "keep the buzz boys up." They bombed specific houses that were fortified as strongpoints on the northeast corner of Bergstein facing Brandenburg. These strongpoints had a clear field of fire against the attacking American troops, but not for long, as the 391st demolished the strongpoints. Smoke then marked the area where the troops needed heavy strafing to quiet the German rear guard. By the time the 391st left, they could see American tanks and troops in the center of Brandenburg. The 391st also arrived back at the base completely out of ammunition.

The ground troops anticipated a counterattack from Bergstein to retake Brandenburg, so the 389th with eleven aircraft bombed Bergstein to spoil the German regroupment. They also bombed a castle in the town of Nideggen, across the Roer River from Bergstein, which was probably an observation post and/or headquarters. Adolph Able confirmed they were mopping up in Brandenburg but that they were concerned about an expected counterattack from Bergstein. He mentioned that the Germans never relinquished a position without mounting a counterattack, and requested the air cover remain overhead as long as possible to help foil the expected attack.

The last mission of the day consisted of twelve aircraft from the 390th squadron, which relieved the 389th. Adolph Able requested continued harassment of the assumed German regroupment, so they again bombed and strafed Bergstein. They also expended four bombs on a castle-like building housing a German command post in Nideggen. This mission returned about 1230 and spent the next 10 minutes landing in very bad weather. It was chaotic as aircraft tried to land any which way, but fortunately all landed safely. I believe this was the time we had two aircraft, on their landing roll, headed in opposite directions, meet in the middle of the runway without colliding. We all looked on the impending collision in open-mouth horror, followed by back-slapping exuberance as they missed each other. While the weather in the battle area was satisfactory, at our field 40 miles away it was socked in with low clouds and a visibility of not more than a half mile.

This Siberian high-pressure area kept the German airfields and battle area clear and, with fog and low clouds grounding us, freed the Luftwaffe to strafe the American troops in the Hürtgen Forest, including those who had just captured Brandenburg. It was a novel experience for the American ground forces, and the antiaircraft units responded with exuberant fusillade fire, claiming the shoot-down of nineteen German fighters. No counterattack against Brandenburg occurred from Bergstein, so perhaps our vigorous bombing and strafing during the morning kept the Germans off-balance long enough for the Americans to consolidate their newly won positions.

As a change of pace it may be interesting to know what the other six fighter groups of IX TAC were doing that day. On 3 December IX TAC ran the following missions in very inclement weather that covered the air bases with fog and low clouds. The 368th Fighter Group flying P-47s supported the 1st Infantry Division slogging through the Hürtgen Forest near Gey. They accomplished three squadron missions before their field, A-84 at Chievres, Belgium, was closed down by fog.

The 365th Fighter Group, flying P-47s, supported the 104th Infantry Division driving through the northern fringes of the Hürtgen Forest. Two squadron missions bombed a factory-like structure that concealed tanks just north of Düren. They also ran one mission that destroyed a railroad bridge on the rail line from Düren to Cologne and shot up some trains. The 365th was also stationed at A-84.

Three P-38 fighter groups assigned to IX TAC—the 370th and the 474th, both stationed at A-78, Florrennes, Belgium, and the 367th stationed at A-71, Clastres, France—had the unusual mission of helping the Eighth Air Force Fighter Command escort a major bomber strike in Germany, so they were unavailable for close air support that day. No mission results were presented in the IX TAC report of operations. As a matter of record, the 370th did get a call to launch their alert flight to investigate bogeys approaching the Hürtgen Forest battle area. Multiple cloud layers prevented any visible contact.

No mention was found in the combat operations report on the activities of the 10th Photo Reconnaissance Group, also a part of IX TAC and stationed at A-94 at Conflans (near Metz), France.

These missions, along with those of the 366th previously outlined, present the weather-shortened 3 December missions of IX TAC. Destruction (not counting the 366th) included four locomotives, five railroad cars, four railroad track cuts, and a factory building harboring tanks. It was a very slow day indeed for IX TAC.

For a short time we had an F-5 (P-38) photo-reconnaissance aircraft stationed on our field. He flew several missions with us to obtain action movies of our bombing and strafing. On one mission he was right with us on bombing and then went back into the alerted flak gunner sights and buzzed the target after we completed our mission. He must have obtained some good movies of a typical mission. Unfortunately it was usually so dark and dreary that most photos were useless. This was also the period we were loaded with color film in our gun cameras, with the same disappointing results. I later found this experiment was to try to make a movie similar to the one the Navy produced, *Fighting Lady,* on aircraft carrier operations. It turned out great, but it was also filmed in the bright sunny skies of the South Pacific.

After we were grounded by weather for a day, 5 December dawned slightly better, allowing the launch of seven missions to help the troops now assaulting

Bergstein. Weather allowed only four of the missions to work with Stanza and Adolph Able. The others were sent on an armed reconnaissance, each reporting some more German equipment destroyed. Each of the four missions to Bergstein reported that they could see the ground battle in progress, and all were asked to bomb and strafe the southeast part of Bergstein and/or the town of Nideggen or Castle Hill.

A typical mission that day was the one run by the twelve aircraft of the 391st squadron. After they reached the battle area, Stanza said they were attacking within Bergstein, but it was slow going because the Americans were continuously under German artillery fire directed on them by observers on Castle Hill or the castle-like building in Nideggen. While circling around, the pilots became quite confused and got caught in an air/ground controller misunderstanding between Stanza from 8th Infantry Division and Adolph Able from the 5th Armored. Both controllers gave conflicting bombing instructions on what targets the squadron should bomb. Because of the dispute the 391st squadron almost bombed our own troops. It was a serious dispute that could have resulted in tragic consequences. An excellent account of that episode can be found in the book by Charles MacDonald, *The Siegfried Line Campaign*.[3] The 391st was finally told to bomb Nideggen and that castle housing the German observers. During dive-bombing they welcomed an antiflak barrage, courtesy of the U.S. Army Artillery, substantially eliminating the flak. They saw what looked like a tank battle in progress near Castle Hill. Adolph Able confirmed they had a tenuous hold on Bergstein.

During a quasi-static front-line situation, as in the Hürtgen Forest, the ground forces would sometimes be able to lay down an antiflak barrage of artillery fire on known and suspected flak positions. It wasn't always possible, since the artillery could be otherwise engaged, but when they did we greatly appreciated it. It didn't stop all the flak but it eliminated a great deal of it. They tried their best to accommodate us whenever possible.

In another one of the Bergstein missions, eleven aircraft of the 389th were directed on a road reconnaissance south and southeast of Bergstein to look for supply wagons or any other movement. The Germans controlled only one road and probably some trails that were accessible for German supply columns to Bergstein. When that reconnaissance turned up nothing, because it was impossible to see through the pine trees, Stanza requested that they bomb a church steeple in Nideggen, probably being used as an observation post. Pilots again reported seeing American troops and tanks in Bergstein.

The reader may wonder how a handful of Germans could stymie the mighty army arrayed against them. The battle raged over a terrain that is impossibly rugged and forested, and is extremely difficult to negotiate even without a well-dug-in and camouflaged enemy. From the air everything was hidden by the trees, even the roads. The Germans were also under a direct order from Hitler to stand fast and not let the Americans reach the Roer River. He needed that river barrier to protect his right flank for the winter offensive slated to begin in a few days. The fighting at Bergstein was somewhat analogous to the Spartans resisting the Persians at Thermopylae.

Only one late hurry-up mission was run on 6 December to aid our troops re-pelling a determined German counterattack to retake Bergstein. Weather was bad but ten aircraft from the 390th were able to get through to bomb and strafe the woods just west of Bergstein. Adolph Able commented that the bombing and strafing were right on top of the Germans. Bergstein was finally, firmly in our hands. Landing at our field was very difficult in fog and haze, but we all got down using the low cloud and visibility landing scheme we developed (described later).

Weather on 8 December had an overcast at 2,000 feet, but visibility under-neath was 10 miles. Runway alert was scrambled just at dawn. They sent two aircraft each from the 389th and 391st squadrons aloft to intercept bogeys com-ing from the east. They were vectored to patrol along the Rhine River, but saw nothing except a few friendly squadrons prowling the cloudy sky.

The 390th, unable to engage the primary target, performed an armed recon-naissance. A German town, having active military traffic, obligingly appeared through holes in the clouds. The 390th was getting ready to dive-bomb when Sweepstakes ordered them to jettison their bombs and hurry northeast of Cologne and engage a swarm of enemy aircraft. They jettisoned all the bombs armed, but were unable to find the enemy in the cloud-pocked sky. Extremely dis-appointed, they released their frustration by strafing the Cologne area, destroying seven trucks and four locomotives and damaging a bunch of railroad cars.

The weather lifted for the twelve aircraft of the 389th squadron and they bombed on red smoke outlining a factory-type building in the small town of Zerkall. The small village is situated at the confluence of the Kall River with the Roer River, nestled alongside Castle Hill. It was hardly visible from the air, hidden within a forest of tall trees. The ground troops' artillery batteries laid down an antiflak barrage. They obtained a good pattern of bombs on the tar-geted factory building.

Twelve aircraft from the 390th were next to try their luck with the marginal weather. They assigned us the task of destroying a large-caliber gun in a wooded area just north of Düren. We judged the location of that well-camouflaged gun in the woods, and we dropped all bombs in the area. This mission was very memorable for me since it was the first time they assigned me to lead a flight (not withstanding my recent goof-up). What a revelation I experienced when dive-bombing. I was lead man down to dive-bomb that gun position and I hardly

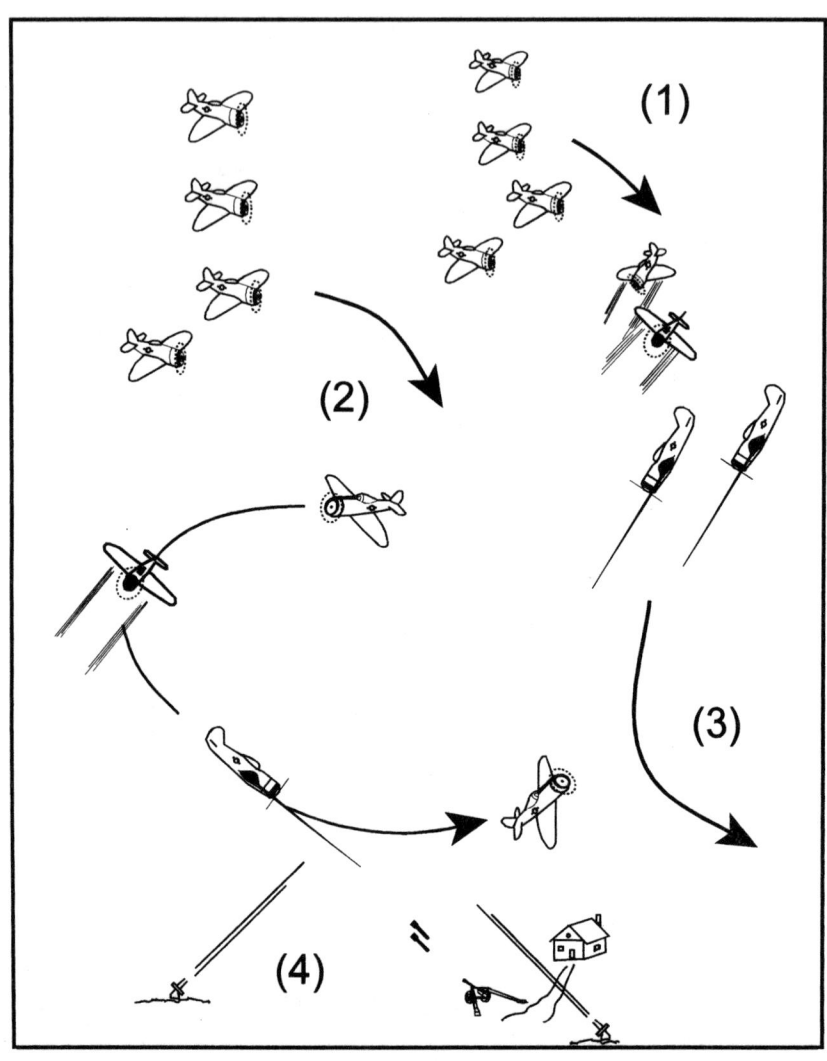

Flak-busting Technique. Top cover Yellow flight (1) dives and sprays area to suppress flak. Red flight (2) follows spraying area and then dive-bombs. Yellow flight pulls up at 3,000 feet and re-forms to dive-bomb. (4) Sometimes flak gunners would get in their foxholes.

experienced any flak. What a pleasant surprise, until I pulled up and saw what the rest of the flight was getting. We knew the Germans weren't leading us enough, but it really didn't strike home to me until I was first in and saw all the flak behind me. After bombing, we strafed the woods there and around Zerkall, but could not determine any results of our attack.

The flak we received in the Hürtgen Forest missions was very intimidating. There was no way to escape it, and it took a lot of courage and determination to commit to dive down into that inferno of fire and shrapnel. The intimidation of the flak undoubtedly reduced our dive-bombing accuracy (at least it did mine), as it reduced our concentration and precipitated a higher altitude and airspeed bomb release to facilitate getting the heck out of there. To try to combat that flak we developed a dive-bombing tactic that appeared to help (see opposite page).

An eight-aircraft mission had two flights, coded "Red" and "Yellow." Yellow flight would fly top cover at Angels 11, while Red flight at Angels 10 contacted the air/ground controller and identified the target. On cue from the Red flight leader, Yellow flight would dive down through Red flight and at about Angels 7 start spraying the entire target area with their guns. With all the tracer bullets flying through the air from four aircraft, some German gunners would scramble for their foxholes, thinking they were the target. Red flight would peel off right behind Yellow flight. At Angels 3 Yellow flight would pull up without dive-bombing. Red flight would continue spraying the immediate target area and at the last possible moment line up with the target for their dive-bombing pass. Yellow flight would quickly re-form and commence their dive-bombing pass while Red flight would strafe the flak positions they may have discovered during their dive-bombing. Once the German gunners were in their foxholes it appeared all the tracer bullets intimidated them, and they were reluctant to get out again to man their guns. At least this was what we hoped would happen. This technique was not used when close to the front lines since it was too risky to spray bullets indiscriminately, not knowing where they went. A twelve- or sixteen-aircraft squadron mission of three or four flights would adopt a similar technique.

We think the flak-busting tactic helped; however, it may just have been a psychological satisfaction that we were shooting back at those persistent gunners. In retrospect, it is surprising that more aircraft were not shot down, considering the heavy flak we encountered. Flak hit many aircraft, at least one on every mission to the Hürtgen Forest, but that old Jug took the damage in stride. We sometimes flew with superficial damage, like a hole through the skin of the tail, to keep enough aircraft flying to meet our mission schedule. The ground crew had a herculean task to keep enough aircraft in service, and they performed it in admirable fashion even though they had to work outside in all kinds of weather.

I finally had enough seniority to get assigned a brand-new aircraft, a P-47D-28, serial no. 42-28608, with a squadron designation of B2-J. This was a replacement aircraft for the one lost when Capt. Al Jennings was shot down on 8 November. The crew chief was S.Sgt. Al Czaplicki who survived the Pearl Harbor attack, assistant crew chief S.Sgt. Jim Hizer, armorer Sgt. Ray Johnson and radio mechanic Sgt. Charles Wood. I immediately arranged to get the cowling painted with a Varga girl picture and named my aircraft "Virginia," for the girl I had dated in high school. The Varga girl picture I used was the centerfold of the February 1941 issue of *Esquire,* which I had cut out and saved for that purpose. I kept the picture for years and finally sent it to the U.S. Air Force Museum at Wright-Patterson AFB for display as a pinup in their World War II Nissen hut.

After being grounded another day due to weather, the group received a very specific assignment for 10 December. The 2nd Ranger Battalion (they captured Pointe du Hoc on D-day by scaling the 150-foot cliffs) finally evicted the Germans from Castle Hill in a 7 December early morning surprise attack. Klaus Schulz researched this attack and found the rangers were aided in part by a provisional battalion of the 153nd Field Artillery using eighteen pieces of German 105mm howitzers and 12,000 rounds of captured ammunition. Unfortunately, the Germans didn't withdraw across the Roer River after losing Castle Hill but stubbornly held onto another, slightly lower, companion ridge that included the small town of Zerkall. The German units stubbornly defending that ridge and Zerkall were elements of the 272nd Volks grenadier Division. They were reluctantly withdrawn from refitting for the upcoming Ardennes offensive and were recommitted to the Bergstein battle to prevent the American army from gaining the Roer River. Begrudgingly, we have to admit that they did their job well.

The only supply route for the Germans on that ridge was a winding secondary road, almost impossible to see from the air. It followed the Roer from Zerkall to Brück, a small hamlet just opposite Nideggen where the road crossed the Roer River over a small stone bridge. IX TAC targeted the group to destroy that small but extremely sturdy stone bridge.

It was not an easy assignment. The embankments on both sides of the Roer are steep and high, which meant a steep dive-bombing pass was necessary for our bombs to clear the embankment on the way to the bridge. A steep dive requires a high-altitude bomb release to allow room for the pull-out to clear the high ridges, which would degrade our bombing accuracy. The Roer River is also very curvy at that point, precluding a more moderate approach along the river. Reducing dive speed was not an attractive alternative since the flak was extremely heavy in that embattled region.

The first squadron to try its luck was the 391st. They were airborne at 1110 with twelve aircraft. They achieved one hit on the east and one hit on the west approaches to the bridge, but no hits on the bridge itself.

Next was the 389th with twelve aircraft. An antiflak barrage from the artillery helped them, but they only achieved one direct hit on the east approach road.

The twelve aircraft of the 390th were next. It was the inaugural mission of my newly assigned aircraft, B2-J. We dive-bombed the bridge one flight after the other, creating a rain of bombs aimed toward the bridge. I was one of the first to bomb, and as I observed the others bombing I noted that most bombs were hitting the embankments. We generated a tremendous dirt cloud, and as the cloud began to clear we could see that there was either a hole in the center of the bridge or a large boulder blown on the bridge; verifying it from altitude was impossible. A flight leader volunteered to go down and see. He told the other flight members to perform some localized flak-busting as he looked over the bridge. He reported a four-foot hole in the center of the bridge and possibly another on the west end. The approach roads were well cratered from the seventy-two bombs aimed toward that bridge. It would be unusable for horse-drawn or other vehicles for some time.

My buddy Chuck Bennett was almost a statistic on this mission. We were forming up for the return to base, and when he formed up on my wing I saw him waving his finger at me through a hole in the canopy. With hand gestures he indicated there was another hole on the other side of the canopy, and when they were lined up, they went straight through his head location. Flak hit him on his dive-bombing pass. When diving down a pilot naturally sort of hunches forward to concentrate looking through the sight. The shell went through the canopy while he hunched over and just grazed the back of his neck. He said it felt like someone hit him with a two-by-four. He received the Purple Heart but was too embarrassed to wear it since it was such a minor wound. Chuck later sustained a more debilitating wound that solved his embarrassment problem.

The 391st squadron was returning with twelve more aircraft to bomb the bridge when Sweepstakes diverted them to help the 83rd Infantry Division wrest Gey from the enemy. They were directed to bomb and strafe a wooded region marked with smoke. One building, at the edge of the woods, exploded in a large orange fireball. They also destroyed two large trucks hiding in the woods.

The operations order for 11 December was also quite unusual. The 366th group was ordered to bomb four towns a few miles from the front lines, south of the Hürtgen Forest area. The towns were Steckenborn, Strauch, Konzen, and Rollesbroich, all northeast of Simmerath except Konzen, which was southwest. According to the operations order, these towns were filled with German troops. They further requested a maximum effort of sixteen aircraft per squadron, and to run as many missions as possible. Besides bombing we were directed to strafe vigorously. It makes one wonder why the American commanders were surprised by the German Ardennes offensive, considering that G-2 (intelligence) recognized the massing of front-line troops in the towns for us to bomb and strafe.

The weather on 11 December did not cooperate. The first mission of only twelve aircraft from the 389th squadron did not get off until 1000 with Steckenborn as their target. Finding a dense overcast that completely obscured their target, they tried a pickle-barrel mission, but the radar broke down halfway through the run. Finally they found a hole in the overcast and identified the town they saw as Wollseifen, another town on the list. They went ahead and bombed it, only to discover with horror that they were bombing Lammersdorf, a town in our hands. Lammersdorf is about nine miles west-northwest of Wollseifen. The Report of Operations mentions twenty-six casualties, with some fatalities.

Konzen was the target for the 390th, but they too found it cloud-covered. They also found a town through a hole in the cloud layer and definitely identified it as Rollesbroich. Half the squadron bombed before the hole closed while the others brought their bombs back. The fickle weather cleared enough for the twelve aircraft of the 391st to clobber their Rollesbroich target. Attack results showed several buildings demolished, but other than that they knew nothing.

The twelve aircraft of the 389th could not bomb their primary target, the town of Steckenborn, because of weather, so they elected to make a pickle-barrel mission to Zulpich. It was interesting to the pilots because a hole opened up as they bombed the town, and they saw their bombs were on target, achieving a good pattern on the eastern edge of Zulpich. It alleviated, somewhat, our skepticism of hitting anything with ground radar bombing.

Weather also frustrated the 390th mission. The eleven aircraft were directed to bomb Konzen, but it was completely cloud-covered. They were, instead, sent on an armed reconnaissance. It was a fortunate circumstance as through a hole in the clouds they found a train speeding down the track, pulling about twenty-five flat cars, each car carrying two tanks. The whole squadron bombed and strafed the entire train. They were elated when they returned to base. Assessing the damage was difficult, but they felt they destroyed at least four tanks and perhaps as many as thirty.

Frustrating weather diverted another mission from its primary target. Twelve aircraft from the 391st squadron were to bomb Rollesbroich but were forced to their secondary target, Zulpich. It was the same for the twelve aircraft from the 389th. They settled by bombing the marshaling yard at Euskirchen.

The twelfth of December was a replay from the previous day. We had the same mission, the same weather, and the same unknown results of our effort.

It was back to close ground support on 14 December after another day of being grounded by weather. The operations order specified support for the 2nd and 99th Infantry Divisions, part of General Gerow's V Corps, making the first concerted attack to capture the approaches to the Roer River dams. The 2nd and 99th Infantry were attacking in the Monschau Forest area, a southern extension of the Hürtgen Forest. The air/ground controllers were Hoptide for the 2nd Infantry and Blankwall for the 99th Infantry, both at Elsenborn. It was back to the same missions with the same weather, just another forest.

The 389th Squadron sent up twelve aircraft but could not work with the infantry air/ground controllers because of weather. Marmite directed that they attack railroad bridges on the Green System. Finding several railroad bridges in the Bad Neuenahr–Ahrweiler area, Marmite gave them the option to select the bridge to bomb. They temporarily put out of commission a three-span double-track bridge by a clean cut at the west end.

The 391st was similarly weather-hampered, so Marmite directed them to the town of Mechernich, southeast of Euskirchen, to investigate a reported train unloading military equipment. They found the train, stopped, but with steam up, and fifteen empty flat cars. Train and track were in a demolished state when they left.

It was the same story for twelve aircraft of the 390th squadron. Since they were precluded by weather from working with the infantry air/ground controllers, Marmite directed they bomb a large heavy artillery position near Düren. We had been there before but evidently did not destroy it. They bombed the area where the position was supposedly located, but again they could observe no tangible results. Weather was closing in fast at the base so they expedited the trip back.

Weather was a continuing problem for the 15 December missions. After being vectored around for a while, the twelve aircraft of the 391st finally performed a pickle-barrel mission bombing an unknown target.

The Report of Operations for the 390th mission seemed familiar when I read it. On looking in my diary, sure enough, I had been on that mission and the entry was quite appropriate, "A flubbed mission to the Ruhr Valley." We couldn't work with the front-line air/ground controllers so Marmite vectored the twelve of us through the middle of the heavy industrial Ruhr Valley area. Mentioning the Ruhr Valley as a target usually brought a collective groan from the pilots. It was a megalopolis of several large cities and numerous smaller ones, all devoted to the manufacture of armaments and munitions. It was the heartland of Germany's heavy industry and of vital importance to the military. Although heavily bombed, industry still flourished with workers on the job in the roofless buildings and it was still a major manufacturer of German weapons. Antiaircraft emplacements abounded in the area and was so heavily protected that it acquired the nickname of "Flak Valley." So here we were, right over the middle of Flak Valley. Usually heavy flak batteries did not fire at prowling fighters because we could usually evade them, but this day we drew heavy-caliber radar-controlled flak as we prowled the sky at Angels 12 over a solid undercast. I found it fascinating that the flak exploded right at our altitude and directly in line where we would have been had we not changed direction every 10 seconds. They tracked us for about three minutes and then gave up. Getting low on fuel and frustrated by the lack of targets, we dive-bombed a working factory through a break in the undercast in the town of Bochum, near the notorious flak-protected city of Essen.

I experienced heavy-caliber radar-controlled flak sporadically from the time of my first mission flown on 10 August. At that time I called it "terrifying" and tried to run away from it. The next occasion mentioned is 11 October, when I had about twenty missions. Then heavy-caliber flak disabled one of our aircraft, and I called it "intimidating." This time, having completed about forty missions, it fascinated me. It shows the progression of attitude as one becomes combat-hardened.

A flubbed mission was also the story for the eleven aircraft of the 389th squadron. One aircraft had a landing gear failure on takeoff. The pilot was not injured although the mishap heavily damaged the aircraft. They performed a pickle-barrel mission bombing an unknown town through the overcast. This was the last mission of the day since that cold, wet northern European winter haze settled in.

So ended the Hürtgen Forest campaign. The next morning the Germans unleashed their Ardennes offensive, and our operations area shifted slightly south to support the troops fighting to stem the German tide. We were to go back briefly to that forest in late January when the drive to the Roer River was finally completed, but by that time the German army and flak were not as menacing. Flak was still deadly, but appeared more subdued. It was a hectic six weeks and the constant and furious effort we expended in fighting the Germans and the European weather will always be remembered by those of us who flew those missions to that miserable and hated Hürtgen Forest.

7.   **Battle of the Bulge**

German Attack

The most vicious and demanding battle American forces fought in Europe began on 16 December when the German forces unleashed their Ardennes offensive. It was bitterly cold, snowing, and foggy that kept us grounded. But in the end it was the finest hour of the American army.

The sixteenth of December was no different than any other day. The weather was lousy and our operations order briefing spelled out the same type of missions we had been flying for the past month. The intelligence officer did mention that this morning some front-line army units, south of our operations area, were experiencing heavy German shelling and strong attacks with tanks, but that was all the information he had. The weatherman thought we might get off but would see very little if we did. It looked like we would have another day to keep up the winterizing of our tent and improve our living conditions.

Winter weather hit us with a blast just as the German offensive started. It turned bitterly cold and snowed heavily. They installed small potbelly stoves in our tents, but they constantly needed stoking to keep burning, which wasn't practical during the day. We usually started a fire in the early evening and then let it burn out during the night. By morning, when we were roused for a mission, it was freezing and our canteens of water were solid blocks of ice. The operations tent had a stove burning all day that kept it above freezing, and it was a good place to get out of the elements.

The group arranged for the delivery of two prefabricated buildings to our site, one for the CO's office and operations and the other for our briefing room and lounge. We all pitched in to help erect them. In the lounge we were determined to install a fireplace, constructed with the correct building materials this time. I'm not sure, but I believe Wally Lundie volunteered to build it. Several of us pitched in by mixing mortar and hauling bricks. Finally the lounge with a fireplace was finished and we threw a grand opening party. With a great fanfare we started a fire that promptly drove us all outside; the chimney wouldn't draw and the room filled with smoke. We gave up on fireplaces. The unused fireplace did become a shelter for a couple during our New Year's Eve party when German aircraft strafed and bombed us.

I was a veteran of forty missions when the Battle of the Bulge started. Surviving that many missions enhanced my belief that I had the luck to make it through the war alive. I knew I was fooling myself, because I saw my friends going down, but it still gave me hope—so much so I became a cocky and "hot" pilot. To nonpilots that expression may sound peculiar so I will attempt an explanation. The *Webster's Dictionary* defines "cocky" as being arrogant or jaunty. A cocky pilot is certainly that, but in addition he is sure of himself and his aircraft. He understands and knows the aircraft's capabilities and, when flying, achieves a perfect welding of the man/machine combination. Being a hot pilot implies the ability to do any type of flying better than most other pilots, and exhibiting an attitude similar to that expounded by the song, "I Can Do Anything Better than You," from the musical *Annie Get Your Gun*. Now even though a pilot is cocky and hot, it doesn't mean he has become disrespectful of the enemy's capability or the flak, but he knows the limitations and defense against it. In other words, a cocky and hot combat pilot has become combat-hardened and finally knows what he is doing.

The first day of the German offensive, 16 December, was routine weather frustration for us. For the last several days we had supported the 2nd and 99th Infantry Divisions attack to push through to the Roer River just south of the Roer River dams, but lousy weather had frustrated our missions. The weather on 16 December was no better, and only the 391st squadron of twelve aircraft completed a pickle-barrel mission. Reports of enemy aircraft in the area caused two alert scrambles to try to intercept them. Both flights were uneventful.

They scheduled me for a couple of stand-down days and I took the opportunity to visit my relatives in Oordegem. While there, I heard the news over the radio about a German offensive in the Ardennes region of Belgium. I immediately returned to base, arriving back in the early evening of 17 December in the midst of a German air raid. Oh, what a day to miss. I still hadn't seen a German aircraft and on several missions that day German aircraft had been the aggressor. The squadron was all agog since many fellows had scored in the melees.

The missions I missed on 17 December were continued support for the 99th Infantry Division, now on the defensive and being vigorously attacked by the I SS Panzer Corps, consisting of the 1st and 12th SS Panzer Divisions and three infantry divisions. They were part of the Sixth Panzer Army, comprising the northern flank of the projected German breakthrough. Overwhelming German strength was pushing the 2nd and 99th Divisions back, but they were fighting furiously to hold their positions at Elsenborn Ridge. It was the group's mission to help blunt that German attack.

As the squadrons reached the 99th Division area around Büllingen and Krinklet, Belgium, swarms of Me 109 and FW 190 aircraft attacked them. In all, they attacked six of the fourteen squadron missions dispatched on 17 December. Sometimes the Germans disrupted the squadrons' dive-bombing attack, forcing them to jettison their bombs. In other attacks the Germans forced an air battle. The claims for German aircraft destroyed that day totaled seventeen shot down, one probable, and fourteen damaged. We lost three aircraft and two pilots. While engaged in a dogfight, Lt. Robert F. Boehn from the 389th squadron incurred severe damage and crashed while making an emergency landing at A-89 (Le Coulot, Belgium). He died a few days later. Lt. John Crawford was seriously wounded but returned to base and was hospitalized. Another aircraft sustained extensive damage, forcing the pilot to bail out over the base. Several more aircraft were heavily damaged, forcing one to make a belly landing at our field.

My good friend Stan Sobek was the pilot that bailed out over the base. In a dogfight an Me 109 ruffled his tail feathers, requiring him to hold full right rudder and stick to keep the aircraft level. Just northwest of the base he unbuckled his shoulder harness and seatbelt and prepared to bail out. When he let go of the controls, the aircraft snap-rolled and tossed him out. He landed a few miles from the field and was picked up by members of the English antiaircraft battalion guarding Y-32. The aircraft crashed in a sparsely settled area a few miles northwest of our field, between Y-29 and Y-32, where we jettisoned safe bombs. The next day he returned and retrieved the aircraft name plate from the crash as a souvenir. Stan said the aircraft serial number was 43-25514. To clear up all the paperwork, they required him to sign for losing the eight machine guns and for a while he was concerned they would charge him for them.

The operations order for 18 December specified support to the hard-pressed and nearly encircled 106th Infantry Division in the St. Vith area. Weather prognosis was poor, predicting multiple cloud layers from the deck up to 10,000 feet, and a winter haze and snow giving a visibility from zero to five miles. They scheduled four aircraft per mission throughout the day. They put me for the morning alert duty since it would be dedicated to engaging enemy aircraft and was active the previous day.

Wouldn't you know it, the first mission on 18 December—four aircraft each from all three squadrons—ran into a hornet's nest of enemy aircraft near Cologne. They became entangled in a dogfight against a swarm of about 90 Me 109 and FW 190 aircraft. Fortunately several other Allied squadrons entered the fray, evening the odds. In the resulting 10-minute dogfight, twelve German aircraft were shot down by the 366th against a loss of two aircraft and one heavily damaged. Lieutenants George Demmon and Matt Slaven bailed out safely to POW status.

The next mission of four 390th squadron P-47s were also involved in a dogfight. They entered a melee of Me 109s and FW 190s mixing it up with Spitfires, P-38s, and some other P-47s. They shot down two Me 109s but lost one aircraft.

The P-47 lost has an interesting conclusion. The pilot was Bob Goff, the pilot who lost his teeth in the latrine at A-70 two months before. As he applied war emergency power to enter the engagement, he saw his manifold pressure go off scale. Before he could react, the engine blew a cylinder and quit. He speculated that the one of the exhaust waste gates, which regulates the turbo supercharger rpm, went to the full closed position. He arrived back at the base that evening and related the following story.

After his engine quit, he dove out of the battle and started to glide west as far as he could, planning to make a belly landing. He couldn't see a clearing large enough to do that in the rugged terrain of the Ardennes, but he didn't want to bail out yet since he wanted to make sure he was out of enemy territory. In desperation he selected a road through a small village to make a belly landing. Unfortunately he didn't have enough altitude to reach the road and went straight into the second story of a house. The engine, as a battering ram, hammered a hole through the typical European thick brick-walled house, broke off, and fell down to the basement, narrowly missing a lady living in the house. When the dust settled, he found himself balanced on the wall with half the fuselage inside the house. When he moved to get out of the cockpit, the fuselage swayed and rocked so menacingly he was afraid it would fall, trapping him in the gasoline-soaked rubble. Some American medics driving by in a jeep helped him out after tying down the fuselage. He was well strapped in and suffered only some heavy bruises from his shoulder straps. The rugged P-47 saved another pilot. Bob has been exchanging Christmas cards with the two medics since that meeting in a small Belgium village.

This is the only case I know of a Pratt and Whitney R-2800 engine failing while using war emergency power because an exhaust waste gate regulator failed. This also happened to our piggyback P-47, made by replacing the auxiliary tank with a seat. Our squadron flight surgeon, wanting to gain first-hand experience, came on a mission riding in the piggyback seat. Fortunately the pilot was able to react; he retarded the throttle and got home. I can't recall the surgeon going on any other mission.

After watching several other missions depart while sitting in our aircraft anxiously awaiting a scramble call we were finally ordered to take off about noon. The flight consisted of twelve aircraft, four from each squadron. We were vectored east of Aachen to the Rhine River to Cologne but did not meet any hostile aircraft. We reluctantly returned to base for a belated cold lunch.

The group launched fifteen missions that day, and in five of them contact with enemy fighters occurred. They scrambled the afternoon alert flight at 1430, and a few minutes later they engaged enemy aircraft overwhelming a group of Spitfires. They claimed one Me 109 shot down and another probably destroyed. I didn't even get to see any enemy aircraft. I was really cussing my luck.

The missions that enemy aircraft did not attack proceeded with their ground-support task of helping the 106th Infantry Division. Unfortunately they ran into weather problems. Clouds were down to only 500 feet over the ground, precluding the identification of targets. Some missions even brought their bombs back. It was the start of the miserable weather that stopped our attacks just when the ground troops needed them the most. Not only was the weather bad, but the days were very short, lasting a little over eight hours from official sunrise to sunset. Fortunately the northern latitude had a long twilight period that extended our flying period another hour or so. The ground forces started calling it "Hitler's weather."

We sent up three missions on 19 December in very bad weather. The twelve aircraft from the 391st squadron did a little bombing and strafing, claiming a few vehicles, but losing Lt. Jim Colbroth. Flak hit him while he was dive-bombing and he crashed into a hillside. Not everyone could bomb so they brought back twelve bombs. The 389th squadron ran a pickle-barrel mission but on the way back to base found a hole in the clouds and clobbered an enemy column of 150 tanks, trucks, and other vehicles with their rockets and guns. They were cussing their luck for having expended their bombs on an unknown target. The twelve aircraft of the 390th squadron were directed about 20 miles east of the battle area to bomb, rocket, and strafe the town of Marmagen. All they could claim was a half-track vehicle destroyed and a large secondary explosion in the town.

For the next four days weather grounded us with fog and heavy snow. The only flying during that time was a two-aircraft weather reconnaissance by the

389th squadron on 22 December. The weather reported at two points in the battle area was a 700-foot ceiling and a visibility of three miles, and a 100–200-foot ceiling with a visibility of one-half mile. The top of the cloud layer varied between 8,000 and 9,000 feet. All we could do was follow the ground battle through the situation map in our operations shack and hope for good weather to plaster the German columns.

The German offensive caused our front lines to buckle inward into Belgium, creating a bulging salient. Our situation map usually displayed a red line signifying the location of the bomb line. We noted that within the breakthrough area there was no longer a solid bomb line displayed, only some arcs indicating where American forces still had a coherent defense against the attacking Germans. The intelligence officer, Capt. George Wilcox, said that was all the information he had and no one knew where the German armored columns were. It was about this time that the American army started referring to that battle area as "the Bulge." The name stuck and forever this German offensive will be known to Americans as the "Battle of the Bulge."

We heard rumors and speculation that the German offensive was aiming for Antwerp, and that the northern pocket cutoff, including our field, was to be annihilated. I recall that we weren't unduly worried for we knew that when the weather cleared we would devastate their attacking columns. Weeks later, when we read what the newspapers back home had to say about Germany's latest offensive, we were amused and dismayed by their remarks. We were amused by their sensational headlines such as "American Disaster in the Ardennes," and their exaggeration on the extent of the German offensive. However, they dismayed us by the way they belittled the American army reaction, and by their maps that had bold arrows depicting the German drives and small arrows for the U.S. Army response. They neglected the gallant stand on the northern flank that held the breakthrough to a narrow corridor, dooming Hitler's offensive. We knew newspaper reports were inaccurate but didn't realize the extent of their sensationalism.

Major credit for limiting the German corridor width must go to the 2nd and 99th Infantry Divisions' heroic stand in the Elsenborn Ridge area. They stopped the 12th SS Panzer Division and forced the 1st SS Panzer division into side roads and trails where they became bogged down, collapsing the main spearhead of the Ardennes attack. These two Panzer divisions, part of the Sixth Panzer Army, were to break through the American lines and race to Antwerp. The rest of the Sixth Panzer Army of five infantry divisions were to follow to consolidate the breakthrough. Hitler's crony, Gen. Josef "Sepp" Dietrich, commanded this formidable army. He lost face in the debacle that followed.[1]

We took no chances about German intentions. They tightened security around our base and, for a short while, even helmets and side arms were required apparel. As a contingency plan, in the unlikely event of a German armored-column approach, we were to take off and fly to England and either land if an open field was available or bail out. These were just precautionary measures, and no one took them seriously.

The weather cleared over the southern part of the battle area on 23 December, and the Ninth Air Force took to the sky, leaving a trail of destroyed German forces in their wake. The aerial onslaught created bedlam throughout the German command structure as all the field forces clamored for Luftwaffe help to stop the devastating air attacks. Many fighter groups pounded the German spearheads, while other groups patrolled and held at bay the German aircraft that tried to intervene on behalf of their own troops. Fighters of the Ninth Air Force hounded German aircraft and shot down ninety-one for the loss of nineteen fighters. Ninth Air Force medium bombers pounded the German communication centers, but lost thirty-five to flak and aircraft during the raids. The Eighth Air Force joined in the melee and claimed another seventy-five German fighters, losing seven of their own.[2] It was, quoting General Patton, "What a glorious day for killing Germans." Unfortunately, we were one of the few fighter groups that could not participate as our field remained socked in with fog until the next day.

Early that cold clear 24 December morning, the group dispatched the first squadron at 0905 on a fighter sweep to interdict German aircraft trying to enter the battle area. They surveyed several German airfields but could spot no aircraft in residence, although tracks in the snow showed they were in use. They did not see or claim any German aircraft shot down, but in their frustration did destroy several train locomotives and strafed the boxcars as they sped down the track. We dispatched two more alert fighter-sweep missions. One was uneventful, but the other encountered seventy-five enemy aircraft. They attacked and shot down an Me 109; however, Lt. J. K. Jones, 391st squadron, became separated from the flight and was in turn shot down and killed.

The operations order for our ground-support missions specified a battle area armed reconnaissance as directed by Marmite. The 390th sent up eight aircraft at 1000 hours, although only seven became airborne. One pilot lost control on an ice- and snow-crusted runway, damaging the landing gear and wing. After we reached the battle area, Marmite assigned us to perform a reconnaissance along the northern end of the German breakthrough in the Malmedy area. We spotted and dive-bombed German vehicles parked just along a road bordering some woods by the town of Ligneuville. As I pulled up from my dive-bombing pass, I caught a glimpse of a command car off the road, parked next to the

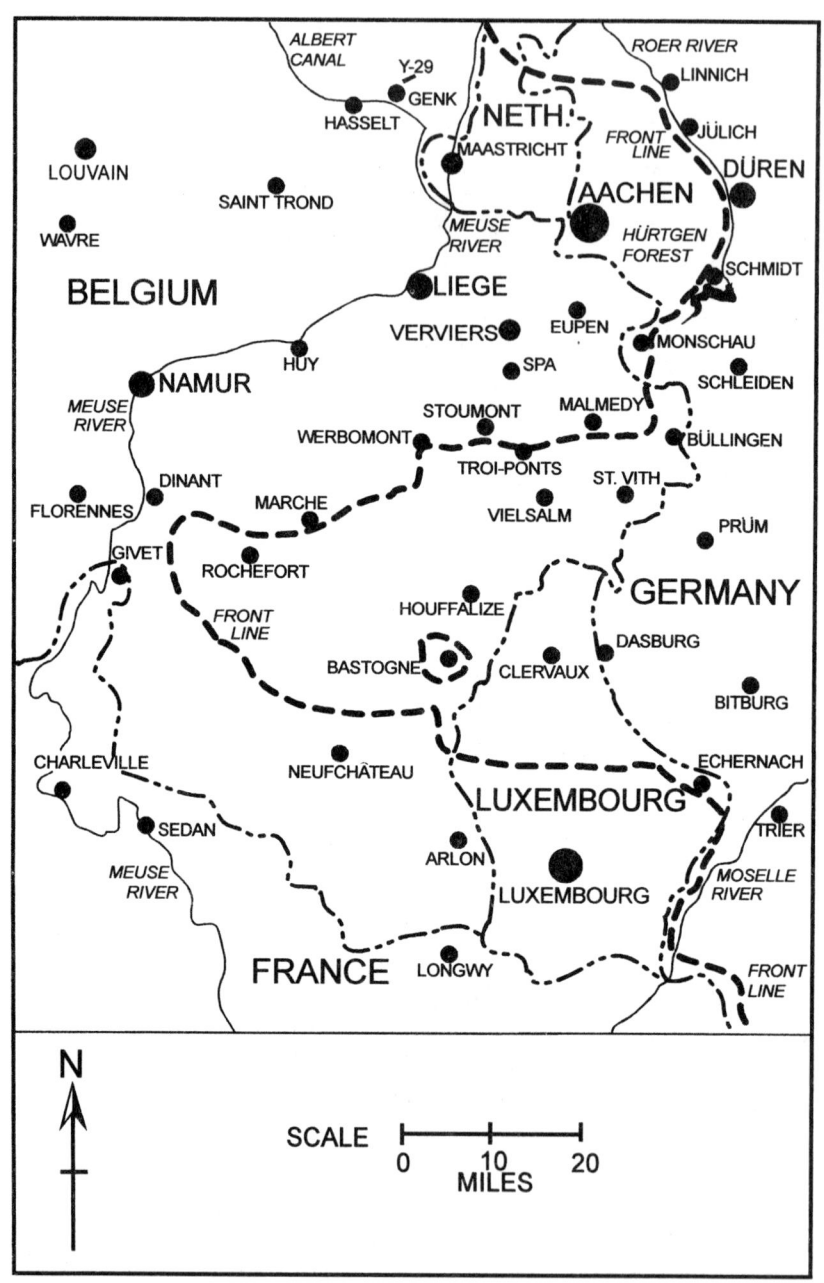

The Ardennes Area, Front Line, 25 December 1944

trees by some buildings. I reported the find and mentioned that we might have found an enemy headquarters. Several others confirmed this as they reported spotting a truck with radio antennas and a tank parked by a house. Records indicate this was probably SS Obersturmbannfüher (Lt. Col.) Otto Skorzeny's headquarters of the 115th Panzer Brigade trying to seize Malmedy. He was attached to the First Panzer Division and his so-called Operation Grief, German soldiers dressed in American uniforms, had collapsed. (Actually he was just starting to walk back in retreat. The hodgepodge of ground troops at Malmedy had stopped him cold.)[3]

I kept my eye on the command car as I made a wingover into a strafing pass. A few bursts from my guns saturated the area, but the car wouldn't burn. At the last moment I realized the predicament I was in because I was rapidly approaching the ground in a 30-degree dive. Strafing passes were not normally that steep, being only about 15 degrees, but I had to steepen my dive to keep that barely visible target in sight in that forested region. My concentration on shooting at the target had blocked my other perceptions and I had encountered what they then called "pilot fixation in destroying a target." I sucked the stick in my gut to pull out and just before blacking out from the G loads was relieved to see I was in level flight just a few feet off the ground. I noted with concern, though, that I was heading toward the tall pine trees towering above me. When the fellows viewed my combat film and saw those pine trees right in my flight path, they gasped as they recognized my predicament.[4]

Although I was blacked out, I managed to keep a strong steady pull on the stick. Suddenly the aircraft shuddered and my feet left the rudder pedals. I realized that I had flown through the trees and was relieved to feel the sturdy Jug still flying, although in a horrendous sideslip. I relaxed back pressure on the stick and screamed and shook my head to try to clear the blackout. My vision returned while my head was facing the right wing. To my surprise there was a two-foot hole in the wing and hydraulic fluid was all over everything. The German gunners had had target practice while I was in my ground-hugging pullout. My cockpit was full of cable and my rudder pedals limp.

I reported, "I'm hit and heading home." My wingman, who accompanied me, appraised my damage as a large hole in the right wing just aft of the gear. However, it appeared they did not hit the gear and it would function. He also reported several holes in the fuselage and that the tail area was a mess. My aircraft controls were entangled with rudder cable that must have snapped back violently when severed. I cleared the cable away from the controls as best I could, but it was coiled and looped over everything. Although the aircraft was in a sideslip, it flew satisfactorily, so I would be able to reach our base. However, I didn't know if I could land safely without a rudder or ground-control capability because I could not depress the brakes on the limp rudder pedals. When I mentioned that I might have to belly in because I had no ground-control capability, Major Martin (leading the mission) firmly requested I land it if possible. We were going to need every aircraft we had.

On the way back to base I experimented to find some way of controlling the aircraft on landing. If I lowered the seat all the way down and loosened my seatbelt, I could slouch down, allowing me to reach and depress the toe brakes on the rudder pedals. This was necessary since the rudder pedals hung free and stopped only when they were forced against the fire wall that separated the cockpit from the engine compartment. This would at least give me some ground control to correct the swerving caused by landing in a large sideslip. I could only hope that the separate brake hydraulic system was functional.

The landing gear locked satisfactorily when I shook it down so I passed that hurdle. I set up a long approach and tried to pump down the flaps, but the pump went limp after only 15 degrees came down. I made certain it was a perfect three-point landing so the tail wheel would be on the runway to help control the aircraft. On touch-down I cut the engine, bottomed the seat, and slouched down and applied the brakes for control. The wide landing gear and tail wheel lock of the P-47 proved their worth as I successfully controlled the aircraft and rolled straight down the runway even though I touched down in a large yaw angle. Once the aircraft was under control, I raised up to see where I was. With the seat lowered and me slouched down, my head was below the canopy sill. When the aircraft was almost stopped, I unlocked the tail wheel and let it go off the side of the runway so the others could land.

My crew chief, along with several others, ran over to offer assistance. When I circled the field they saw I was damaged and came up to the runway to stand by and help if needed. They saw me touch down, fight for control, and then roll past them with apparently no one in the aircraft. They couldn't see me and they were wondering what the heck happened. They thought I may have collapsed from being wounded and were quite relieved as I climbed out. It was my forty-second mission and my first flak damage.

Inspecting the aircraft later, I blanched when my crew chief pointed out the 20mm shell path and how close the rudder and elevator cables were in that area. If the shells had hit two inches over they would have cut my elevator cables, and I would not be writing this story. It was comforting to know my guardian angels were still with me, plural because I must have worn out one.

Claims for that mission amounted to three half-tracks and fifteen other vehicles destroyed. Also a radio truck and a tank probably destroyed, and the house, thought to be a headquarters, demolished by bombing.

Three of the five missions sent up on 24 December were alert flights to investigate bogeys and interdict German fighters. The two ground-support missions conducted were by the 390th, as narrated above, and by the 391st squadron. They were able to dive-bomb German troops in the St. Vith area, claiming several trucks destroyed, but losing Lt. Al McKinley to flak. It appeared the German troops were well supplied with our nemesis, the German Zugkraftwagen eight-ton two-centimeter Flak-Vierling (German eight-ton halftrack with a quadruple-mounted 20mm antiaircraft system), which we called the "flak wagon."

The flak wagon was not only used for aircraft defense but was employed as an offensive attack weapon. When the four 20mm guns hit a ground target it just pulverized it. Gen. James M. Gavin, commander of the 82nd Airborne Division, mentioned several times in his book being taken under fire by that fearsome weapon.[5] He noted it wasn't very accurate because the halftrack chassis vibrated so much, but it had a long effective range and the volume of fire intimidated the infantry.

The next several days were clear and we really pounded the Germans. On 25 December we flew eight missions, the next day ten missions, and the following day eleven. During these three days, we shot down twelve enemy aircraft, seven of those in a big dogfight by the 389th squadron on 27 December, and we destroyed numerous German tanks, trucks, and troops. The cost to the group was the loss of four pilots (three killed and one wounded), three aircraft lost, ten heavily damaged requiring service group repair, and an untold number lightly damaged, meaning they could be repaired using squadron maintenance. By the end of the week, six, seven and eight aircraft squadron missions were common. The seventy-five aircraft assigned to the group, and twenty-five more spares from the service group, were used up.

The following quote is from a then-secret report on the number of sorties flown by fighter-bomber groups in IX TAC for the first ten days of the battle, 17-27 December.

Close support was given to the Ground forces in the break-thru area, the [366th] group utilizing all available daylight hours. From 17th December to the 27th December a total of 600 sorties were flown by the group. During this period there were four days that no flying was done due to the field being closed in by weather. Of all the groups flying under control of IX TAC, this was the highest number of sorties flown by any one group. It is interesting to note that the other groups were grounded only three days, one day less than the 366th, and [366th] performed more sorties in six days than the others in seven.

During this period (17–27 December), the 366th Group claims amounted to (partial list of only destroyed military equipment):

Enemy aircraft 43
Tanks and armored vehicles 55
Motor transport 328
Half-tracks 15[6]

The Germans were aware of our field and, I suppose, looked at it as a vicious thorn upsetting their latest offensive. German bombers periodically bombed and strafed our airfield in night attacks, but the fighter-bomber attacks these last few days must have hurt them. On 26 December the Germans subjected our field to a serious night-bombing and -strafing attack. During the night they made four separate attacks with antipersonnel bombs and cannon-fire strafing, the first at 1918 and the last at 2330. They caused minor damage and wounded several personnel, only one seriously. They killed two British soldiers in a nearby town that bore the brunt of one bombing. It would take more than a few nuisance night-bombing raids by some Ju 88 bombers to knock out our operational capability.

The aggressive attacks by the German Luftwaffe were very effective in disrupting our ground support. This was evidently their purpose since reports of German aircraft diving through fighter-bomber formations, and withdrawing when they saw the bombs jettisoned, were common. Generals Hoyt Vandenberg and James Doolittle, respectively the Ninth and Eighth Air Force commanders, recognized this dilemma and took appropriate action. The Eighth Air Force mission was changed from its strategic role to hammer the German logistical support and communications systems behind the Ardennes front. In addition, the Eighth Air Force Fighter Command transferred two fighter groups to the continent. Their task was to conduct fighter sweeps along the Rhine River and prevent German fighters from reaching the battle area, leaving us free to do our job. We, the fighter-bomber pilots, were admonished that if a timely warning of an attack by enemy aircraft was given we were to retain our bombs and turn into the diving enemy. Only if they stayed around to fight were we to drop our bombs and engage them. This edict was not popular and affected our egos as fighter pilots. For the past week the fighter-bomber pilots of the Ninth Air Force proved that in air-to-air combat they could clobber the enemy at a greater than 10 to 1 ratio. Not bad for inexperienced air-to-air combat pilots still using the reflecting ring and bead sight. All Eighth Air Force fighters were now equipped with the new gyro-controlled K-14A computing gunsight. It eliminated a lot of guesswork on obtaining the correct lead to nail a German aircraft. As the Eighth was oriented more to air-to-air combat, it made sense to let them have first priority for the new sights, but it made us jealous. No matter, we accepted the new dictate and vowed to make up by really blasting the German columns.

Weather interfered for two days and it was barely flyable on 31 December, but we ran eight missions. They were not very productive, but we knocked out some more German military equipment and soldiers out of the battle. That day I learned they appreciated my efforts as they promoted me to first lieutenant.

The year ended with a most spectacular display of the P-47's rugged construction. Lt. Karl Hallberg of the 389th was forced to land with a hung-up 500-pound bomb that he was unable to jettison. This was not uncommon and many of us had found ourselves in the same situation; the essential survival condition meant landing as gently as possible so it wouldn't get jarred off. Unfortunately, the swampy ground of our airfield was not a good base, even for the sturdy pierced planking used for this runway, and hard use had made it bumpy. We could see he had a hung-up bomb and we watched his landing intently. He made a long approach, landed smoothly, and was rolling along the runway when the bomb came loose, hit the ground, and tumbled into the air, minus the tail fin that had broken off. Even if the bomb was dropped safely, the loss of the tail fin armed it, and it could explode the next time it hit the runway, which it did. What was left of the aircraft came skidding out of the explosion debris. When it stopped, we saw Karl climb out and clear the area in a record-breaking sprint. He suffered head wounds that hospitalized him for a few days, but the armor plate and sturdy P-47 construction saved his life.[7]

Landing with bombs on was a fairly common occurrence. Besides having to land with hung-up bombs we also returned with them whenever a suitable target could not be found. The 389th had two additional pilots, Tom Durham and Bob Stinson, who survived dropped bombs on landing explosions. I dropped one in landing on the runway, but it didn't explode.

8.

Battle of the Bulge

Americans Strike Back

The German bulge in American lines was contained by heroic defense that upset the German timetable and stopped their drive short of the Meuse River. Hitler refused to admit defeat and threw the last reserves into the battle to regain the initiative. The air war heated up as the Luftwaffe appeared in great strength to wrest control of the air from us.

The last several days of flyable weather buoyed our spirits as we saw that Hitler's offensive was doomed. That must also have been the feeling of our commander, since helmets and side arms were no longer required apparel. The air battles fought the past few days provided a high point of a day when the gun camera film was viewed. Unfortunately, the dark cloudy skies did not result in good pictures, so much of the film was worthless. It was very gratifying to hear the comments and cheers from the enlisted men when a German aircraft was seen being destroyed by their P-47s. My own thoughts were muted as I cussed my luck, not even seeing a flying German aircraft.

We ushered in the new year 1945 with one wing-ding of a New Year's Eve party, arranged by Harry Wildhaber. I was having a drink with my crew chief S.Sgt. Al Czaplicki, bemoaning the fact that if I never saw any German aircraft, I could never shoot one down. At that moment another serious German air raid occurred. It was just at midnight, so the new year was welcomed in with the always spectacular display of antiaircraft fire. They dropped several sticks of bombs but they exploded a mile east of the field in the town of Eisden. Continuing our drink, Sergeant Czaplicki remarked that it was a new year and maybe my luck would change and I would meet up with some German aircraft.

Let me digress a bit to record an interesting occurrence. On the fiftieth anniversary of the Battle of the Bulge I was featured in a local newspaper article. A few days later I received a call from a Mr. Anowski, who lived in the town of Eisden during the war. He mentioned that he used to come to Y-29 to pick up the wash from the airmen for his mother. He was jarred by the German bombs that New Year's Eve and witnessed the dogfight the next morning where several German aircraft were shot down. It's a small world.

The next morning, 1 January 1945, I was one of eight on the early mission. I was very miffed that they scheduled me to fly our group commander's aircraft B2-H, the "Flying Carpet," an old razorback aircraft (nonbubble-canopy) instead of my own B2-J, which was out of commission for a hydraulic leak. At that time there were only a few razorback P-47s left in the group; all others were bubble-canopy types.[1] The weather was clear with a 4/10 cloud cover at 3,000 feet. Capt. L. B. Smith led the eight aircraft taking off toward the southwest at 0915. Waiting at the southwest end of the runway were twelve P-51 aircraft from Col. John C. Meyer's 352nd Fighter Group; they would take off to the northeast after we left. The Eighth Air Force 352nd Fighter Group, one of two groups temporarily assigned to work with the Ninth Air Force, had moved in on the other side of Y-29. They took over the interdiction role to prevent the German air force from interrupting and harassing our dive-bombing and strafing. This relieved the Ninth Air Force from that task, which allowed more of the P-47s to be used in the ground-support roll. Their continuous high cover and patrolling well east of the battle area practically eliminated German air force interference with our ground support.

After takeoff we made a 180-degree turn and formed up into a close comfortable formation as we set a course for the front lines. At that point we saw antiaircraft fire on our left. Turning to investigate we saw a large gaggle of German fighters, flying at about 200 feet and heading toward our strip. Other German fighters were already strafing Y-32. We met the fifty or sixty Me 109 and FW 190 German fighters head on as we dove down. As I did a wingover and dove down to attack, I caught a glimpse of our field and saw the P-51 aircraft lining up for takeoff. During this initial attack we were busy getting our aircraft cleaned up by jettisoning bombs, turning on our gunsights and guns, and switching the gas back to main tank.

A lone FW 190 near the front of the gaggle was my target. It took only a moment before I was on his tail and I had not yet turned on my guns and gunsight. He dove down to the deck, skimming the ground at full throttle. I tried to slide right behind him but his prop wash almost flipped me over into the ground. I could not depress my nose to bring my guns to bear and it was hard, because of my eagerness, to hold fire, even though my bullets were going over him. At one point I noted a puff of white smoke from his engine, and I quickly retarded the throttle. I thought, I'll bet he chopped the throttle. I almost overshot him, and for a few moments we were in tight formation together, with me stepped up and slightly behind. The vision of the pilot crouched over his controls is still vivid. I entertained the thought, for a moment, to fire my Colt .45 pistol at him, but dismissed it as impractical. As he accelerated I returned to my position on his tail. Finally some trees loomed ahead. As he made a turning pull-up, I hit him with a good burst and he blew up, hitting the ground in front of me. The crash site was about five miles northeast of the field but I had no time to pinpoint the crash site to visit later. There would be very little to see as he hit the ground at about 350 mph in nearly level flight so the aircraft would be widely scattered.

I flew through his explosion, which jolted my P-47 with a severe whomp and covered my windshield with oil, making it quite opaque for a few moments. Spotting another FW 190 I maneuvered behind him, and just as I started firing I saw cannon shells flying over my canopy (captured on my combat film as fireballs coming from behind and curving down in front of me). Instinctively I started a roll to the right, our best turning direction, but since I was already in a slight left turn, snapped back into a steep left turn. My unplanned feint into a right roll and snap-roll reversal to the left probably confused my antagonist, an Me 109, because when I saw him behind me he had not yet reached a steep left bank turn. The slow flashes of the cannon firing through the propeller hub and the faster winking of the machine guns on the cowling fascinated rather than scared me. By practically dragging my wing tip on the ground in a near vertical bank turn, and using war emergency power to maintain my high airspeed, I kept his occasional bursts of shells streaming behind me. After completing about a full 360-degree turn, the Me 109 suddenly broke away, leaving me alone to chase another target. I fired a few bursts at another FW 190 that pulled in front of me. Some hits were observed and I thought I saw smoke swirl from his engine, but I ran out of ammunition and broke off the chase. Aircraft were darting in every direction, all at full throttle and below 300 feet. Also some frantic calls came over the radio for help in getting aircraft off their tails.

The moment I ran out of ammunition I scurried away in a westerly direction and happened to fly right over our field at 200 feet. That stirred up a hornet's nest of excited, trigger-happy, antiaircraft gunners as they all opened up on me. Wagging my wings violently stopped them from shooting as I zoomed to 3,000 feet just below the cloud cover. It was safe there since I could duck into the clouds to escape any enemy aircraft. Circling there I had a front-row seat to the battle below.

I observed an Me 109 heading back toward Germany, pursued by two P-51s about 1,000 feet behind him. As the Me 109 started to go below my wing I rolled over so I could keep my eye on him. The German pilot must have seen me and, thinking I was going to attack, chandelled toward me so I couldn't close on his tail. That allowed one of the P-51s to turn inside him and get close enough to set up a beautiful deflection shot that nailed him. I always felt they should have given me an assist for shooting down that enemy aircraft.

When there was a lull in the battle I went in and landed. Just as I was turning off the runway, two Me 109 aircraft roared right at me to strafe our field. I shut off the engine and scrambled out of my aircraft, running away as they roared overhead, strafing the other side of the field. A P-51 was close behind the Me 109s and undoubtedly had them lined up for a sure kill. Of course the antiaircraft gunners all opened up, missing the enemy aircraft but hitting the P-51. In spite of the danger, spectators crowded the field to watch the dogfight, and when we saw what was happening, we all screamed "*No!*" at the gunners. The P-51 pilot just dropped his gear and landed.

The unlucky and very mad P-51 pilot was Dean M. Huston from Ames, Iowa. He said, "I had them in my sight for a sure kill when they [antiaircraft gunners] hit me in the oil system. My only recourse was to drop my gear and hope to land before the engine freezes up. My engine froze up during the landing roll."

Walking back to our operations area I met Dave Johnson, one of the eight P-47 pilots on this mission. He was riding a bike and carrying his opened parachute. A couple of Belgium civilians accompanied him on another bike. He rode over and asked me to thank the Belgium civilians for letting him use their bike to get back to the field. He had shot down an Me 109 that had shot down his own aircraft three miles north of Y-29, forcing him to bail out. Landing near the German fighter's crash site, Johnson walked over to see it. The pilot was dead, probably from loss of blood since he was wounded but crash-landed his aircraft prior to expiring. The identity card identified the rank of the German pilot as equivalent to a lieutenant colonel. Johnson brought back the identity card and showed it to several pilots. He was then asked to return it to the authorities for disposition. For many years we thought that Dave shot down the CO of the attacking force; however, records indicate that Lt. Col. Gunther Specht, CO of the attacking force JG 11, was lost during that raid flying a FW 190.[2] Dave died several years ago from a heart attack, and none of the pilots he showed the identity card to could remember the German pilot's name, so Dave's claim of a lieutenant colonel flying an Me 109 is unresolved.

One at a time our aircraft returned. German aircraft damaged Lt. John

Feeney's aircraft so badly he was forced to belly it in. Lt. Jack Kennedy landed his P-47 while missing half his rudder and without a hydraulic system. We therefore lost one aircraft and had two damaged, but lost no pilots. We claimed twelve German aircraft shot down. Later, after gun film review and resolution of ambiguous claims, they credited us with eight German aircraft destroyed. My gun camera film captured the explosion of the FW 190 I shot down. All the action lasted about 30 minutes. The Eighth Air Force P-51 group of twelve aircraft (it was the 487th squadron of the 352nd group) claimed twenty-three aircraft and the 792nd Anti Aircraft Battalion, stationed around Y-29, claimed four aircraft destroyed. I was finally in an air battle, and one where they outnumbered us at that. This air battle over Y-29 was written up in many articles and books.[3]

The German raid on Y-29 was part of a general air offensive to destroy the tactical fighters devastating the German troops in the Ardennes. About 800 German fighters participated in Operation Bodenplatte (Baseplate) as they called it. The Germans achieved surprise and destroyed many aircraft at several tactical fields in Belgium. We were fortunate to be in the air just in time to spoil their planned attack. The attack on Y-29 was carried out by a Jagdeseschwader (JG) 11 commanded by Lt. Col. Gunther Specht, and joined by some elements of JG 4 that could not find their assigned target of A-89 at Le Culot, Belgium.

Just recently I found out that JG 11 had just been re-equipped with brand new Me 109Ks, some even having pressurized cockpits.[4] The 109K variant had an up-rated Daimler-Benz engine generating 2,000 hp and sported an up-gunned armament system. The nose cannon caliber was increased from 20mm to a 30mm, and instead of two 13mm machine guns it carried two 15mm machine-gun/cannons. This awesome armament was tailored to shoot down heavy bombers with just a few well-aimed shells at a vital area. I was fortunate that the German pilot missed me on his first attack.

Although we didn't know it at the time, Operation Bodenplatte spelled the death knell for the Luftwaffe. They destroyed a large number of Allied aircraft, but sustained debilitating losses themselves in aircraft and pilots, especially in the hard-to-replace squadron and group commanders positions. Allied aircraft losses were quickly replaced and operational sorties experienced only a small dip immediately after the battle.

From my observation of the battle while circling around, it was obvious that the German attack lost all cohesion from our unexpected slashing head-on attack. German aircraft were just meandering around, not knowing what to do. Only a few aircraft maintained their rotte flying unit (the two-aircraft fighting formation that allowed the leader to concentrate on fighting while the wingman guarded his tail), and most were flying singly, making easy pickings for any Al-

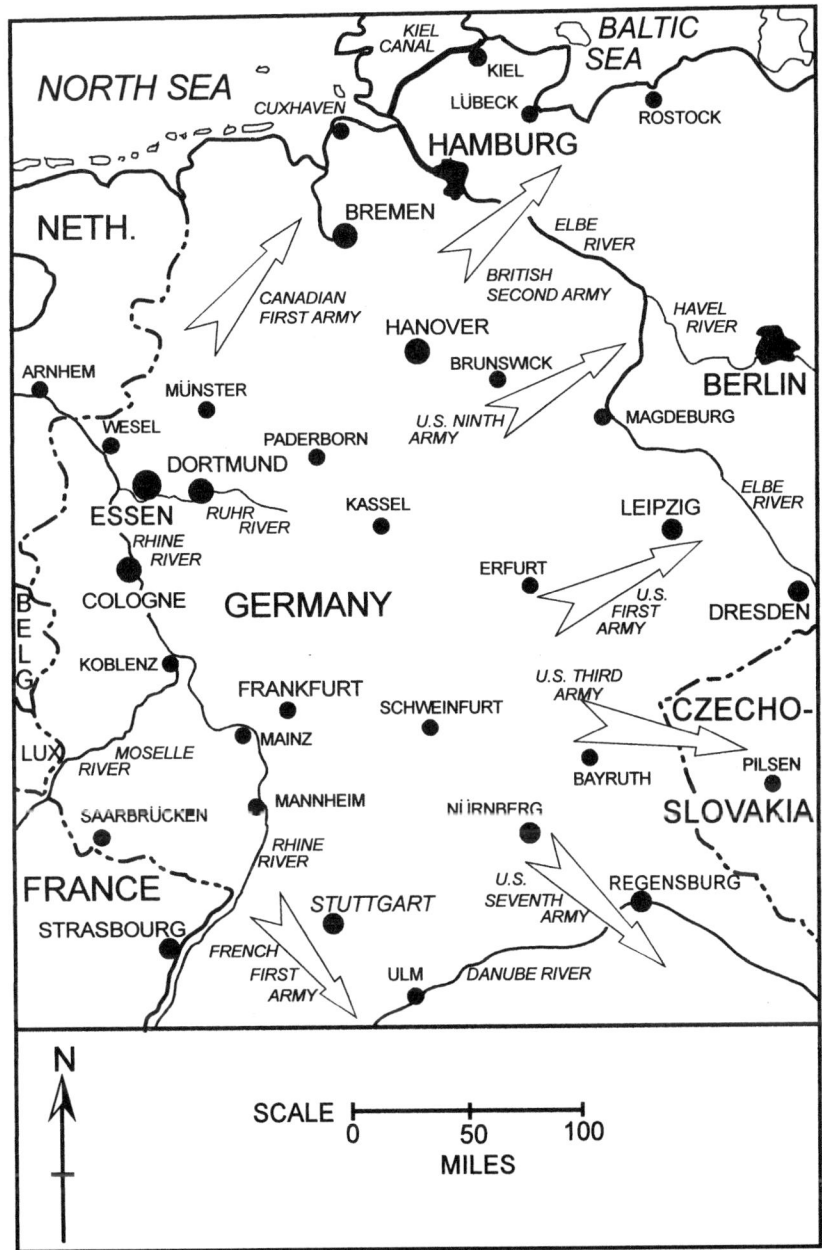

Allied Sweep of Western Germany, April 1945. (This map also refers to the material recorded in the last two chapters, espec. ch. 9.)

lied aircraft catching them. When I saw those juicy targets just milling around, I cussed at myself for squandering my ammunition. I could have become an ace-in-a-mission if I had heeded the admonishment to hold fire until there was a good setup. Even though I was a veteran combat pilot with forty-five combat missions, it was my first (and only) air battle, and there is nothing like experience to develop the calm calculating skill needed to be an air-battle tiger.

It should be noted that our squadron also scattered and did not maintain its fighting formation. After the battle I asked my wingman why he didn't stay with me. He said, "So many aircraft were milling around that I had my hands full trying to avoid a collision, and in the process lost you." I believe another reason was that most of us had never been in aerial combat and were anxious to get into a good dogfight, regardless of the odds. When suddenly presented with a swarm of enemy aircraft, we threw caution aside and slashed into them. If the relentless air battles had not decimated the German Luftwaffe the previous years, I don't believe we would have done so well.

Historians have compiled various statistics of both German and Allied losses from Operation Bodenplatte. Werner Girbig's research of German casualties lists 151 fighter pilots who were killed or still missing, and 63 who were shot down and became prisoners of war, giving a total loss of 214 German pilots.[5]

The loss tally of Allied aircraft and pilots is more confusing. The various participating Allied Air Forces, comprising the U.S. Eighth and Ninth and RAF 2nd Tactical Air Command, have quoted losses, but it is unclear whether they include those lost both by strafing and in the air, or if they also include damaged aircraft. Danny Parker summarizes the losses as 300 Allied aircraft. Norman Franks quotes a breakdown of 169 RAF aircraft destroyed or seriously damaged, and the U.S. Air Force with 55 destroyed or damaged. About 19 Allied personnel were killed and another 95 wounded. The casualty breakdown between pilots and ground personnel was not given.[6]

To present the reader a more vivid picture of the battle than just my account, I have related some other pilot narratives herein.[7] The transcribed copy of 366th Fighter Group mission report on the 1 January 1945 mission is presented to provide an overview.

Even after the standard New Year's celebration eight planes were airborne at 0915. Through a pure matter of chance they were airborne fifteen minutes early which may have played a vital role in the events of the day. Immediately after take off, fifty plus FW 190's and ME 109's were sighted on the deck approaching the field. These enemy aircraft were engaged immediately and the ensuing dogfight raged over and around the field. The eight P-47's kept the enemy aircraft engaged and enabled a squadron of P-51's to become airborne. In the encounter the P-47's, P-51's and Ack Ack [antiaircraft fire] destroyed 39 enemy aircraft. There was some strafing but little damage was done and only one casualty resulted. S/Sgt Widmeier was hit in the leg in a strafing attack. One P-47 was lost when Flight Officer Dave Johnson was forced to bail out because of damage. He returned to the field on a bicycle before the fighting was over. Lt. Feeney made a wheel-up landing and one other plane was damaged quite badly.

The individual score claims were:

Capt. Smith	2-0-0	FW-190
Lt. Brulle	1-1-0	FW-190
Lt. Davis	1-0-0	FW-190
F/O Lackey	0-0-1	FW-190
	1-0-1	Me-109
Lt. Paisley	3-0-1	FW-190
	1-0-2	Me-109
F/O Johnson	2-0-0	Me-109
Lt. Feeney	1-0-1	FW-190
Lt. J. Kennedy	0-1-0	Me-109

Lt. Paisley was the high scorer for the squadron as well as achieving distinction by claiming the destruction of an enemy aircraft with a rocket.

Capt. Lowell B. Smith was the squadron leader, and I remember him leading our diving attack as he hollered over the radio, "Tally ho." He probably wanted to give that call of the huntsman since he heard that RAF pilots shouted it as they attacked the German bombers during the Battle of Britain. Here is his story.

On 1 January 1945 I was leading Relic Squadron on a close support mission. We had just taken off, and as we joined up, Relic Red 2 called in flak bursts just northeast of our field. I led the squadron to investigate. As we approached the flak, we sighted enemy aircraft strafing strip Y-32. Another force was sighted heading toward Y-29. We attacked immediately.

I got into position on the tail of a FW 190 and observed a few strikes around the cockpit. I overshot him but noticed that he was burning. My wingman stated that he saw this enemy aircraft crash.

I then got on the tail of another FW 190 and chased him 20 to 30 miles to the east. I was unable to overtake him. I fired several bursts at extreme range but observed no strikes. I broke off and returned to Y-29. Just north of the field I was bounced by a FW 190. I broke right and succeeded in out turning him. We were below 500 feet when he snapped rolled and dove into the ground.

Jack Kennedy was the first pilot to notice the flak to our left after takeoff, although he was probably the groggiest of us all. The flak piqued our interest and all of us were anxious to check it out. Events happened quickly after that point, as narrated by Jack.

If you remember we had a New Years Eve party, and had I known I was on the first mission the next morning, I probably would have not partied as much as I did. We had some Belgium girls at our party and the Germans dropped some fragmentation bombs that night. I can remember me and a girl crawling in the fire place (no fire) for protection during this raid. These nightly nuisance raids by the Germans did some damage and there were some casualties; however the raids always got us up and in the slit trenches and this is what they wanted. Back to the mission. I don't know what time we took off but it had to have been quite early. I don't know if I got to bed or not. I must have because I put my flight suit on over my pajamas. My tent mate, Judge McLean says he went to the flight line with me and after I got in the aircraft I asked him how to start the thing. I was flying Red 2 wingman for Capt. L. B. Smith who was leading the squadron.

We all got off quite fast and I had just got on Smith's wing when I saw the flak and then Paisley spotted bogeys at 9 o'clock on the deck. I looked and I did not see them at first. Then I picked them up just north of our air strip. I don't know if an order was given to drop our bombs, but I did. I don't know how many German planes there were, but I guess there was 50 to 60. We were in the midst of them in seconds. I don't know if I lost Smith or he lost me. With all the aircraft just off the deck who could tell. I got on the tail of a ME 109, which at first I thought was a spitfire. This 109 really filled the gun sight and I just got off a few rounds when I was hit in the tail end. I found two ME 109s on my tail. I broke to the right and of course those guys followed me still firing away. I got hit again in the right wing and a hell of a fire started with the hydraulic fluid burning. My first thought was to bail out and I unhooked ready to jump. They always told us to go out the right side and when I looked at the flames I thought I can't go through there. I broke to the left and was flying around a slag pile [coal mine slag heap about 500 feet high] with those guys still firing away. I did turn inside those devils and finally two 51s from the 352nd group got the 109's off my tail. We had a low ceiling that day and I ran for the clouds. By that time the fire had burned out and the plane was still flying. I came out of the clouds and most of the fighting was over. I found the field and called Burdock (tower) telling them I had some damage. I shook the gear down and came in pretty fast—hit the flaps—no flaps—hit the strip at over a 100 mph. I hit the brakes—no brakes—I ran out of runway doing 30–40 mph—I was not going back up—it finally stopped.

Melvyn (Mel) Paisley was high scorer for our squadron, including one claimed by firing his rockets. At the time of this letter he was assistant secretary of the Navy in Washington, D.C.

It was after I shot down my second aircraft that the 352nd got off the ground and got involved in the fray. Colonel J. C. Meyer gives an account of the 352d part of the battle in the book "American Aces" by Edward H. Sims where they take credit for the repulse of the German attack. I talked to "Colonel" Meyer when he was a four star general, Vice Chief of the Air Force, about this whole raid. He reflected on the fact that if we had not spotted that German sweep made up of about 80 aircraft, they probably would have gotten his group on the ground.

Next is an excerpt from the letter from Lowell B. Smith, Relic squadron leader during the battle. He sent this letter to all the surviving pilots sometime in the 1980s.

Deep in my heart I will always believe that you and the other officers under my command won great air battle over Y-29, who with great courage did not hesitate to attack against overwhelming odds. General Meyer was wrong in claiming all the glory for himself and his Eighth Air Force unit [referring to the Meyer's account in E. H. Sims, *American Aces*]. Moreover, our record speaks for itself. Another aspect of this affair was that the 390th had been heavily involved in the Battle of the Bulge. Casualties were heavy during that period and the eight aircraft we hit the Germans with were the ONLY serviceable aircraft in commission—all others were under repair for battle damage or were destroyed during our sorties against the German armored divisions. Had we gotten a full 12 aircraft airborne, I know our record would have been even more impressive.

Our attack went smoothly and we came in on the tail of our targets who apparently were concentrating on hitting our airfield and destroying our fighters on the ground. We hit the lead wave and I am sure accounted for some of their leaders as shortly after we had shot down the first of our victims, the thrust at our airfield was dulled as some of the Germans turned to fight.

It was a good show for us all.

An interesting follow-up from the battle around Y-29: The Belgium air enthusiasts and historians are now recovering the remains of the aircraft that were shot down during that battle. My friend and local historian Lucien Bogers from Genk, Belgium, sent me a map of the Y-29 area. The map plotted where German aircraft have been recovered from the 1 January battle, and within a small eight-kilometer radius from Y-29 (4.8 miles) eleven German aircraft had crashed.

One conclusion we made after the battle was the antiaircraft gunners' obvious inability to identify aircraft. To us that was incomprehensible. They saw our flying P-47s day after day and still shot at us. The Unit History for the 792nd Anti Aircraft Artillery Battalion (the unit defending Y-29) claims that they did not shoot at friendly aircraft during that raid.[8] I was not the only P-47 to get shot at and missed by our gunners, but they did score and severely damage a P-51, requiring the pilot to make an emergency landing. Because of our complaints, they detailed us to instruct the gunners in aircraft recognition. They also required us to stand watch at their observation posts to identify flying aircraft for them until the lessons were completed. This duty lasted about two weeks.

The second mission that day was a return to ground support. We struck the German columns in the Bulge area. The next several weeks were productive, as we destroyed many German armored and transport vehicles while the ground troops gradually pushed the Germans back to their border. Some pilots reported seeing the new German jet aircraft go screaming by but, as a whole, the German Luftwaffe was not very active. Some fellows got lucky and not only saw German aircraft but even got into another dogfight. Unfortunately I was not that lucky, and the 1 January battle just described was the only time throughout the war I saw a flying German aircraft. The missions again became routine, if anyone could call any wartime combat mission that. We were fighting the weather and flak, having problems identifying the ground targets, and sometimes even finding some.

One mission that I recall happened on 16 January. We were unable to find a suitable target and were vectored by the air/ground controllers from one sector to another, but no one had a target. With our gas getting low they released us to find and attack any opportune target. We knew that the German troops used woods for camouflage, so when we spotted a wooded area near the front lines we went to look it over. From Angels 10 we could see nothing, so I volunteered to go down and drag the woods for a closer look. Imagine my surprise when I found the woods filled with German soldiers. A P-47 suddenly flying over them at treetop level obviously surprised them, and I vividly remember their terror-stricken eyes as they scurried for cover. While dive-bombing and strafing the woods I felt kind of sorry and pitied the poor German foot sloggers.

The furious combat the last few months, first in the Hürtgen Forest and then in the Battle of the Bulge, seriously depleted our inventory of aircraft, which degraded our combat effectiveness. To speed up delivery of new aircraft we had pilots who went on leave in England pick up a new airplane at Burtonwood Field (near Liverpool) and fly it back. It also solved our problem of getting back to the continent from England. An incident happened to Saul Faktorow, one of the first pilots to initiate this procedure. His flight from England was uneventful until he reached the vicinity of Brussels. There the weather turned foggy, and, you guessed it, he missed our airfield and wandered over the front lines, getting the new aircraft all shot up. He nursed it home but it was junk. Chalk up another one for Saul.

To relieve mission tension, we started to frequent the cabarets in the town of Hasselt, Belgium, about seven miles from Y-29. One evening Chuck Bennett and I were talking to two girls at a small cabaret and asked them if they would like a beer. Most Belgium girls by now understood enough English so that we could carry on a reasonable conversation. The girls answered no—they would rather have a glass of wine. One girl then turned to the other and in a boorish, rapid-speaking Flemish said, "If you drink too many beers you have to go the toilet too often." I burst out laughing, since I understood her and answered in Flemish, "G spriekt te rap voor m te voorstaan. Spriekt a bettje trager" ("You speak too fast for me to understand. Speak a little slower"). When they realized that I could understand them, both turned a crimson red. It was interesting understanding and speaking a language that very few Americans do. The native population felt secure when speaking Flemish in front of Americans.

Another evening tension reliever was to gather in the lounge or a tent and have a few drinks and start a bull session. Sometimes we even had a movie. These relieved the boredom and helped us develop a camaraderie. What we liked best, though, was to have some kind of party. In that respect the 390th squadron was fortunate to have Lt. Harry Wildhaber, an avid party man. At the drop of a hat he would somehow arrange a party; in fact, we started calling him, "Harry, Let's Have a Party, Wildhaber." He arranged our Christmas party and scrounged up delicacies we hadn't seen in months. For New Year's he even arranged to bring in a group of girls from Hasselt. The best party he organized, though, was a 390th squadron officers' party and dance in a Hasselt hotel on 19 January. Various drinks and snacks, an orchestra, and plenty of dance partners made it a gala affair. I accompanied Harry on his arrangement rounds and translated his request to the Belgium merchants. He was an indispensable asset to the squadron and I recommend that every squadron have a billet for a person of that talent.

An incident occurred on a sojourn to Hasselt that pursued several fellows for almost ten years. After supper the squadron CO would usually approve a liberty run by a weapons carrier (a small pickup truck) to Hasselt. This particular evening about ten of us piled in, drove to Hasselt, and parked the truck in the town square. For security we removed the distributor cap and rotor (there were no keys on Army vehicles), and arranged to meet at 2200 to go home. At the appointed hour we found someone had stolen our truck. A short distance away another group of soldiers were futilely trying to start their weapons carrier. To protect their truck they chained the front axle to a lamp post. The resourceful thief(s) removed their distributor cap and rotor and put it in ours to make a clean getaway.

The British MP detachment in Hasselt provided a small British vehicle to take us back to Y-29. Our group squeezed aboard. Jack Kennedy must have had a very precarious perch because over the years he told the story at every reunion on how fortunate he was that he wasn't killed by falling off that careening vehicle. We arrived in one piece to face an irate Maj. Marty Martin. It was a brand-new truck, and Marty charged us with negligence and ordered us to pay for it. By a quirk of fate I escaped having to pay up. Shortly after this incident they assigned me on temporary duty with the 5th Armored Division as an air/ground controller. While I was gone, they filed the paperwork and I was left off the list. Each fellow was eventually presented with a bill for $72.00. Chuck Bennett received his while in the hospital recuperating from severe battle wounds. Most paid up promptly. However, Sandy Ross felt that the bill was unfair and tried for many years to get it canceled. He finally paid up in 1954 when the Air Force threatened to take legal action. Since I escaped the charges, the fellows have threatened to expose me. So far nothing has happened except at our reunions where I occasionally buy a round of drinks for them. Finally, at our 1986 reunion, I heard Mel Paisley brag that he also did not get caught and have to pay up. I therefore served notice to the twenty or so who claim they were on the truck that they have a new patsy.

No party or other diversion allowed us to escape the fact that we had a war to win, and every morning a new operational order awaited us. By mid-January 1945 Hitler recognized the collapse of his offensive in the Battle of the Bulge and allowed a withdrawal back to Germany. The German forces had so far escaped the wrath of the fighter-bombers by traveling at night and when the weather prevented air attacks. Reconnaissance aircraft achieved glimpses of the withdrawal, but attacking them was just impossible due to the fog and low clouds covering that hilly, forested region of the Ardennes. Pilot reconnaissance showed that the protracted bad weather had apparently dulled the German troops' constant vigil and countermeasures against fighter-bomber attacks, and they were bunched up, bumper to bumper, on the roads. This was a fighter-bomber pilot's dream situation—if we could just get to them. It was going to be difficult, but our dream situation was about to become a reality.

The twenty-second of January dawned no different from the previous days, dismally cold and foggy. The weather was, however, improved over the last several days since seeing the trees at the other end of the field was possible. Intermittent layers of ragged scud clouds, ranging from 500 to 1,500 feet high, swirled over the field, but it appeared we could get off. The prognosis was for more of the same but a possible slight clearing could occur by this afternoon.

The operations order for that day specified that three squadrons of the 366th group would provide column cover and support for the 7th Armored Division pressing the retreating Germans near Malmedy, Belgium. They scheduled flights of four aircraft per mission, the first taking off at dawn, followed by other flights at 20-minute intervals throughout the day. Missions of four-aircraft flights were specified on account of the weather. A small group of aircraft is easier to control and keep together when it is continuously in and out of clouds. The radio call sign of the 7th Armored Division air/ground controller was Wetrag and he was in the vicinity of Malmedy.

The first mission airborne that day was a four-aircraft alert flight of two aircraft each from the 389th and 391st. They took off at dawn, 0830 hours, to patrol around the field while the first few ground-support missions got underway. Following the alert flight, two aircraft from the 391st took off for a weather reconnaissance near Wetrag. Lt. Floyd N. Hass led the mission; his wingman was Lt. Ray Hunt. After being vectored above the clouds to the Wetrag area by Marmite, Floyd Hass let down through the overcast to check the cloud ceiling. As he let down, Ray reminded him not to go below the high ground level of 1,750 feet. Ray heard only one other transmission from him, reporting he was at 2,000 feet. After not hearing from Floyd for a while and not getting a response when called, Ray Hunt also let down. He found the clouds consisted of multiple layers of 9/10 broken clouds with the lowest layer between 300 and 700 feet above the ground. He then returned to base. Postwar records indicate Floyd Hass crashed into a hillside 10 miles northeast of Malmedy.

The 389th squadron sent out four aircraft led by Lt. Joe A. Kelley at 0946. Weather prevented them from attacking in the Wetrag area, so Marmite vectored them about 30 miles east-southeast of Malmedy. There they glimpsed, through holes in the clouds, German vehicles on the roads and around some small villages. They dive-bombed and strafed by coming down through the hole in the clouds and then zooming back up through 500 feet of clouds to regroup and do it again. They destroyed four vehicles and damaged twelve others. They also exploded what they thought was an ammunition dump. Two P-47s sustained major flak damage. One pilot returned to base, but the other, piloted by Lt. Frank Smith, was last seen heading west. Frank described his ordeal after returning to base several days later.

A 20mm shell exploded in his left wing gun bay, blowing the door open so it draped over the flap. Several belts of ammunition also were blown out and were swirling around in the slipstream, further banging up the wing and flap. To maintain level flight required full right aileron and rudder and an airspeed above 210 mph, which took full power. Smith was unable to climb over the Ardennes hills to get back to American lines so he bellied in about five miles from St. Vith. He was in German-occupied territory but evaded the Germans for four days before meeting up with American troops.

Weather frustrated three missions of four aircraft each from the 390th, 391st, and 389th. They bombed and strafed several small convoys of armored vehicles under extremely difficult conditions, probably destroying twelve half-tracks and fifteen to thirty trucks. In some places the weather was tolerable, while a short distance away it was socked in.

At 1100 the 390th launched a mission with Major Martin leading and Lt. Sandy Ross as his wingman, while I was the element leader with Lt. Curry

Davis as my wingman. On takeoff we entered the clouds at 800 feet and climbed through several layers until we topped them at 5,000 feet. Marmite vectored us to an area south of St. Vith where, through a hole in the clouds, we saw fifty or more trucks and other vehicles clustered within a small town. After advising Marmite, we dive-bombed through the hole and claimed eleven vehicles and two houses destroyed. Being vectored further east we suddenly came upon a long German convoy of trucks and other vehicles taking advantage of the cloud cover and heading back toward Germany. The overcast consisted of several layers of broken clouds that from the ground looked like a solid ragged overcast. This probably lulled the Germans into believing the weather was too nasty to fly in, and they were safely screened from the Jabos by a very low, solid overcast. From the air, however, the holes in the various layers would line up enough so we could catch a glimpse of the ground. It was through one such hole that we discovered that long German convoy. While circling and coming down lower to keep in visual contact with that column, we noted that the bright low-lying sun was finally breaking and raising the overcast, improving ground visibility each minute.

Marty directed I stay up with my wingman and have Marmite get a good fix on our position. We were to advise that the weather was improving and to send all available aircraft to clobber that long column of trucks. Marty and Sandy then dove down to strafe. After instructing Curry to keep his eyes open for enemy aircraft, we climbed to 9,000 feet so Marmite could get a good radar fix. It took about five minutes to confirm our position and then Curry and I joined Marty and Sandy strafing. We made a run over the column and I can still remember the sight of the terror-stricken, surprised German troops jumping from their trucks to escape our strafing. Suddenly Marty advised us to terminate strafing and head home. I could not persuade him to get in a few more runs so we joined up and started back to base. As we left, the weather over that truck convoy had improved from almost completely fog covered to a 7/10 broken cloud layer, varying from 500 to 1,500 feet above the ground.

Upon landing we found out why we had terminated our mission prematurely; a 20mm antiaircraft shell exploded in Marty's main gas tank, rupturing the tank beyond self-sealing capability. He lost all his main tank fuel. Fortunately our base was only 20 minutes away, and he just had enough fuel in his auxiliary tank to make it back to base. The only explanation we could figure for why he didn't explode was that the main tank was almost full when they hit him, and the shell must have exploded within the fuel itself. Without any gas fumes around to sustain the burning, there was no explosion. We knew the gas tanks provided protection against nonexplosive bullets but never thought they could contain an explosive shell.

Recently I talked with Sandy and he recalled boring down through the overcast holes and surprising that long convoy of vehicles. He commented that the bunched-up troop-filled trucks were so close together it was possible to concentrate his gunfire through several trucks on each strafing pass before having to pull up. He estimated that he and Marty hit more than 200 troops and destroyed thirty-four trucks.

Our opportune sighting of the German motorized convoy and the verification of improving weather started an avalanche of tactical aircraft attacks on that long German convoy. Improving weather revealed other jammed convoys of retreating Germans in the Schnee Eifel road network. The Schnee Eifel is a high tree-covered ridge, part of the Ardennes massif, lying east of St. Vith. The four aircraft of the 391st, led by Capt. Vince Kramer, were just airborne when they received a vector from Marmite to the area just discovered by the 390th. They were armed with two 500-pound bombs on the wings and a 260-pound fragmentation bomb on the belly shackle. They continued the destruction, claiming twenty trucks destroyed and many more damaged. During their attack they had the unusual experience of being fired on by an 88mm heavy flak battery while strafing. They reported that it was very inaccurate but quite intimidating. Unfortunately another P-47 sustained major damage from flak, again reducing the number of serviceable aircraft.

The 389th, led by Capt. Elten Diehlman, continued the destruction by destroying seven more trucks and a three-gun light-flak battery. That battery was one of many that harassed our strafing. Of greater importance was that the 389th cut the main road the German convoy was on with several direct bomb hits, stalling the whole convoy. Snow and mud restricted the Germans to the few good roads in the area so they were stuck there a while. From all indications we were presented with the best hunting since the Falaise pocket in Normandy. The German withdrawal area was greater than the Falaise pocket carnage area, giving us some maneuver room to attack without having to queue in line. The only drawback was the weather, varying in a few minutes from being barely acceptable for dive-bombing and strafing to being completely socked in.

Note that the selected narrations are the missions of only one group out of a dozen or so operating along the entire Belgium-German border. All types of aircraft were observed attacking the weather-obscured German forces. I personally saw P-47s, P-38s, Spitfires, and Typhoons attacking the Germans.[9] Conspicuously absent were German aircraft. We had, without a doubt, absolute air supremacy.

It was evident at this point that we had caught in the open a large portion of the German army that stormed into Belgium just a few weeks before. They had gambled on the weather being too bad for us to fly in, but hadn't considered our training in instrument flying. In contrast, German fighters did not even have the instruments, nor were most fighter pilots trained in instrument flying.[10] Perhaps that had a bearing on the decision to gamble on the weather; they figured that since German fighters wouldn't fly in that weather, we probably wouldn't either. Another consideration was our determination not to let the brash German army that had surprised us with their attack escape our bombing and strafing. If there was a slim chance to clobber them, we would take it.

We were running missions as rapidly as the ground crew could get four aircraft ready. Each mission lasted about one hour and 20 minutes. If the weather would only hold, we had the opportunity to destroy most of the German forces. While weather remained marginal over the battlefield it was deteriorating fast over our airfield.

This day turned out to be frantic for both the pilots and ground crew. Although most missions were four-aircraft flights, we ran them so frequently that each squadron had two flights airborne at any one time. The experienced ground crew could turn around an aircraft in 30 minutes, refueling, bombing up, and replenishing the ammunition. When an aircraft left on a mission, that crew would help wherever needed to turn around any other aircraft. It was a team effort that everyone should be proud of. The pilots meted out the destruction, but the ground crew made it possible.

Each aircraft had a four-man ground crew, a crew chief, assistant crew chief, armorer, and radio mechanic. There were also some groups of roving mechanics, a sheet-metal specialist to patch nonstructural flak damage, a propeller specialist, instrument specialist and others. In a pinch, however, each would lend a hand where needed.

The ground crew worked under difficult conditions as everything was done outside. At a recent 366th Fighter Group reunion crew chief S.Sgt. Ralph Woolever still dreaded the memory of having to change the thirty-six engine spark plugs on a cold, windy, snowy day. It was a challenging task as it had to be done without gloves. So in addition to the skinned knuckles they had frozen hands. S.Sgt. Jim Hizer heartily concurred with Woolever's comment and added the memory of his fingers freezing to the cold metal parts. Tents were set up around the flight line where the crew could warm up for a few minutes, but during a hectic flying day, as this was, there was no time to take advantage of that luxury. Recall that the days are short during a European winter, and since no lights were permitted during the night the maintenance was completed that day or waited until the next one. The spirit of "Keep 'em flying" was not just a war bond rallying cry, but was wholeheartedly implemented by the ground crews.

The afternoon missions continued the carnage. Some missions encountered fair weather and could really pound the Germans, while low clouds completely frustrated other missions. As the afternoon wore on it wasn't the weather over the battle area that concerned us, but the weather over our field. We could recognize the onset formation of that cold hazy fog that seems to permeate the entire European area during winter. We hoped it would hold off until we got the job done.

As the afternoon wore on the battle area became more congested as more aircraft were thrown into the battle. A common complaint echoed by Ray Hunt and others when returning from a mission was, "So many aircraft were working over the same area it made the cloud shrouded sky quite crowded and hazardous, filled with diving and zooming aircraft interspersed with multiple flak bursts." At a recent reunion several of us swapped stories of those missions. An underlying theme expounded by all was, "It was so damn frustrating to see all those juicy targets, but so damn difficult to get down to dive-bomb and strafe them." Also recalled was the trepidation and excitement we felt, as we sort of lined up our aircraft with the target through a hole in the clouds, and then came screaming down in a dive through the clouds to strafe it. No safe haven from flak existed below the clouds, so we had to pull back up above them to do it again. As we now reflect back on those days, we agreed that it's a good thing that we were young and invincible then, since diving down in a 30-degree dive, hoping to break out at 500 feet above the ground to strafe the German forces, seems quite foolhardy now.

Lt. Eber Simpson, 391st squadron, led his flight to the long convoy of German vehicles discovered earlier. He verified that German traffic was stopped, bumper-to-bumper, in a double lane on the road and all types of aircraft were pummeling them. They contributed their ordnance and estimated twenty trucks destroyed and 200 damaged. Pilots felt that claim was conservative but weather made it hard to assess the destruction.

The next four missions were repeats. Targets were scattered throughout the area and our group went after them with a vengeance. The claims for destroyed vehicles for the four missions totaled fifty-one trucks, eleven large vans, five artillery guns, seven tanks, and four half-tracks. Several missions complained that smoke from burning vehicles was obscuring other targets.

The 389th squadron went on a flak-busting mission in the area to reduce the intense light-caliber flak that was taking a dreadful toll of our aircraft, limiting some missions to only three aircraft. On return they claimed that they destroyed a 20mm flak gun position and strafed others, claiming sixteen damaged. They also accounted for another eight trucks. Pilots again reported deteriorating weather at our field, making landing hazardous, but operations said to ignore it. (I have this to say about our operations staff. They just didn't tell us to ignore the weather while staying safe themselves. They flew the missions and experienced the risks with us.)

Back-to-back missions of three aircraft by the 390th, two four-aircraft missions by the 391st, and a three-aircraft mission by the 389th completed the day's attacks by getting in one last punch. These late missions claimed another fifty trucks, six half-tracks, two scout cars, four houses, and 100 troops. The 389th flying the last mission found 100 more untouched trucks and other vehicles on a secondary road system. They strafed but could only account for a few vehicles as they had to return to base. Landing for these late missions was chaotic. Aircraft milled around, trying to get down any way possible in that restricted visibility caused by a snow haze and fog.

The evening field alert mission landed in the gathering darkness, barely getting down before it became completely fogged in. They estimated the visibility was half a mile. The time was 1730 hours. So ended a hectic day of combat with the 366th Fighter Group. It was a maximum effort flown in very marginal weather.

During the day, ninety-four aircraft were dispatched on twenty-five missions. Of these, two were destroyed (those of Lieutenants Floyd Hass and Frank Smith). Five others sustained major flak damage and many others minor damage. One pilot, Lt. Floyd Hass, was killed. The day's tally of destruction was:

Trucks	284	Large vans	11
Tanks	9	Scout cars	2
Half-tracks	25	Houses	10
Flak guns	5	Ammunition dump	1
Artillery pieces	5	Train	1
Troops	350		

These are, of course, estimates. It is quite difficult to ascertain whether a vehicle is destroyed unless it blows up or burns.

The weather stayed marginal the next several days as we continued the destruction of the German forces. On 23 January we dispatched 115 aircraft of eight- and ten-aircraft missions to clobber the Germans. The cost was six aircraft damaged by flak and one shot down. Flak heavily damaged the aircraft of Lt. Gordon Steele (389th squadron) while he was strafing and he crash-landed in enemy territory. His wingman saw him get out of his aircraft and run into some woods. He was quickly captured and spent the rest of the war in captivity until liberated by American troops on 28 April 1945.

On 24 January we dispatched only sixty-four aircraft in four-aircraft flights because the weather worsened again. Flak heavily damaged another four aircraft and Lt. John Feeney from the 390th squadron was lost. He was last seen on fire heading west. They terminated all flying in the afternoon of the twenty-fourth when our field became completely socked in. After the war we learned of John's fate. He was hit in the gas tank. The explosion tore the left side of the cockpit off and the aircraft caught on fire. He was unable to bail out over the side but fortunately had enough altitude and control to roll over and fall out into captivity. He suffered only some burns around his eyes. He was liberated 6 May.

During those days, 22–24 January, the U.S. Ninth Air Force, helped by the British Second Tactical Air Force, demolished a large part of the withdrawing German forces. The total claims over that three-day period were 6,600 motor transport and innumerable tanks, guns, and trains.[11] The actual destruction was undoubtedly much less than the claims; however, the size of the claims shows the tremendous loss meted out to the Germans. Had the weather been clear I think we could have destroyed the greater portion of the German army that had fought in the Battle of the Bulge. But, of course, they wouldn't have taken to the roads so recklessly in clear weather. The Tactical Air Force received a commendation from the commander of the U.S. Air Forces in Europe, Gen. Carl Spaatz, for a job well done under extremely adverse weather conditions.

Having to fly in all types of atrocious weather those two months led to the development of an approach and landing scheme that at least gave us a chance of making a safe landing. Normally we would let down through the clouds in a tight formation. Y-29 was in flat country, but many coal mines in the area sprouted slag heaps about 500 feet high. Letting down when a ceiling was near that height was precarious. Fortunately the slag heaps were clustered within the northern quadrant from the field. This left the southeast quadrant leading to the runway as the safest in which to let down. The question was how to find the field when we were above the clouds so we could let down in the safe area. To do that we utilized our only navigation aid, the radio direction finder (RDF) station located on the field.

We would first get a homing and ask the RDF operator to listen for us going over the field. When notified we were over the base we would turn to a heading of 240 degrees. Then in trail and 10 seconds apart we would let down through the overcast at a specific air speed and rate of descent. We made a procedure turn when half the altitude was lost, and continued letting down on the reciprocal heading of 60 degrees. It was always hoped that before we descended to 500 feet we would break clear. A very visible white-marble church was fortuitously located about one mile from the runway threshold, right along the runway centerline, which made it an excellent landing aid. When we broke through the overcast and could see the white church, we maneuvered to fly over it on a heading of 60 degrees. We were then on final approach so we lowered the gear and flaps and waited for the runway to appear. Obviously, it didn't always go as planned. In hazy, low ceiling days (and there were many) it would sometimes deteriorate to utter chaos, with airplanes trying to land any way possible.

I received a picture of that Catholic church, still there, from Lucien Bogers. It is located in the town of Wiemismeer. In 1995 I visited the church and, looking up at the white steeple, thanked it for leading me to the runway during that miserable winter.

Not only were we flying in downright treacherous winter weather, the runway and field conditions were at best chancy. Our pierced-steel plank runway was slick even when it wasn't covered with a coating of ice. Fortunately when we rolled over the springy runway the ice would crack and the propeller slipstream would blast the pieces away. After a squadron or two took off, the runway would be quite clear except some low areas where standing water would freeze. I recall one mission where dawn revealed another eight- to ten-inch overnight snowfall accumulation. I was scheduled for the first morning mission, and when I got to my aircraft a half-dozen men were shoveling to clear a path to the taxiway while crew chiefs Al Czaplicki and Jim Hizer were busy chipping the last of the ice from the wings. Two trucks with a snowplow attached were busy clearing the runway, having already cleared the taxiways. When I pulled on the runway and lined up for takeoff, the width of the plowed section was less than the wing span. Not only that, the preceding aircraft taking off had generated a blizzard, requiring a near instrument takeoff. I got off okay, but after the mission some fellows related how they swerved the gear into the snowbank and had some anxious moments as they recovered their takeoff roll.

We knew combat flying was exciting, exhilarating, and dangerous and were readily aware of our mortality. We were committed to do our duty but any help we could evoke to keep us safe was readily seized upon. I acquired a superstitious act I performed every mission. Our flying gear was in individual wooden boxes, stored in a tent on the flight line. After getting out my flying gear for a mission, I habitually closed my equipment box and knocked on the wood door twice. I remember forgetting to do it once when rushed to get ready for an urgent mission (6 December), and it bothered me throughout the flight. I wasn't the only one; some wore their lucky shoes or carried some charm. By the way, some English pilots followed the same ritual, but instead of calling it "knocking on wood" called it "touching wood."

9.   The Final Battles

The final battles are anticlimactic, but the killing continues. We cannot understand why the Germans don't surrender, as they must see they have been vanquished.

My first experience firing rockets occurred in late January. Gradually they were outfitting all our airplanes with an adjustable sight and four zero-length rocket launchers to fire five-inch high-velocity aircraft rockets (HVAR). A chart that listed the sight settings as a function of dive angle, air speed, and range to the target accompanied the new sight. Correlating all the factors and setting the sight was extremely difficult to do on a firing pass. When we fired the rockets, they almost disappeared below the nose, making it hard to even see where they went. I just couldn't hit anything with them. Later, on 30 March to be exact, they finally scheduled some training sessions on a practice range. They released one squadron per day from combat flying for rocket practice. The key was to preset the sight for a set of flight conditions we strived to meet at rocket fire. Accuracy improved to where I could hit the target if I got close enough. Under combat conditions, with flak flying around, I don't think I ever hit anything but a large target, like a barge or house.

Our rocket installation had a very serious drawback; we could not use our guns until we fired the rockets. The rockets were placed under the chutes that ejected the machine-gun belt links and shell casings. If we fired our guns before firing the rockets, the ejected links and casings could break the rocket-firing wire. We didn't like that at all since we used the psychological effect of tracer bullets to intimidate the German flak gunners and chase them to their foxholes. Unfortunately, that objection became moot because shortly thereafter a new ammunition that eliminated the tracer rounds was introduced.

We all recognized that tracer bullets were not to be used for aiming, and they served no purpose other than the psychological one. They were not reliable incendiary devices, compared to an incendiary bullet, so since every fifth round was a tracer bullet, we lost 20 percent of our destructive power. To increase our guns' effectiveness and provide a greater incendiary potential, they introduced a new ammunition. Our guns were now being loaded exclusively with armor-piercing incendiary (API) ammunition instead of the 2-2-1 loading where every fifth round was a tracer. The first time I fired API ammunition it surprised me on two accounts. First, not seeing the tracers flying toward the target made me feel the attack was ineffectual. The second surprise was more dramatic. When an incendiary bullet hits, it flashes. I was strafing a truck and gave it a one-second burst. Suddenly the truck and surrounding area lit up like a Christmas tree as the 120 or so rounds flashed when they hit. The effect was a sparkling display, which in a macabre way was quite beautiful. It really brought home the admonishment we continually received—a short burst is all that is needed to destroy a target.

My turn for air/ground controller duty finally rolled around. I was not looking forward to that two-week duty in a combat tank. Having pilots along in an armored division tank or half-track was born of necessity as close air support evolved. Having someone who could not visualize the way the ground looked from Angels 10 to 15 direct pilots to a target was not practical. Vision at ground level is very limited and has a different perspective as opposed to looking at the same area from the air. Directing pilots to bomb an antitank gun concealed in a barn with a red roof is ridiculous since from a pilot's viewpoint many red roofs are usually visible. Because ground personnel were not familiar with pilot jargon, the radio technique was formal and drawn out. This further aggravated the severe congestion we had on our four radio channels. Putting pilots in the tanks solved both problems. The pilot on the ground could visualize how the area looked from the air and by starting with prominent landmarks he could first get the squadron oriented. From there he could gradually lead them, by relating to visible features, to the right barn. Also, especially when working with one's own squadron, voice recognition and curt statements speeded up the target acquisition, further reducing radio chatter. Another advantage was that a pilot was available to evaluate the feasibility of an air attack on a specific target. As such he could advise the ground commanders and express an opinion about attacking it with an air strike.[1]

On 28 January 1945 Jim Pinkerton of the 391st squadron and I reported to IX TAC headquarters in a Maastricht (Holland) school for our assignment. While walking through the corridor we met General Quesada, CO of IX TAC. He asked if we were coming or going (referring to the front). When we told him going, he wished us luck and said that so far no pilot casualties had occurred. I didn't feel very reassured since there always has to be a first one.

I met General Quesada again in San Antonio, Texas, when he attended the reunion of our fighter group in September 1986. When I told him, "I came back," and then explained about our previous encounter, we sat and had a pleasant chat. He was 82 then, but still spry and alert. He asked how I liked being an air/ground controller and, without waiting for an answer, said, "I'll bet you didn't like it." Of all the pilots he asked, only a few felt comfortable in that duty. One, he remembered, liked it because he got a chance to engage a strafing Me 109 with a half-track-mounted antiaircraft machine gun. It was an honor to chat with that great aviator.

They assigned us to Combat Command A (CCA) of the 5th Armored Division in the line at Neudorf just south of Aachen, Germany. One of us would be assigned to the command post and the other to a tank. I lost the coin toss and drew tank duty. On my second day I attended a briefing on the battle strategy for an infantry and armored attack to take the town of Eicherschied, in the Kesternich-Konzen area of the Siegfried Line just above the Roer River dams. That night we moved to the attack jumpoff point near Lammersdorf. Two feet of snow covered the ground and the night was bitterly cold. The weather report for the next morning predicted more snow.

About midnight the company of tanks I was with pulled up to a wrecked house being used as the forward command post. It was perfectly clear and bright, and we could see at least a half mile of the snow-covered landscape. In the distance I heard a short machine-gun duel with the slow staccato rhythm of the American gun answered by the faster burp of the German gun. Not having any immediate duties, I sacked out on a settee in the building and grabbed a couple of hours sleep. The next morning I found I was sleeping over three German "potato mashers" (grenades). I just left them where they were.

At 0530 our five-minute artillery barrage opened up and we could hear the shells screaming overhead. It was a short barrage because they rationed the shells to make sure they had a plentiful supply for the next major operation to cross the Roer River. The supporting 78th Infantry Division jumped off shortly after the barrage lifted. The engineers moved in behind the infantry to clear the antitank minefield for the armored assault. The hip-deep snow hampered the operation, which delayed the armored assault about 45 minutes. While packing my gear on the tank I noticed that the attacking force had two British Churchill flamethrower tanks attached. They called them "Crocodiles," and they were sure ugly pulling their petroleum wagon behind them. The supporting tanks jumped off about 0900 and we followed shortly afterwards. It was snowing hard again and the clouds were low. The weather will ground air support, I thought.

My temporary home was an M4 Sherman tank mounting a 75mm cannon. I occupied the assistant driver's seat on the right side and was in charge of the .30-caliber forward-firing machine gun. My access hatch contained a swivel-mounted periscope; however, it was frozen sideways and no amount of coaxing or pounding could free it. This gave me two choices, sit bottled up not seeing anything, or leave the hatch open and see but get covered with snow. I chose to see.

As I watched the driver manipulate the controls, he gave me a few quick lessons on how to drive a tank. The tank slipped and bogged down in the snow several times as the driver rocked and coaxed the tank along an infantry trail in the snow. It was interesting to listen to the battle conversations over the tank commander's radio. From our location there wasn't much to see. The only evidence that we were attacking was the firing just forward from us. Once when we were stopped so the captain tank commander could confer with the infantry, I climbed on top of the tank to try to pick up some landmarks to orient myself. At that instant the Germans sent a few artillery shells toward us. When the first shell came over and impacted about 100 yards away, I scrambled back in the tank and closed the hatch. The tank crew, standing outside, laughed. The next shell was closer, and the third closer yet. Before the fourth shell came over, they were all inside the tank with me. It burst on a house just behind us.

About midmorning a flight of P-47s roared overhead. When I turned on the radio, I found it was the 389th Slipshod squadron of our group. They were talking to a rear area air/ground controller, trying to obtain some target information. All I could hear were snatches of conversation. They were only at 1,000 feet, in and out of snow showers, and at that low an altitude, with the short antenna on the tank, I could only receive and transmit when they were nearly directly overhead. Shortly I heard them say they were returning to base. The weather was too bad and they were uncertain of their exact position looking down on a deep snow-covered landscape. They gave it a good try.

From the air a pilot has a view of the entire battle area, but on the ground he is limited to just the immediate location. I learned later that all three squadrons tried to support the attack, but two squadrons failed due to weather. The 391st bombed a road bridge, marked by smoke, just east of the battle line. From my position I never saw or even heard that squadron overhead. It was a revealing experience for me.

Later that afternoon the tank radio ecstatically proclaimed that a group of

German soldiers had surrendered. Shortly afterwards I saw them being herded back. One had no pants on—he was just in his long johns. When I asked about it, the tankers said he probably was wearing American uniform pants when captured and they cut them off him. Several other prisoners were in sad shape—one obviously had frozen hands and several elderly ones were very haggard and exhausted. I was a rabid Nazi hater, but I couldn't help feeling sorry for them.[2]

The soldiers cleared the town of Eicherschied about dusk and patrols sent forward to the Roer River that night. The Roer above the dams was in our hands. Two women wearing German uniforms were among the 230 captured prisoners. After moving up to the town we pulled next to an abandoned house to spend the night. That evening I reflected on the day's events, and the incongruity that after being trained as a pilot here I was in a small German village in the middle of winter with a tank crew. Exhausted from the day's events, I slept like a baby on the floor of a German house though it was bitterly cold.

They fought this little battle in horrible weather of deep snow, cold, and a biting wind. Capt. Richard Biederman, commander of A Company, 34th Tank Battalion, 5th Armored Division supporting the attack, answered my request for stories on the battle. He related an incident that epitomizes the harsh conditions combat soldiers endure, and the fickle nature of combat.

After we captured Eicherschied we went through the town and seized the high ground just beyond. On this high ground was a small shed where the medics set up an aid station. While I was there, they brought in a soldier from the 46th Infantry who were working with us. They hit this man in the chest with a piece of shrapnel that tore up his combat jacket. The medics cut away his clothing to get at the wound. If you will recall it was bitterly cold, and this man had put on all the clothing he could find to keep himself warm. When the medics cut away his jacket, they found another jacket, and then some sweaters, etc. When they got to his undershirt they found that was as far as the shrapnel had penetrated. The hit had been so violent it had knocked him out, but all the clothing had protected him.

After returning to our bivouac area, Division Headquarters summoned me to a secret briefing. I don't remember for sure, but I believe Maj. Gen. Lunsford E. Oliver, commander of the 5th Armored, chaired the briefing. I do remember that I was the lowest-ranking officer present and was singled out by the general to assure that front-line air support would be available. My answer was in a wavering voice, "Yes, sir, weather permitting," answered by a "humph." In the briefing I learned that the 5th Armored was going to spearhead a crossing of the Roer River. This was part of a general Allied offensive slated to begin up north in the Canadian sector on 8 February 1945. Our attack was to begin on 12 February by forcing a crossing of the Roer River near the town of Linnich.

Cannon fire by the tanks was to support an initial crossing of infantry and engineers by boats. The engineers were to construct a foot bridge to allow more infantry to cross and expand the bridgehead. Then the engineers were to span the river with a heavy equipment bridge able to support tanks. They slated my assigned command tank to cross the river early in the consolidation phase, to enable direction of front-line air support. Air support and long-range artillery were tasked to isolate the bridgehead during the build-up.

During the next night deployment for the assault began by moving about 30 miles north of our bivouac area to the town of Baesweiler, Germany, but before we could get into position the operation was postponed. The Germans had destroyed the penstock of the Schwammenauel Dam, releasing a torrent of water down the Roer and flooding everything in its way. This dam is a short distance downstream from Eicherschied, where we had pushed through to the Roer a few days ago. Continuation of that attack was threatening to capture the dam so as the Germans retreated they destroyed the penstock. Forcing a crossing of the Roer was just physically impossible while the river was up. They postponed the operation until the torrent dispersed, estimated to take about two weeks.

The remainder of my tour with the 5th Armored was spent bivouacked in a small German town with nothing to do. We used the time to visit the local coal mine where we showered and cleaned up. Boy, it sure felt good to take off week-old clothes and stand in the hot shower. My instinct for exploring also led me to examine the Siegfried Line of interlocked pillboxes and bunkers. During my explorations I unknowingly walked into a field that had not been cleared of mines. After walking through the field I saw the signs warning about the mines facing the road. The engineers who put up the signs probably never thought some curious, naive, and stupid pilot would walk through the field from the Siegfried Line dragon's teeth side. Divine intervention through my guardian angel was surely with me that day.

Upon my return to Y-29 on 14 February, Major Martin immediately summoned me to his office. Marty notified me that since I was privy to the offensive plans for crossing the Roer River, I was barred from flying combat missions until the offensive was well under way.

Recently I acquired a report titled, "Letter Report, After Action Against Enemy—March 1945, Headquarters 5th Armored Division. Use of Fighter-Bomber Pilot as Forward Controller."[3] The report was harshly critical of assigning pilots as air/ground controllers for only two weeks. The two-week period was hardly enough time to acclimate the pilot to his new environment and duties. Then, just as he was becoming proficient, he was replaced. The quick pilot turnover degraded the efficacy of the air/ground controller concept.

When I read that report, it made me feel guilty that I had not stayed to complete the Roer River crossing assignment. The captain of the tank company I was with had asked me to consider sticking around for "the interesting time we're going to have on crossing the Roer," but I respectfully declined. Fighting a war cooped up in a lumbering steel monster did not appeal to me. I now feel I let them down. I might just as well have stayed since I was grounded until the operation was under way.

The report remarks:

During the past eight months of almost continuous operations it has become increasingly apparent that the policy of changing the Fighter-Bomber pilots with the forward VHF radio in tanks every ten (10) days does not maintain the efficiency necessary in Air-Ground cooperation. It usually takes several days for a new pilot to become familiar with the ground picture and his new job. It takes a few more days for him to feel sure of himself in his vastly different role. By that time his replacement is on hand, which often times occurs in the middle of an operation, and the pilot must return to flying status. Then, too, pilots working with the ground troops and aware of certain operations are necessarily grounded for a few days upon return to their base because of this knowledge.

It goes on to note that an armored division requires six pilots for air controllers, two for each of the three combat commands in a division. In each combat command one pilot is stationed with headquarters and the other with the task force front-line combat command. The report recognizes that that number of pilots is unavailable and proposes authorization of special air officers, to be jointly trained by air and ground, and then attached to the armored units. If it is not feasible to authorize those special officers, the report recommends a detached service (semi-permanent) pilot assignment to the armored command for two to three months.

We certainly deserved the well-directed criticism for the quick pilot rotation. While I was glad to get back to base from my front-line tour, I have always regretted not having had the opportunity to direct an air strike. I'm sure if I had remained with the ground forces I would have had my desire fulfilled.

The only flying I did until 2 March was slow timing and combat flight testing various aircraft. I took the opportunity to fly to various parts of Belgium, Luxembourg, and Holland, and buzzed my hometown of Oordegem several times. I even wrangled a few days' leave to visit my relatives.

While I was up front, the group was busy performing rail cutting and armed reconnaissance missions from the Roer to beyond the Rhine at Cologne. These more northerly missions consummated the transfer of our group to XXIX TAC under Brig. Gen. Richard E. Nugent, and we were now providing support for

Lt. Gen. William H. Simpson's Ninth Army attached to the 21st Army Group commanded by Field Marshal Bernard L. Montgomery.

I sat in on most mission and interrogation briefings during my forced grounding, and noticed how the pilots grumbled about just busting up a few railroads on some missions. When I think about it, we grumbled about most missions. We didn't like cutting railroads because it didn't seem like we were accomplishing anything. We didn't like the Hürtgen Forest missions because of the flak and the lack of visibility in that forest. About the only missions we liked were finding German armored column to shoot up, getting into a dogfight with German aircraft, or seeing tangible results of our bombing and strafing, like when we helped the troops capture Brandenburg. In that respect, I guess, we were like most civilian soldiers, we grumbled and complained, but we did the job.

Finally, after a two-week delay, the offensive to cross the Roer River, named Grenade, started on 23 February. The day before the ground offensive started, the Ninth Air Force unleashed a massive air interdiction campaign against the German transportation system behind the projected Grenade attack. They called the air portion of the attack Operation Clarion. Clarion was actually an attack by the entire European air force stretching from England to Italy. General Spaatz initiated it and used 7,000 Allied fighters, fighter-bombers, light bombers, and medium bombers. The purpose was to underline the fact that Germany was defeated and emphasize that fact to the German populace by simultaneously attacking railroad and communication stations in hundreds of towns and villages. The fact that it coincided with our immediate area attacks to isolate the battlefield for crossing the Roer River made it more fascinating.[4]

The operations order specified a maximum strength strike with each squadron launching a minimum of sixteen aircraft per mission. Each squadron was to escort a group of medium bombers to and from a cluster of railroad bridges just east of the industrial city of Hamm. They were then to dive-bomb and strafe the same target the bombers attacked or, if the bombers destroyed the target, attack other railroad bridges in the area. The order read, in part, "The bombers will attack their targets at high enough altitude to bomb accurately, yet low enough to strafe effectively. As the bombers approach their target the fighters will fly slightly ahead and strafe flak positions which are firing at the bombers." It was an unusual escort mission, having to carry bombs and strafe flak positions ahead of low-flying bombers. Also, if the group was attacked by enemy aircraft, only sufficient aircraft to ward off the attackers were to jettison their bombs and belly tanks. Listening to the briefing, I was disappointed on not going on such an unusual mission.

The mission turned out to be uneventful for the fifty-four aircraft dispatched. They rendezvoused with the bombers on time and the escort went as planned.

It was unusual to escort the bombers at low altitude and, after bombing, see them drop lower so they could strafe the area with all guns blazing away. Of the five bridges attacked, they destroyed one, probably destroyed another, damaged two. Only one was undamaged. Railroad tracks leading to the still-standing bridges were all cut in several places. In addition the marshaling yard at Beckum, holding at least fifty boxcars, was dive-bombed and strafed, claiming six boxcars destroyed and eight others probably destroyed.

The second mission of thirty-five aircraft performed an armed reconnaissance in the area from Dusseldorf to Bonn. They destroyed many railroad cars, including five oil-tank cars, which were left burning, and several flat cars carrying tanks. As a bonus, strafing destroyed several locomotives. Roselee (XXIX TAC radar controller) urgently called the 391st squadron to attack fifteen to twenty Me 262 jet aircraft bombing American forces. Diving down on the strafing German jets allowed the 391st to get close for a firing pass. One Me 262 was claimed destroyed by David B. Fox. The American antiaircraft gunners were jittery after being bombed by the German jets and they subjected the 391st to a heavy antiaircraft barrage as they drove off the Germans. Fortunately the American gunners were not very accurate and all 391st aircraft flew through the unnerving barrage unscathed.

Missions over the next several days halted all German transportation and denied the Germans access to the Allied bridgeheads established across the Roer River. Fifteen missions were run on 23 February and thirteen the next day. The same pace was continued for the next week. One casualty was my new aircraft, lost on 28 February. Just that day I had borrowed Chuck Bennett's camera and took a few pictures of my aircraft while the ground crew was rearming it between missions. Lt. Claude Halterman flew it on that mission and never returned. Records indicate that a flak burst made a direct hit and Claude didn't have time to bail out. He crashed two and one-half miles northeast of Grevenbroich, Germany, about 20 miles northeast of Cologne. Claude was the fourth fellow lost whom I had gone on leave with in October. In a few days they assigned me another new P-47 (B2-J no. 3), but I never did get the cowl painted— it just wasn't the same.

When I returned to base from my front-line tour, it appeared everyone had a motorcycle. Motorcycles of every description were running around, from the big Harley Davidson types to small ones more aptly classed as motorbikes. To this day I don't know where they all came from. I took an interest in a one-cylinder English bike and became part owner. After a few days of practice I became proficient in handling it. Our squadron had a cute cocker spaniel mascot named Turbo (after the turbo-supercharger in the P-47). He was actually Marty Martin's dog but he adopted the entire squadron as his domain. In the evening he would investigate each tent and usually spend the night in the one that had some goodies available. He also loved to go for rides on the motorcycles. If anyone started one, he was there begging for a ride, and would hop aboard and sit on the gas tank when he heard, "Okay, Turbo, hop on." I gave him many a ride around the base. Marty brought Turbo back to the States after the war and he became part of the Martin family for many years. One day he just disappeared walking down a country road.

We felt proficient enough riding the motorcycles that one evening five of us, riding on three bikes, decided to go to Hasselt. By this time we knew some girls in Hasselt and could park the bikes in their courtyard while we all went to the cabaret. About 2230, being pleasantly drunk, we started on our way home. For some reason we decided to exchange bikes. In the trade I drew the Harley Davidson, an American bike. An English bike has its clutch on the right and the brake on the left; a Harley is exactly the opposite, with the clutch on the left and brake on the right. I was in the lead since the Harley was the only one with a working light and I was carrying a rider.

Everything went fine until we came to the temporary bridge over the Albert Canal. (The original one was rubble.) What I didn't know was that on the far side of the bridge the tram line ran on the left side of the road but it crossed to the right just before the bridge. We approached the bridge and I saw a single light approaching on my left. Suddenly, the light veered right and crossed over the road. I tried to stop but got confused with the bike controls, and while trying to remain to the right of the light I found myself jammed between the tram and the bridge railing. At that point we up-ended. The fellow I traded bikes with experienced the same problems with his bike controls. He drove right over our up-ended bike before he also spilled. By that time the tram had stopped.

Miraculously, no one was even bruised. I yelled in Flemish to the tram conductor that everything was okay and for him to go on, which he did. We picked ourselves up and found the only damage was the Harley's handlebar, which was twisted about 15 degrees. We continued and reached the base safely. The next day, when sober again, I was struck by the seriousness of the situation. We could easily have been badly hurt or even killed. To this day I have not ridden another motorcycle.

I finally resumed combat flying after a month's delay, on 2 March 1945. My log says only that it was unproductive. The second mission I flew that day was to bomb barges on the Rhine River. In fact, the next series of missions were all directed at Rhine River traffic interdiction and hitting trains in the Ruhr industrial valley (Flak Valley).

A heavily bombed railroad marshaling yard contains many usable boxcars stranded on the rails between bomb craters. Intelligence learned that the Germans were using the stranded boxcars for material storage. Using heavy or even medium bombers to carpet-bomb the remaining cars was impractical, so they gave us the mission. On 3 March the marshaling yard at Hamm, Germany, was our target. We dive-bombed and strafed the stranded boxcars, and since we experienced only light ineffective flak, we set up a training-type strafing pattern. This pattern brought us over a foreign worker or prisoner-of-war camp, and as we flew over we saw all the captives outside cheering us. We rocked our wings to acknowledge their waving and jumping, and then strafed the yard. Discussing this back at our base that evening gave us an uneasy feeling; we were so close to them, rocking our wings, and yet so far away. It made us realize how fragile our position was since any of us could have been a POW in that camp.

German aircraft were still quite active at night, trying to bomb our field. We had air raids quite often and the antiaircraft boys claimed several night raiders shot down. On 3 March they assigned me duty as group airdrome officer (AO) for the night. This duty was usually quite routine and boring. The only important activity occurred late in the evening when we received the mission assignments for the next day in communications. Received with that were the latest weather reports and bomb-line information. As group AO I sorted and parceled them out to the squadron AOs. I was also in touch with the local military police (MP) detachment and other tenant organizations on the field.

During the night the antiaircraft battalion stationed around the field called to warn that German night intruders were again flying around, and we would probably have an air raid. Several air-raid alerts were issued and I duly sounded the air-raid siren. Several times the antiaircraft guns opened up with their spectacular sight of crisscrossing tracers. About 2300 hours, after a particular heavy barrage, a phone call from the local MP unit informed me that they picked up an English airman who just made a parachute landing, and they wanted to know what to do with him. I told them to bring him to group headquarters and we would decide the next course of action. I was somewhat concerned since the Germans were still trying to get saboteurs installed within our lines.

All concern disappeared when the MP and an obviously very English airman arrived. He was a young boy of eighteen (I was now twenty-one), very frightened and shook up. Fortunately he wasn't hurt so I had him sit down, relax, and talk about it while having a cup of coffee (I didn't have any tea). He was a crewmember of a Wellington bomber on a night interdiction mission. German night fighters had chased them, and while evading they had wandered off course and were shot down by our antiaircraft fire. The aircraft carried five crew members but he didn't know what happened to them. I alerted the MP detachment to be on the lookout for other survivors and then called TAC headquarters to report that our antiaircraft detachment shot down an English Wellington bomber and I was hosting a surviving crewmember. They acknowledged the information and said they would be in touch. I then turned him over to the Red Cross detachment on the field so that they could provide him temporary quarters and food.

About 0300, two bird colonels from TAC headquarters showed up to investigate the incident. Since I had sent the fellow to the Red Cross, they said they would just hang around. In the morning I duly reported the night's events to the group operations officer, Maj. Perry Lusby, and warned him that there were two bird colonels lurking in the area. He acknowledged my report and I never heard anything more of the incident. While researching material to verify several remarks made throughout this book, I got in touch with my friend in Genk, Lucien Bogers, who provided an additional insight of this incident. Quoting from his letter (I took the liberty to Anglicize it somewhat):

About 2200 hours on the evening 3/4 March a RAF bomber was wounded on his mission and on return was finished by AA [antiaircraft] from your Y-29. The crash was in Genk-Waterschei area behind the Stalenstraat (the street with several cafes and dancing), near the coal pits of Waterschei. I have found out that several of the crew parachuted safely, but three were killed. Your fire trucks were quickly on the scene and they removed the bodies to Zutendaal.

I recently received a message from a former member of the 792nd Antiaircraft Artillery (AAA) Battalion, Homer Yeakle, concerning this incident. In it he stated that our fighter group commander got so mad about the shootdown of the Wellington bomber that he ordered their AAA battalion to be transferred. They changed locations with the neighboring battalion guarding Y-32, which was now in the American sector.

The Allies enjoyed such overwhelming air superiority that we saw few German aircraft, especially after their disastrous 1 January debacle, but occasionally they would make an appearance. Such an appearance was devastating for an eight-aircraft mission by the 389th squadron on 1 March. An aggressive swarm of FW 190 fighters attacked them as they were pulling up from their dive-bombing pass. In a few moments, four P-47s were shot down and several others heavily damaged; several pilots were wounded. One damaged aircraft was lost when the pilot bailed out safely after nursing it to the American lines. The surviving pilots claimed only one FW 190 destroyed, although German records show that three German pilots were lost.

A week later, 9 March, a swarm of Me 109 and FW 190 aircraft hit the 391st squadron while they were attacking a partially destroyed bridge over the Rhine at Wesel that was the only escape route open for German troops still fighting on the west side of the Rhine. Two P-47s were shot down and several more were heavily damaged. The squadron claimed six FW 190s shot down although German records show only three German aircraft and pilots were lost.

In eight days the 366th lost seven aircraft in air battles. Out of that, four pilots were killed and two were prisoners. The pilots killed were Lieutenants William McCauley, Steve Pease, and Ed Downs, all from the 389th, and F/O Bill Dufford from the 391st. Prisoners were Lieutenants Perry Kaylor (389th) and Bennett Fuller (391st). The German fighter unit that attacked so aggressively was the foremost fighter unit in the west since the beginning of the war, JG 26, otherwise known as the "Abbeville Kids."[5] Although JG 26 was not as formidable as it was during 1943, it retained an experienced cadre of pilots who could exact a large toll on the unwary. We redoubled our vigilance and kept a sharp eye on our tail and up sun.

We ran an escort mission for a group of Martin B-26 medium bombers on a strike in the northern part of the Ruhr Valley on 11 March. German jet aircraft had become very active and were pressing home vigorous attacks on the medium-bomber formations, devastating several formations of them. We met the bombers over the German border and escorted them to and from the military supply dump target that they bombed from Angels 13.5. We flew top cover for the bombers and we climbed to Angels 18 so we would have some diving altitude to get our speed up to strike back at any jet aircraft. Although we were eager to tangle with some jets, and hoped they would show up, they disappointed us. The entire mission was uneventful. It turned out to be the highest combat mission that I flew during the war.

The elite Me 262 jet fighter group JG 7, commanded by fighter ace Maj. Theo Weissenberger (with 200 victories), was stationed at Osnabrück, about 60 miles from the bombing target. At the time, however, they were using the German autobahn as their field. They had the best of the remaining German fighter pilots and ran roughshod over the U.S. Air Force in several battles. Adolph Galland, dismissed as General of Fighters, also formed an Me 262 squadron, JV 44 (Jagdverbande 44) fighter unit, but both units were too little and too late to affect the outcome of the war since they were overwhelmed by sheer numbers of allied aircraft.

The hazard of low-level flying nearly did me in on a fighter sweep on 12 March. We caught sight of a train speeding down the tracks in the same area as the escort mission of the previous day. Speeding down the track during daylight signified that it was probably carrying an urgently needed and important cargo, and probably had several flak cars attached. The squadron commander detailed our flight to strike it.

We dove down to Angels Zero about five miles from the train and proceeded toward it on the deck in a loose line abreast formation. Coming over a good-sized hill and pushing down over the top, we saw the train appear right in front of us, and I was aimed directly at the engine. It was a perfect setup. I centered the gunsight piper on the engine and then wondered if I should lead it slightly since it was really roaring down the track. I dismissed the thought since it didn't seem significant. When I was in range I gave it a short burst and saw my hits were concentrated on the cab and tender area. Before getting off another burst I noticed I was perilously low. My fixation on shooting at the train had blocked out my other perceptions and I was really close to smashing into the hilly ground. I pulled up just as I hit a bush or some small trees with my left wing.

As the flight pulled up to rejoin the squadron, we received a formidable fusillade of antiaircraft fire from flak cars coupled on the train. One aircraft was severely damaged. Looking back we saw the train had stopped steaming, but we were uncertain of attack results. I still curse myself for failing to lead the moving train slightly to assure some good hits on the engine. This was the second time I experienced pilot fixation by concentrating on hitting the target, and both times I just barely survived. This fixation might explain how we lost some pilots who crashed into the ground for no apparent reason.

They assigned a Polish pilot, Marion Cheslaw Glowczynski, or "Chaz," to temporary duty with us to become indoctrinated in ground-support tactics. He fought in the battles of Poland, France, and England. In the process he was shot down several times, once horribly burning his hands. Glowczynski probably had over 1,000 combat hours and was an exceptional pilot.[6] On one Red flight mission he was flying Red-2. The four aircraft made several passes to strafe a target in the Ruhr Valley while under intense antiaircraft fire. Since they had lost their excess speed during the dive they needed about a minute to climb back to a safe altitude. Rather than try to get back to a safe altitude in the middle of Flak Valley and be subjected to a terrific volley of flak, they elected to stay on the deck, since it was safer there, and get away from the Ruhr before climbing. We gave them a vector to get them away from that dangerous area.

There was very little radio chatter. Suddenly we heard Red leader say, "Watch it—high tension wires." A short time later Red leader came back with, "Did you get them?" Red-3 answered, "Yep!" A few minutes later they were safely out of the Ruhr area and could pull up without having to go through the very intense antiaircraft fire. As Red flight approached our formation Red leader cautioned, "Stay away from Red-3. He has several hundred feet of wire cable trailing from him." Sure enough we could see it swirling behind him.

After Red-3 landed safely, he told us what happened. He had heard Red leader call to watch out for the high-tension wires and saw him pull up over them. He then saw Chaz go underneath the wires. While he contemplated which way to go, he flew through them. He didn't even feel the aircraft jar as he flew through the wires. It was funny afterward, but it could have been tragic.

In the middle of March a critical shortage of .50-caliber ammunition developed. We were ordered to conserve ammunition by only strafing "lucrative targets." The orders did not define what a lucrative target was, but left it to our discretion. Shortly thereafter, we saw a motorcyclist speeding down the autobahn. We easily saw him from Angels 12 as a black dot racing all alone in the middle of the white concrete road. Since we received no orders to attack him, I presume he was not a lucrative target. None of us was disappointed since he was roaring down the road in the middle of Flak Valley. Afterward we laughingly admired the daring motorcyclist for his courage, having a squadron of the dreaded Jabos above him, yet he just kept going on his way. In reality he could easily have pulled off the road and hidden himself by the time we would have reached him.

Marty was on a 30-day stateside leave, so deputy CO Capt. Lowell B. Smith was now in charge of the 390th. We received word that they had promoted Marty to lieutenant colonel and reassigned him to XXIX TAC. Smitty soon received a promotion to major and became commander of the 390th.

Chuck Bennett and two others borrowed a jeep for a souvenir-hunting expedition. They came back that evening with a jeepload of souvenirs and quite a story to tell. The Ludendorf bridge across the Rhine at Remagen, seized a few days ago, was the center of a furious battle as the Germans attempted to evict the Americans from their bridgehead on the east bank of the Rhine. Using their charms, Chuck and company conned their way across the damaged bridge. They traded some flying equipment for several Luger and Walther P-38 pistols, and a jeep full of other German weapons and material. They said the bridge was unsteady, swaying menacingly as they went over, and was under constant artillery fire. They returned on a floating treadway span installed by the engineers several hundred yards downstream from the Remagen Bridge, but it was a wide double-track one for heavy vehicles. For the jeep to negotiate it, they drove with one set of wheels on the inner wheel guide of one treadway. It was a perilous, slow journey back across the Rhine. Chuck gave me a machine pistol (burp gun) and some other booty I sent home.

On 18 March Ray Kennedy and I went for a five-day leave in a rest home in Southport, England. After the leave we were to pick up two new P-47s at Burtonwood Field and fly them back to base. The rest home was the Palace Hotel, a big resort hotel right on the beach, and it hosted at least 500 air crewmembers. They had many interesting activities but it was just too crowded to be enjoyable. My other rest-home leave in Oxford was much better. I enjoyed walking on the wide sandy beach, and one day I walked out about a mile at low tide.

When the tide turned I was forced to run all the way back to keep in front of the incoming ocean. When I returned to the beach a finger-shaking local Englishman admonished me on the dangers of strolling on the tidal flats. They contained many sink holes that could have trapped me.

Ray and I picked up the new P-47s at Burtonwood and received a weather briefing for a direct flight to the ferry-flight staging field at A-81 at Creil, France, just north of Paris. A weather front was located just in the middle of the channel, and the weather officer advised us to penetrate and go through it at Angels 15. He estimated it would only take us about 10 minutes of instrument flying to go through the front. Talking it over with Ray we chose to ignore him and stay below the weather.

While we lugged our parachute, helmet, and oxygen mask with us, we had for some time given up wearing our inflatable Mae West life jackets and replaced our uncomfortable dinghy pack seat for more comfortable cushions. Consequently, we were going to fly across the channel with no survival gear. We agreed that if one of us ditched, the other would drop his then-empty belly tank for flotation (a futile gesture in the near-freezing channel water).

We had an uneventful pleasant flight until just west of London where the weather started to deteriorate. To stay below the overcast we had to fly lower and lower; by the time we reached the channel we were on the deck. Our estimated channel crossing time was 20 minutes. We were not really aware of how restricted visibility was until the cliffs of France suddenly appeared in front of us. We both pulled up and immediately disappeared into the overcast. The jarring pull-up caused Ray's radio receiver to fail. I could hear him frantically calling me, but he obviously wasn't receiving my replies.

I set a course and started climbing, breaking into the clear at Angels 12. Within the next 15 minutes the clouds started to break and I descended to Angels 3. Ground visibility was now about five miles. I had only a large-scale (1/1 million) chart, not wanting to carry a bunch of smaller-scale ones, but I was unable to find my location using a chart showing only a few landmarks. Fortunately, I chanced upon an airfield occupied by a Martin B-26 group. Rather than expend time trying to orient myself, I landed. A puzzled AO met and informed me I was at A-60 at Beaumont-Sur-Oise, which wasn't even on my chart, about 10 minutes flying from my destination. Ray happily greeted me when I landed. We spent the night at A-81 getting the paperwork cleared and Ray's radio repaired, and flew the aircraft to our field in Belgium the next day.

In retrospect, that flight was obviously a foolhardy thing to do. We violated all safe piloting principles but got away with it. At the time we were young and cocky, and never even gave the flight a second thought. I survived with my stupidity, but many others didn't.[7]

When we returned to our base, I was horrified to learn that Chuck Bennett had been shot down on 24 March. Our group was supporting the 30th Infantry Division in the big push over the Rhine River at Wesel. Chuck was leading his second squadron mission, strafing about 10 miles east of the Rhine, when flak hit his aircraft. Blazing furiously, he nursed it back over the American side of the Rhine before bailing out; however, the wind carried him back so he landed in the middle of the Rhine. This was a few miles south of where the river crossing was in progress. A few minutes later an American liaison aircraft came and circled him and, as the squadron left, they saw a rescue boat coming downstream. The only word received was that he was badly wounded and in a hospital. I was finally able to find out he was in a hospital in England, and that he might lose his leg, which was broken when he hit the tail on bailout. I was now the only one left out of the six who had gone on operational leave together a few months before. It was a sad day packing Chuck's personal belongings to send home. I still had many good friends in the squadron, but Chuck was special. At least he had not been killed.

Chuck confided to me later that his rescue was just in time. He didn't think he would have lasted another minute. The discarded Mae West life jacket would have come in handy for him, but who would have thought a 100-yard-wide river would be a water hazard. He was in and out of hospitals for two years. However, they saved his leg and he returned to flying status.

Until that time I was anxious to fly, hoping to get another chance to shoot down some German aircraft, but now I just didn't care anymore. It was obvious the war was going to end soon, so why take unnecessary chances? I only flew seven more missions from then until the end of the war in Europe.

Even at this late date the Germans were still resisting tenaciously and firing their V-2s to London and Antwerp. Suddenly seeing the trail of a V-2 curving up into the sky from northern Holland was a common sight while flying in the clear spring skies of northeastern Germany. We idly speculated on the possibility of shooting one down. We also wondered why the Germans just didn't surrender and stop the carnage. They certainly had to see that their cause was hopeless.

The ground forces were really pushing ahead now and the length of our missions increased to where we again had to carry belly tanks of extra fuel. We needed the extra fuel not for extending the range, but due to a lack of suitable targets. We would be vectored from one spearhead to another looking for targets. Usually we ended up bombing suspected enemy concentrations in wooded areas where the Germans might make a stand or a town that showed an inclination to resist. I flew my longest mission of four hours during that time.

On a 5 April mission we were vectored around on a wild goose chase in the heavily defended Ruhr area. We were running low on fuel when finally they told us to bomb Soest. This was a fair-sized city and the Germans were putting up a stout ground resistance, resulting in a street-by-street battle. We were directed to just hit a certain section of the city to try to discourage the defenders. I noted that the city was mostly rubble from RAF and American Eighth Air Force raids. We released our bombs quite high, generally aiming to just hit the German section of the city. It seemed like it was a good place to experiment on how far a bomb would travel when released horizontally at high speed. I watched how my bombs arced down after release and noted with horror that they hit an aid station or hospital since a big red cross was on the roof. In my playing around with the deadly bombs I had not aimed at any target and didn't even see the red crosses until my bombs hit. I reported the bombing mishap but I'm still bothered by that episode of indiscriminate bombing.

On 7 April an incident occurred that reminded us it was still a brutal war. The mission was to cover the 2nd Armored Division, but they had no targets and had advanced practically unopposed into Germany. They released the squadron to bomb the alternate target, the Halberstadt railroad marshaling yard. On bombing, Lt. Walter Barnard hit an ammunition train or ammunition storage dump, and it blew up with a tremendous explosion. He was pulling up from bombing and was at 5,000 feet when the explosion occurred. The explosion disabled his aircraft and he had to bail out. The flight leader orbiting at 11,000 feet felt the concussion. The blast leveled about half the town.

The squadron saw Walt land safely and then run away from the area. Twelve days later he showed up back at the base. He landed unhurt but hung up in a tree about eight feet off the ground. In the distance he saw some angry farmers coming after him with pitchforks. He had the presence of mind to take his cigarettes and throw them as far as he could. While the Germans went for the cigarettes he hurriedly cut himself down and ran away. He hid out for several days until American troops arrived. We heard about angry German civilians killing downed pilots, but this was our first confirmed probable incident. Although I didn't smoke, I always carried a couple packs of cigarettes with me from then on—just in case. Walt had been saving a bottle of bourbon to celebrate the approaching end of the war. When we didn't hear from him after a few days, his tentmates Fred Keys and Don DeWyke finished off Walt's bourbon, thinking he was a prisoner of war. Walt was quite upset that his bourbon was gone and that he couldn't drink it to celebrate when the end finally came.

On 14 April 1945 we moved from Y-29 to Y-94, a Luftwaffe field at Handorf, five miles northeast of Münster, Germany. The Germans constructed the airfield in 1936 with three intersecting runways about 4,500 feet long. It had a long war history as a bomber base and was last used during the Battle of the Bulge by

KG 76 flying the new jet bomber, Arado (Ar) 234. We were now going to take up residence. We flew our aircraft to our new home loaded with three empty 150-gallon external tanks to save trucking space.

The engineers had repaired only one side of one runway and were working on the other side when we took up residence. This compelled us to land on a narrow strip of concrete next to several hundred engineers working with bull-dozers, cranes, and concrete mixers on the other side. Although we had to operate like that for a few days in all kinds of winds, we had only one minor runway landing incident. This speaks well of the pilot skill we had in the group. In a landing attitude the P-47 nose blocks out the view straight ahead. We gleaned our side drift by watching out the corners of our eyes. If we ran off the runway on one side, we were bound to run into unfilled bomb craters, while on the other side the engineers still labored. The exigency of war requires extreme risks, and the pilots of the 366th Fighter Group admirably met this one. I also would compliment the engineers laboring on the runway for their fortitude in continuing their task, oblivious to our roaring by, fully loaded with bombs and rockets.

The Eighth Air Force had heavily bombed this base, destroying all the buildings and heavily cratering the entire field. The bombing pulverized the Luftwaffe buildings so our tents were set up in a farmer's newly plowed field. This meant that my entire time in combat I was quartered in tents, except for those few days in Normandy when I lived in an old bakery building. We, of course, had excellent accommodations compared to what the front-line troops had; nevertheless it had been a cold, long winter. I did not get a sleeping bag until late March and had to make do with a couple of blankets. In spite of the cold and spartan living conditions we were in the best of health.

I flew my last combat mission on 19 April. It was an armed reconnaissance in the Wittenberg-Neuruppin-Brandenburg area, reaching within 35 miles from Berlin. We didn't quite get that close to Berlin because Horsefly, a liaison aircraft experimenting as a forward air/ground controller, directed us to bomb and strafe some woods where die-hard German troops were making a stand.[8] The few vehicles we strafed were probably claimed destroyed by several squadrons. I lined up to strafe a truck and, just as I pulled the trigger, saw that other aircraft had already done that. While flying around checking for other targets I must have seen two or three other flights also strafe that truck. It was clearly a case of massive overkill. An interesting note. The small liaison aircraft that directed our strike was to close to the target and along our specified strafing approach direction. Roaring in for our strafing pass, we suddenly came upon him at 500 feet in a vertical dive to get away from the approaching monsters. We all missed him but implementation of a procedure to prevent such an occurrence needs development.

On 21 April Col. Harold N. Holt was relieved of command of the 366th Fighter Group and made Director of Operations, XXIX TAC. He was group commander through my entire period of combat. When I had contact with him, which was only occasionally, I found him to be an excellent military leader, firm, fair, and understanding. Our new commander was Lt. Col. Ansel J. Wheeler, formerly Assistant Director of Operations, XXIX TAC. I met him only once before I left the group. Most of us were very indignant about an outsider being brought in, espousing instead that Lt. Col. Clure Smith, then deputy group commander under Colonel Holt, should have been given the position. Years later I asked Clure about that insult by Ninth Air Force. He said he talked to General Quesada about it and that the general had agreed that he was the best and logical choice for the position. Clure said General Quesada then explained the politics of the situation. Lieutenant Colonel Wheeler was a West Pointer with high credentials and associates, and needed command experience for his record.

The few missions run during the latter part of April were mostly patrol flights that had nothing to report after landing. We didn't even carry bombs anymore. They scheduled me for one such mission but on taxiing out I got a flat tire. Some flights came back saying they ran into Russian aircraft, with each warily circling the other before breaking off. On 25 April we received an order that said we were not to fly across the Elbe River since that was allocated to the Russians. On 2 May an unusual mission was run to provide column cover for surrendering German troops to prevent them from being strafed by other American squadrons. Allied forces had indeed vanquished Germany.

10. Mission Completed

The great adventure came to an end. I wouldn't take a million dollars for the experience, but wouldn't give a dime to go through it again.

The end of the war in Europe was anticlimactic; we just stopped flying missions and started looking over the country. Places that had been prominent in the war news for the past five years were visited. I recall looking over the giant craters where the British dropped 10-ton bombs on the canal system serving the Ruhr Valley. Of particular interest was Flak Valley; however, there was nothing to be seen except the destroyed cities. Some fellows even tried to find particular places where we dive-bombed and strafed to see if we could find the destroyed vehicles or structures, but it was impossible because we had destroyed almost everything.

We weren't supposed to fly over the Russian zone, but I wasn't going home after fighting so long without being over Berlin. On a sightseeing flight, four of us flew there and looked over the entire city at 500 feet. It was nothing but rubble. The people walking around that battered city did not even look up as we roared over their heads. Hitler was certainly right when he made the prediction in one of his speeches that in 10 years no one would recognize the German Third Reich. I still vividly remember flying over Tempelhof, Berlin's airport. Except for a large curved concrete ramp, it was a sod field. Russian aircraft were parked on the field but none took to the air to dispute our flight. I was at Tempelhof, but many of my friends who had jokingly alluded to a meeting at Tempelhof almost one year ago were no longer around.

We were not the only ones to ignore the restriction for flying over the Russian zone. Stan Sobek's parents came to America from Poland, and Stan wanted to see their hometown. He and another fellow flew as far as Poland before they were intercepted by Russian Yaks and signaled to land. Stan told us that when the Russians pointed down to land, both he and the other pilot shook their heads, "No," and did a split-S away from the Yaks and hightailed it back. He didn't see the Yaks again, but didn't quite get to where his parents had come from in Poland, which he really wanted to see.

Sightseeing Eighth Air Force bombers also buzzed us. For several days after VE Day whole groups of bombers would come flying by at treetop level to view the destruction of vanquished Germany.[1] We narrowly missed having a bad accident with the sightseeing bombers. Several of our planes were taking off when a B-17 group came roaring over. Violent evasive action was necessary by both the P-47s and B-17s to prevent a head-on collision.

The 406th group, which set up on the other side of the field, practiced spelling U-S-S-R and C-C-C-P in flight. They were to perform the flyby in a review staged for the Russian army stationed across the Elbe River. The big day came, and when they came back from their function they were in formation spelling S-H-I-T. I got an informal pamphlet titled "Famous Flight," at one of our reunions and for amusement have included it in here.

One of the most famous flights in the World War II time period occurred after the war was over. This flight was performed by the 406th Fighter Group commanded by Col. Anthony (Snag) Grossetta. The 406th had been requested by XXIX TAC Headquarters, located at Braunschweig, to perform a fly-by spelling out U S S R and C C C P for a review requested by Gen. Simpson, commander of the US Ninth Army. The 406th practiced long and diligently with nine aircraft in each flight. The day before the review some guy from TAC called and requested that they fly over TAC Headquarters so TAC could approve the formation. IF IT WAS GOOD ENOUGH [emphasis in original] they would then let them fly it the next day for the Russians. Having to be approved by some flunky miffed the group, so they practiced four more letters.

That evening they flew over TAC Headquarters for approval. They went by first in four flights of three aircraft VEES, executed a 180 and came back spelling out U S S R, a quick 180 and the next pass spelled C C C P. The final pass read S H I T in the best formation you ever did see to make sure their feelings were legible from the ground. They stayed in the nasty formation all the way back to base eliciting a rousing guffaw from all the troops that observed the flight.

XXIX TAC allowed them to fly in the review but held their breath for fear that they might be indiscreet enough to insult the Russians, thus creating an international incident.

Col. Holt added an additional commentary to this amusing episode at our 1993 Fighter Group reunion.

There evidently were some Russian observers at TAC Headquarters and they asked some press reporters what S H I T meant. The reporters told them it was a "family joke," whereupon the Russians laughed and were satisfied since they knew what a "family joke" was.

I requested and was granted a five-day leave to visit with my relatives in Belgium. During this visit I think I met every uncle, aunt, cousin, and friend of my parents. While on leave, I saw my first pictures of the Nazi death camps in a movie newsreel. The gasps of the movie audience as the camera displayed the scenes showed their unanimous revulsion. It made all our fighting and the loss of good men seem worthwhile to eliminate the scourge of such a despotic system.

I was coming back to Münster in a truck when the driver suddenly swerved off the autobahn and stopped. We got out to see what happened and found the windshield shattered and the driver bleeding from numerous cuts from a brick that some Germans threw through the windshield. The war had been over only two weeks, and of fifteen of us traveling through Germany not one of us was armed. We stopped an ambulance to get the driver bandaged and continued to base. From then on, when traveling in Germany, I carried my side arm, just in case.

At war's end millions of refugees started on the long trek home, congesting the German roads. On the autobahn a continuous stream of people on both sides of the road walked in both directions. They were mostly women and children pushing or pulling a small cart, baby buggy or wagon. When we stopped to bandage the driver after being hit with a thrown brick, the stream of refugees discretely stopped about 100 feet away and only continued their trek when we resumed our journey. It was a pathetic sight but we could personally do nothing. I hope most found their homes and family.

Back at Münster the Air Force unveiled a new toy, a mobile van that sported a precision radar installation. The radar and specially trained personnel were going to guide us through the clouds for a landing in bad weather. All we had to do was follow their instructions and they would direct us on approach to the runway threshold. We pilots were very skeptical and couldn't visualize how this would work. They called it GCA—ground-controlled approach. Little did I know it then, but in later years I would use GCA many times to land in extremely bad weather. Some pilots practiced with it, but I never did while in Germany. It certainly would have been useful the past winter at Y-29 when we were flying in that horrible weather.

The group acquired a pile of souvenirs. Guns of all descriptions showed up, from small palm-sized revolvers to a large .60-caliber elephant gun with a five-foot barrel. I never knew where or how all that war booty was accumulated. I purchased a Luftwaffe officer's dress sword from a fellow for twenty dollars that I still have. Also I brought back some colorful German propaganda books that I gave to my nephew to show in school.

I was told my orders to return to the United States were forthcoming, so I started getting ready. I packed a box of souvenirs and extra clothing to send home. I also gave my hometown in Belgium one last buzz job with some unexpected consequences. Two big trees stood on each end of the house at my aunt and uncle's farm. I paced off the distance between them when visiting and found they were about 45 feet apart. The wing span of the P-47 is about 40 feet, so I figured I could probably fly between them. Until now I stayed above them. For this last buzz job I was determined to fly between those trees.

I came over at Angels 12, picked out the house, then split-S down and applied war emergency power. I was roaring along more than 500 miles per hour as I zoomed over the house between the trees. I pulled up, rolled a few times, and then came around and flew slowly, wagging my wings to say good-bye. Relatives and neighbors were all outside waving at me (I thought). Little did I know the havoc I had caused.

Six weeks later, when I arrived home in Chicago, a letter from my aunt was already there. She had written to my mom and dad to write to me and tell me not to do that anymore. (My relatives could not write directly to me since we had no local European address.) My roaring over the house so low and fast caused the ceiling to fall in. The cow stopped giving milk, the chickens quit laying eggs, and, worst of all, the dog that pulled their milk wagon ran away and hadn't come home yet. I caused them a severe economic burden. They still talk about it when visiting and admit they will never forget it. I have never asked about the dog so I don't know if he ever returned. So ended my last buzz job in a P-47.[2]

My last flight in a P-47 was on 2 June 1945. I left an undeveloped roll of film in Hasselt and I flew back to Y-29 to pick up the developed pictures. That completed my flying in Europe. My tally over the past year of flying was seventy combat missions with 156:30 combat flying hours. During that time I shot down one FW 190 aircraft and destroyed enough military hardware to equip a sizable military force. I probably shot 120,000 rounds of ammunition and dropped 30 tons of bombs. I know I received the Air Medal with about 12 clusters, but never checked to see if they awarded me any other medals.

On 3 June I hopped a B-17 for a flight to England on my way home. While we were waiting to board the aircraft the Chief came by and shook hands with us, wishing us a good flight home and a successful career. He was on his way to fly a just-delivered new AT-6 aircraft for use in instrument training. We watched as he took off and flew out of sight with the gear down. We all laughed since he had obviously forgotten to push the hydraulic power button to energize the system prior to retracting the gear. Years later at a reunion I reminded him about forgetting the power button on that flight. An embarrassing smile and a shake of his head greeted that reminder. He said, "I couldn't understand why that sleek trainer was so sluggish, it must have taken me 15 minutes before I remembered we had to push that hydraulic power button to energize the system." We still laugh about it, especially when admiring that sleek trainer at various museums we have visited together.

The B-17 flew at a low altitude from Münster to Paris, and we had an excellent view of the places that had figured so prominently in the news. Some cities and towns were practically untouched, while the war left others almost completely demolished. There was an interesting contrast on the activities of the people in the various countries. Over Germany there was a mass effort on clearing rubble, almost all by women, cleaning bricks and then sorting and stacking them in neat piles. Over Belgium the same was true, but there was also a determined effort to clear the destroyed bridge rubble from the rivers using farm tractors and manual labor. Over France we saw very little effort to clean up the debris of war. No one was working on clearing the bridge rubble from the rivers. Some large bridges needed heavy equipment to clear them, but nothing was being done to clean up the stone piers or approach roads. I heard some other passengers speculating on the reason, and they agreed that the French were probably waiting for American aid to arrive before beginning the cleanup.

Upon my arrival in London a remarkable transfiguration had occurred; London was lit up and we could see where we were going at night. The lighting was sporadic, with a few signs and billboards lit up, but it was enough to cause one to stop and wonder at the change. Truly the lights were on again in Europe.

I spent several weeks in Chorley, England, while waiting for transportation to the United States. England was then in the throes of an election for prime minister. Winston Churchill, leader of the Conservative Tories, governed the British empire during the war, but Clement Attlee of the Labour Party was waging a serious challenge. One evening Churchill was scheduled to make a speech in the town of Chorley. I debated with myself about going to see and hear that great wartime leader, but decided against it. I have regretted that decision ever since.

Finally on 14 July 1945 they bused us to Warton Field, and ten of us were assigned to a B-24 bomber to fly back to the States. It was a damaged war-weary airplane that had made an emergency landing and spent a year in Sweden. They replaced a couple of the engines and it was flown back to England. We now had the privilege of flying it back to Bradley Field, Connecticut. We met the pilot, copilot, and navigator, and off we went. Our first stop was at Valley, on the northwest tip of Wales. This was the jumping-off spot for transatlantic flights. We waited a day for a weather front to leave Iceland before being cleared to go.

At Valley I met some training companions I hadn't seen since we parted on our assignments to the combat units. There I learned that Bob Hartman didn't survive the flak over the Hürtgen Forest. Hartman, Tanselle, and I had gone through flight training and received our wings together. We shared many good times and made arrangements to meet after the war. Now I was the only one left.

From Valley we flew to Meeks Field, near Keflavik, Iceland, through clouds most the way. Only occasionally did we glimpse the raging North Atlantic on which so much violence and death had occurred these past five years. After landing we noticed gasoline dripping from the wing while the tail surfaces looked brand-new. The blown-back dripping gas had scrubbed them clean. Only a miracle kept us from blowing up—a trait common to B-24 aircraft. It was found that the wingtip tanks, called Tokyo tanks, were all cracked. They were not used in Europe and hence had dried and cracked. We arranged to get the tanks pumped out, and we all pitched in to remove inspection plates and covers to air out the wing. We let the aircraft sit for two days to get rid of the gas fumes.

Most of our time was spent in the club playing poker. The first night I came out of the club at midnight, and the sun was still up. The morning we left we were up at 0400 and found the sun already up.

Since we couldn't use the Tokyo tanks, we were forced to make a refueling stop at BW-1 Greenland, located at Narsarssauk on the southwest coast of Greenland. BW stood for Bluie West, the code name for West Greenland. As we were flying over Greenland in perfectly clear sunny weather, the Greenland ice cap presented us with the most spectacular shimmering scenery any of us had ever seen. When we crossed Greenland and looked down into Davis Strait, the impressive sight of thousands of icebergs and growlers came into view. It was hard to imagine that they were all floating south in the Labrador Current into the North Atlantic. The reason why the maritime countries began an international ice patrol for sea-lane protection from icebergs was very evident from our lofty perch.

We spent only a few hours at BW-1, just enough to refuel the aircraft and get something to eat. The runway at BW-1 slanted from five feet above sea level at one end to 125 feet above at the other end. Landings were always uphill, from the sea toward the ice cap, and large aircraft were committed to land on their first attempt. The Greenland ice cap reached 10,000 feet just a few miles past the end of the runway, and being inside a fjord limited the room to turn or climb to clear the ice cap. Takeoff was in the opposite direction, downhill toward the sea.

The next leg was from Greenland to Goose Bay in Labrador, Canada, where weather grounded us for two more days. The final leg was from Goose Bay to Bradley Field. We landed there on 24 July. It took 11 days to cross the Atlantic by flying—four more than it took us to get to England by ship. We left our war-weary B-24, which we had named "Clem," at Bradley Field. I still wonder if it ever flew again. We were losing power on two engines all across the Atlantic. On our last takeoff from Goose Bay we could not achieve takeoff power from those two engines, but took off anyway, determined to get that plane back.

I had been gone from Bradley Field a little over a year. It was now a main port of entry for returning airmen from Europe. The building we used for ground school was now a mess hall where Italian prisoners of war served us a big steak dinner with all the fresh milk we could drink. They still devoted a small section of the field to P-47 transition training. I went to visit them and found my old instructor still flying the same aircraft. He was bitter that they had kept him in the training command and he had never experienced combat.

It took four days to get processed, including a train trip to Fort Sheridan, located north of Chicago. From there I used the local streetcar to get home for a 30-day leave. My orders were to report to Santa Ana Army Air Base in California on 30 August for reassignment.

It felt good to be home but after a few days it became dull and lonely. After all the excitement of the past three years, adjusting to the preservice home life was hard. Most of the gang was still away in service. When I did meet a couple of old friends, we were happy to see each other, but none of us had the desire to renew our former closeness. Even the girls seemed different. I was looking forward to dating some I had written to, especially my P-47's namesake, Virginia. We dated once and that was that. Everything was different—I couldn't put my finger on what it was, but it was no longer the same.

I was the star attraction of the neighborhood and had to attend a welcome home party arranged by the wartime neighborhood organization. At the party I had to field many questions on the various aspects of the air war, but the ladies especially asked more personal-type questions on medical care, the food, and living conditions. One lady, after I explained that we were all alone in the aircraft and couldn't walk around, was very curious on how we went to the bathroom while flying. The answer brought a few chuckles and some grimaces.

To urinate we used a pilot's relief tube, a rubber hose with a funnel and an outlet on the bottom of the aircraft. There were several drawbacks to this installation that were especially annoying during the winter. The tube tended to freeze up from either residual urine or the slush splashed on the outlet while the aircraft was on the ground, with a predictable result to the user. In the winter we wore heavy woolen long underwear, a woolen uniform, and a heavy flight suit. We were also strapped in with a three-inch wide lap belt and a connecting shoulder harness that covered our crotch area. Getting everything open and exposed was a formidable operation since we had to do everything with one hand and fly the aircraft with the other. At that time the uniform trousers were not equipped with zippers, but with four small buttons. These buttons were not easy to open, even when standing up. Flying during the winter we were always cold, since we had only an inefficient heater for the unpressurized aircraft. The cold not only stimulated our kidneys, but also affected our body physiology, which tends to protect a man's vital organs by withdrawing them inward, making it difficult to expose it for use. All these factors discouraged the use of the relief tube and made a ritual of urinating, usually behind the tail of the aircraft, the last thing before boarding and the first thing after landing. If one really had to use the relief tube we usually waited until we were over Germany.

No provisions for a bowel movement existed. We had a spell of diarrhea sweep through the group during the Battle of the Bulge, and several pilots had the unfortunate luck to have an attack while flying. After landing they tied a rope around their pants legs so they could at least get out of the aircraft without soiling the cockpit. Going to the bathroom in a fighter wasn't easy and was to be avoided if possible.

Another thing people asked me about is religious counseling and services. A chaplain was assigned to the group, Capt. Howard B. Foram, a Protestant minister and a great guy. Many Saturday evenings he made the rounds of all the tents and reminded us that he would hold church services the next morning. He knew I was Catholic but would invite me anyway. We sometimes had a visiting Catholic priest say Mass, and during Reverend Foram's rounds he would make sure all Catholics knew about it. In the heat of flying combat we sometimes were not even sure what day it was, so attending church services was hit or miss. We did not have services before going on a mission since that was impractical with missions run continuously throughout the day. I must confess that I only attended Mass a few times while I was in combat. I'm sure he also had counseling sessions with troubled soldiers, but I never knew anyone that sought that service. He used to kid us that he was available to punch our legendary TS cards. For the uninitiated, "TS" stood for "tough shit." Whenever anyone had a gripe about the Army, the food, or other matters, admonishing him to go get his TS card punched by the chaplain was usually enough to have him stop complaining. At some point in my Army service I had, as a joke, a TS card issued.

My boredom was fortunately relieved by a telephone call from Chuck Bennett. He was visiting Ruth Kealey, his fiancée in Chicago, and on a hunch called my home. It was a happy reunion. He was using crutches and his right leg was in a cast. Doctors were still not sure he would regain its use to walk normally. He asked me to be his best man at his wedding, scheduled for October in their hometown of Janesville, Wisconsin. I happily accepted, provided the Army would cooperate. I also brought him the Luger and Walther P-38 pistols that he acquired as souvenirs. I did not include those with the personal belongings I sent home since attractive souvenirs of that sort had a habit of disappearing in transit.

While I was home on leave the war ended with the atomic bomb being dropped on Japan. This relieved my anxiety since there was a good possibility they would have sent me to the Pacific theater for the final push on Japan. I had gone through enough war in my life. My journey to Santa Ana Army Air Base in California was pleasant. I shared a compartment with a naval officer and we had two days to relive our war experiences. At Santa Ana they discharged me from the service at my request.

I do want to interject one last viewpoint regarding the use of the atomic bomb on Japan. Many people now in the years 2000s feel that using that weapon was morally wrong, noting that Japan was already defeated and would have surrendered by the end of 1945. Even if that statement was true, it would have been devastating to the 300,000 American, English, Australian, and Dutch prisoners, dying like flies in the Japanese POW camps. These men, with little equipment (and what they had was obsolete and inferior to Japanese material), held the line while America mobilized. After the war I had as my immediate CO Maj. Robert I Leyrer, whom the Japanese captured in the Philippines. He went through the Bataan death march and ended up in Japan working in a mine.[3] He told me that conditions were so inhumane and harsh that if the war had dragged on a few more months, none of them would have been left alive to rescue. America owed them a debt to end the war as soon as possible.[4]

Had we invaded Japan, I am convinced the carnage would have been worse than the sum of all the other battles with Japanese forces throughout the war. Okinawa was the last great ground battle of World War II. In that battle we defeated the Japanese, but they refused to surrender and were annihilated. The losses were stupendous; the death toll amounted to 23,000 Americans, including more than 5,000 Navy personnel from Kamikaze attacks. On the Japanese side they lost 91,000 troops and 150,000 Okinawa civilians—more than the losses of the Hiroshima and Nagasaki atomic raids combined.[5]

The Japanese had the material and the Bushido devotion to fight to the death. Understanding the Bushido, the religious-like code of the Samurai Warriors that requires loyalty and obedience and puts honor above life, is hard for Americans. That the Japanese people were committed to this code is exemplified by the ferocious and sustained Okinawa battle kamikaze attacks, and the large kamikaze and civilian suicide forces recruited for the homeland battle. Even after we dropped the two atomic bombs, the Japanese military fanatics almost succeeded in thwarting the emperor's plans for capitulation.[6] So please, before making a judgment on my generation's use of the atomic bomb, get the facts about that era imbued with our burning hatred of the Japanese and their fanaticism to the Bushido code.[7]

Epilogue

With the great adventure completed, most members of the 366th Fighter Group returned to civilian life. Many reservists who elected to stay in the service, thinking to make a career of it, received a rude awakening when the many reductions in force (RIFs) terminated their service as the United States demobilized. As for myself, I accepted immediate separation from the service so I could enroll in college and get an aeronautical engineering degree. Having seen first-hand the power of aviation I was determined to stay in that field and grow with it. That was one of my better decisions in life. I did become an engineer and had the opportunity to work with many outstanding aircraft designers during my career, including Alexander Kartveli, designer of that rugged well-liked P-47 we flew.

I also pursued that other American dream of a loving wife, family, and home. I pursued and finally won over a cute girl, Margie Roth. We were married in North Hollywood, California, on 19 June 1948. My best man was my flying buddy Chuck Bennett. Over the years Marge and I had four children, Andrew, Robert J., Susan, and Charles. We are proud of them all and the five grandchildren they presented us.

Our beloved P-47s didn't fare as well. Of the more than 15,000 produced, more than any other American fighter, only a handful remain. They immediately scrapped or dumped them in the ocean, an ignominious end to such a gallant aircraft. The damage inflicted on the enemy by that aircraft and the dedicated airmen that flew it is awesome. More than 12,000 enemy aircraft, 86,000 railroad cars, 9,000 locomotives, and 6,000 armored vehicles fell victim to the destructive power of the P-47. It was indeed a major factor in assuring victory for the allies in World War II.

The 366th Fighter Group continues today as an active unit in the U.S. Air Force. Except for two short deactivated periods, the 366th has been on active service since June 1943. Throughout this time the 366th has achieved a record of excellence and dedicated service and has garnered many honors during the Cold War and brush wars that our nation has been forced into. At present it is an elite Air Expeditionary Wing, the only one in the Air Force, stationed at Mountain Home AFB, Idaho.[1] Of interest, the 389th squadron now flies F-16s in the air interdiction role, the 390th flies F-16s in the air-superiority and fighter-support role, and the 391st flies F-15Es in the attack role. The 34th Bombardment Squadron, flying B-1Bs, provides the heavy bomber support and the 22nd Air Refueling Squadron provides tanker and transport support. It is indeed a miniature air force.

I am proud to have contributed my small part in establishing the outstanding record and tradition of the 366th Fighter Group. We have an active 366th Fighter Group Association where we reminisce and relive many of the more pleasant memories, conveniently forgetting the unpleasant and sorrowful periods. We do, however, always reverently drink a toast to those that gave their all and fervently pray the world will come to its senses and pursue a more fruitful endeavor than war.

After the war I had to answer several letters from distraught wives and parents from close flying companions, wanting to know the action details that killed their loved ones. They were the most difficult letters I ever had to write. When I read the following poem I knew I wanted to use it to close this narrative. It says it all.

Letter to St. Peter
Let them in Peter, they are very tired;
Give them the couches where the Angels sleep.
Let them wake whole again to new dawns fired
With sun not war. And may their peace be deep.
Remember where the broken bodies lie—
And give them things they like. Let them make noise.
God knows how young they were to have to die!
Give swing bands not gold harps, to these our boys,
Let them love, Peter,—They have had no time—
Girls sweet as meadow wind, with flowing hair—
They should have trees and bird song, hills to climb
The taste of Summer in a ripened pear,
Tell them how they are missed. Say not to fear;
It's going to be alright with us down here.[2]

Appendix

366th Fighter Group Combat Statistics and Casualties

Pilot mission summary statistics and casualties for the fourteen months the 366th Fighter Group flew in combat are presented in this appendix. I extracted the data from the 366th Fighter Group Report of Operations and the commanders' log.

Table A.1 lists the pilot casualties. Note that the worst month was June 1944, when nineteen pilots were lost. The worst casualty rate was during the November Hürtgen Forest and January Battle of the Bulge campaigns where we lost 5.5 pilots per 1,000 hours, or one pilot every 182 hours of combat flying. The overall average was 2.57 pilots per 1,000 hours, or one pilot every 389 hours the group flew during the war.

Table A.2 presents the group's operational combat statistics for the entire time in combat. It is interesting that we dispatched more than 17,000 aircraft on missions, and in so doing used more than five million gallons of fuel. When one considers that the Ninth Air Force had eighteen fighter-bomber groups in action, the fuel used reaches staggering amounts. The logistics of a world war are truly incomprehensible.

Table A.1. 366th Fighter Group Casualities

Month	Aircraft Lost	Pilots Lost Number[a]	Pilots Lost Per 1,000 flying hours
March 1944	2	2	0.97
April	2	2	0.84
May	4	3	0.89
June	26	19	4.66
July	15	11	5.39
August	11	7	2.37
September	5	3	0.89
October	5	5	2.17
November	15	13	5.47
December	21	10	4.66
January 1945	8	7	5.48
February	3	2	0.92
March	13	9	2.27
April	5	2	0.89
May	0	0	0.00
Total	135	95[b]	2.57[c]

[a]In addition, 26 pilots were wounded, and several were hospitalized and returned home.
[b]Of these pilots, 24 were prisoners of war. The rest were killed in action.
[c]Average

Table A.2. 366th Fighter Group Mission Summary, 12 March 1944–7 May 1945

Total number of missions dispatched	1,258	Hours flown	
Escort	55	Operational	36,983
Fighter sweep	33	Nonoperational	6,713
Dive-bomb	382	Drop tanks jettisoned	4,314
Leaflet drop	2	Ammunition expended (rounds)	4,878,000
Armed reconnaissance	695	Bomb tonnage dropped	5,139
Patrol	51	Gasoline consumed (gallons)	5,010,000
Radar bombing	40	Aircraft damaged	
Aircraft dispatched	17,302	Major (service group repair)	224
Sorties	18,016	Minor (squadron repair)	322
Aborts[a]	436	Aircraft lost	135

[a]Mostly due to weather.

Notes

1. Gen. James H. Doolittle, with Carroll V. Glines, *I Could Never Be So Lucky Again* (New York: Bantam Books, 1991), 370.
2. Jerry Scutts, *P-47 Thunderbolt Aces of the Eighth Air Force* (Oxford, England: Osprey Publishing, 1999).

Chapter 1. Pilot Training

1. Duane R. Baker, "Pursuing a Pursuit Pilot," *USAF Museum Friends Journal* 16, no. 1 (Spring 1993): 9–11, describes the World War I training at Carlstrom. It is now the site of the G. Pierce Wood State Hospital, and many buildings we used as quarters and administration, and several hangars, are still in use.
2. Col. John L. Frisbee, "The Cloud with the Mild Blue Lining," *Air Force Magazine* (July 1981): 88–91. A humorous account of flight training at Carlstrom from a check pilot's viewpoint.

Chapter 2. Operational Fighter Training

1. Robert V. Brulle, "Don't Panic—It's Just a Compressibility Dive," *Air Power History* (March 1996): 40–53, provides a detailed explanation on the compressibility phenomenon and the effort undertaken to alleviate this dangerous dive.
2. I mentioned this years ago to Costas (Gus) Pappas, Republic Aviation's chief aerodynamicist during the P-47 years, and he was appalled it took so long to implement the fix. His comment: "We worked our butt off to design a fix, and then the Air Force didn't even bother to install them."
3. Benjamin King and Timothy Kutta, *Impact: The History of Germany's V-Weapons in World War II* (Rockville Center, N.Y.: Sarpedon, 1998).

Chapter 3. Battle of France

1. Col. Harold N. Holt, "Column Cover," *American Aviation Historical Society Journal* 28 and 29 (Winter 1983): 233–42 and 29 (Spring 1984): 3–15.
2. Ronald H. Bailey, *The Air War in Europe, World War II* (Alexandria, Va.: Time-Life Books, 1979), 123, shows a photograph of that P-38, piloted by Capt. Lloyd K. Cox, skidding alongside the runway, taken just as the right engine propeller walked its way over the cockpit.
3. We used the German term "flak," shortened from *Fl*ugzeug*a*bwehr*k*anone, to denote antiaircraft fire.
4. The entire report is presented in Report of Operations, 366th Fighter Group, 18 August 1944, available from Air Force Historical Agency, Maxwell AFB, Alabama.
5. "*Achtung Jabos:* The Story of IX TAC," *ETO Stars and Stripes Pamphlet,* n.d. (probably about January 1945).
6. Ibid.
7. William B. Breuer, *Death of a Nazi Army: The Falaise Pocket* (New York: Stein and Day, 1985), 281. The author provides a graphic presentation of the destruction meted out by the dreaded Jabos to the German units caught inside the pocket.
8. Holt, "Column Cover," presents several mission profiles detailing the entire procedure, from briefing to landing, in performing a close support mission.
9. Martin Blumenson, *Breakout and Pursuit,* The U.S. Army in World War II: European Theater of Operation (Washington, D.C.: Government Printing Office, 1984), 572–83. The entire Allied force was beset by logistical problems; my conjecture is that the British aggravated theirs by religiously stopping for tea in the afternoon.
10. Ibid., 583.
11. Robert V. Brulle, "Roaring Homecoming," *FlyPast Magazine* (October 1994): 55. It describes my visits and consequences of my subsequent buzz jobs of the area.
12. Ronald G. Ruppenthal, *Logistical Support of the Armies,* vol. 1, U.S. Army in World War II (Washington, D.C.: Government Printing Office, 1953).

Chapter 4. German Border Stalemate

1. Charles B. MacDonald, *The Siegfried Line Campaign,* The U.S. Army in World War II: European Theater of Operations (Washington, D.C.: Government Printing Office, 1963), 260.

   I acquired the information on the mistaken bombing from the Air Force Research Agency at Maxwell AFB for my friend and Belgium historian, Lucien Bogers, in Genk, Belgium, the town bombed that day. We later saw the damage and became friends with many people there when we moved in November to nearby Y-29. For those interested, the errant bombers were two boxes from the 394th Bombardment Group.
2. Thomas A. Hughes, *Overlord* (New York: Simon and Schuster, 1995), 6–8, provides an excellent account of General Quesada and his tactical doctrine in World War II. The reader should beware, however, since there are some glaring errors in the text.

3. We had a single-frequency transponder installed in our aircraft. Named Identification: Friend or Foe, (IFF), it would emit an identification blip on the radar scope as the radar pulse hit our aircraft. We even had a means to destroy the IFF transponder in event we were forced down in enemy territory. The unit was turned on only when requested by the radar operator. So many aircraft flew over Europe, mostly Allied under some type of radar or other operational control, that it made IFF superfluous. To my knowledge, the transponder was used only on pickle-barrel missions. If we wanted a position fix we used our radio and held down the radio transmit button for 10 seconds.

Chapter 5. The Hürtgen Forest Campaign: Initial Attacks

1. That battle has been written up in many books. Several are recommended. Edward G. Miller, *A Dark and Bloody Ground* (College Station: Texas A&M University Press, 1995), vividly describes the hazardous, exhausting, intolerable conditions under which the ground troops had to fight. A more official version is presented in MacDonald, *The Siegfried Line Campaign*. Many photographs on the Hürtgen Forest Battle are shown in Karl Margry, *The Battle of the Hürtgen Forest* 71 (1991): 1–35. A 1998 TV movie titled *When Trumpets Fade* also portrays the brutal aspects of that battle.
2. MacDonald, *Siegfried Line Campaign,* 326–28.
3. Fleig's effort to get to Schmidt were written up in his memoirs, which he generously sent me. Many of his exploits were featured in Miller, *A Dark and Bloody Ground.*
4. Conversations with Dr. William F. Atwater, Director, U.S. Army Ordnance Museum, Army Proving Ground, Md., and Mr. Uwe Feist, historian and author of German armored vehicles. Two of his books are recommended. Uwe Feist and Bruce Culver, *Panzerkampfwagen Tiger* (Bellingham, Wash.: Ryton Publications, 1992), and Uwe Feist and Bruce Culver, *Panzerkampfwagen Panther* (Bellingham, Wash.: Ryton Publications, 1992).
5. Several years ago I answered a request by historian and lecturer Klaus Schulz, from Meerbusch, Germany, for air-support stories during the Hürtgen Forest battle. We have exchanged information and compared notes about the battle since then.
6. Geoffrey Perret, *Winged Victory* (New York: Random House, 1993), 353; and Hugh M. Cole, *The Lorraine Campaign,* U.S. Army in World War II (Washington, D.C.: Government Printing Office, 1997), 389.
7. "366th Fighter Group Operations Order—Operation Q," 9 November, Air Force Historical Research Agency, Maxwell AFB, Alabama.
8. Robert V. Brulle, "Shootout Over the Hürtgen Forest," *World War II Magazine* (November 1995): 31–36.
9. My thanks to Albert Trostorf Jr. of Merode, Germany, for the description of his father's eyewitness experience.
10. Quentin Aanenson recorded his World War II experiences on videotape and titled it *A Fighter Pilot's Story.* This excellent personal presentation was broadcast on public television stations and can now be rented at video stores.

Chapter 6. The Hürtgen Forest Campaign: A Slugging Match

1. MacDonald, *Siegfried Line Campaign*, 490. The surrounded troops were elements from the 26th Infantry Division. They were annihilated.
2. Ibid., 453–54.
3. Ibid., 457–59.

Chapter 7. Battle of the Bulge: Germans Attack

1. Hugh M. Cole, *The Ardennes: Battle of the Bulge*, The U.S. Army in World War II (Washington, D.C.: Government Printing Office, 1993), chaps. 5 and 6.
2. Danny S. Parker, *To Win the Winter Sky* (Conshohocken, Pa.: Combined Books, 1994), presents a well-researched and accurate account of the air war during the Battle of the Bulge.
3. Gerald Astor, *A Blood Dimmed Tide: The Battle of the Bulge by the Men Who Fought It* (New York: Donald I. Fine, 1992), 252; and Cole, *The Ardennes*, 360–63.
4. A gun camera is set to run two to three seconds after the trigger is released to record the flight of the shells fired.
5. James M. Gavin, *On to Berlin* (New York: Bantam, 1992), 263, 295.
6. 366th Fighter Group, Operations Report, Unit History—1 December to 31 December 1944, Air Force Historical Agency, Maxwell AFB, Alabama.
7. Pictures of that destroyed P-47 have been published in many books to illustrate the hazardous nature of combat flying. For example, see Ronald H. Bailey, *The Air War In Europe* (Alexandria, Va.: World War II Time-Life Books, 1979), 112–13.

Chapter 8. Battle of the Bulge: Americans Strike Back

1. Edgar S. Tingley, "The Saga of the Magic Carpet," *American Aviation Historical Society Journal* 29, no. 1 (Spring 1984): 14–15. Colonel Holt's B2-H, "The Magic Carpet," had an illustrious combat record. It was still around at the end of the war, having completed 175 missions without an abort.
2. Werner Girbig, *Six Months to Oblivion* (West Chester, Pa.: Schiffer Publishing, 1991), 100.
3. This particular air battle was written up and published in several magazines and books. One of the best overall accounts of the entire air battle is presented in Parker, *To Win the Winter Sky*, 373–449. Others include: Tom Ivie, "The Legend of Y-29," *Air Classics Magazine* 23, no. 8 (August 1987): 38–41, 52–54, originally published as "The Key Block," *USAF Museum Friends Bulletin* (Winter/Spring 1987): 24–30; Edward H. Sims, *American Air Aces* (New York: Ballantine Books, 1958), 205–22; Girbig, *Six Months to Oblivion*, 73–117; and Norman Franks, *Battle of the Airfields* (London: Grub Street Publishers, 1994), 130–37.
4. William Green, *The Warplanes of the Third Reich* (New York: Doubleday, 1979), 571.
5. Girbig, *Six Months to Oblivion*, 110–15.
6. Parker, *To Win the Winter Sky*, 447–49; Franks, *Battle of the Airfields*, 193–200.

7. I collected these accounts for Tom Ivie's "The Key Block."
8. Unit History, 792nd AAA, Air Force Historical Research Agency, Maxwell AFB, Alabama.
9. Parker, *To Win The Winter Sky,* devotes an entire chapter, "Slaughter at Dasburg: January 22nd," to that day's destruction of German vehicles (chap. 23). He quotes Gen. Erich Brandenberger, commander of the German 7th Army, as saying, "the situation in the air was similar to that which prevailed in Normandy."
10. Adolph Galland, *The First and the Last* (New York: Ballantine Books, 1963), 190.
11. Parker, *To Win the Winter Sky.*

Chapter 9. The Final Battles

1. Hughes, *Overlord,* 183–84, presents the logic and implementation of this practice.
2. An excellent write-up of this little battle can be found in Victor Hillery, *Paths of Armor, 5th Armored Division History Book* (Atlanta: Albert Lowe Enterprise, 1950), 219. Another shorter version can be found in Charles B. MacDonald, *The Last Offensive,* The U.S. Army in World War II (Washington, D.C.: Government Printing Office, 1972), 72–73.
3. The 5th Armored Division, "Letter Report, After Action Against the Enemy," is available from the National Archives.
4. Kenn C. Rust, *The Ninth Air Force in World War II* (Fallbrook, Calif.: Aero Publishers, 1967), 148–53, presents a description of the Ninth Air Force effort in Operation Clarion.
5. Donald L. Caldwell, *JG 26: Top Guns of the Luftwaffe* (New York: Ballantine Books, 1993), 340–43.
6. Jon A. Guttman, "Aerial Oddities," *Aviation History* (November 1999): 16–24, presents an interesting account on Lieutenant Glowczynski in action during the battle for France, flying an obsolete French Caudron CR 714.
7. Robert V. Brulle, "Angels for Co-pilots," *Air Classics Magazine* 34, no. 6 (June 1998), is a fictionalized account of that flight as seen through the eyes of guardian angels.
8. Hq 5th Armored Div, Letter, Report After Action Against Enemy—April 1945, "Horsefly Planes as an Aid to Air-Ground Cooperation," available from the National Archives. This report is the earliest mention I know on using aircraft as forward air/ground controllers (FAC). Today that technique is well honed and uses specially designed aircraft for the purpose.

Chapter 10. Mission Complete

1. John J. Horan, "Our Trolley Mission," *USAF Museum Friends Journal* 19, no. 3 (Fall 1996): 29–31. The bomber buzz jobs were called "trolley missions."
2. Brulle, "Roaring Homecoming."
3. William H. Bartsch, *Doomed at the Start—American Pursuit Pilots in the Philippines, 1941–1942* (College Station: Texas A&M University Press, 1992). 2nd Lt. Bob Leyrer was shipped to the Philippines directly out of flying school, arriving

in late June 1941. He was assigned to the 17th Pursuit Squadron, 24th Pursuit Group. He never got a chance to fly a combat mission and ended up as an infantryman in Bataan.

4. Robert S. LaForte, *Building the Death Railway: The Ordeal of American POWs in Burma, 1942–1945* (Wilmington, Del.: Scholarly Publisher Resources, 1993), gives a first-hand account of twenty-two lucky prisoners who survived the brutal conditions in Japanese prison camps. William A. Berry's *Prisoner of the Rising Sun* (Norman: University of Oklahoma Press, 1993) is another excellent account on being a Japanese prisoner.

5. George Feifer, *Tennozan* (New York: Ticknor and Fields, 1992).

6. Pacific War Research Society, *Japan's Longest Day* (New York: Ballantine Books, 1983), gives the story on how perilously close that military revolt came to succeeding in scuttling the emperor's surrender.

7. Thomas B. Allen and Norman Polmar, *Code-Name Downfall* (New York: Simon and Schuster, 1993). These two eminent authors researched and documented the American and Japanese plans for the invasion of Japan. The invasion battle would undoubtedly have turned Japan into a wasteland. An interesting side note: both sides were considering using poison gas and germ warfare.

Epilogue

1. An Air Expeditionary Wing is a self-contained miniature air force. It has aircraft, support equipment and personnel combined in a quick strike force. It has all of the functions and abilities to independently deploy and conduct air operations anywhere in the world. It combines fighters, attack fighters, bombers and tanker/transport aircraft together in one compact wing. See Tom Clancy, *Fighter Wing* (New York: Berkley Books, 1995).

2. This poem was found in the Philippines during World War II.

Index

01 14